"Writing in the tradition of media-ecology scholars such as Jacques Ellul and Neil Postman, Peter Fallon takes on the subject of propaganda with intelligence, insight, and moral clarity. Coupling historical context with contemporary analysis, *Propaganda 2.1* is essential reading for anyone concerned about the contemporary media environment and where we may be headed in the years to come."

—**Lance Strate**, Fordham University

"*Propaganda 2.1* is a timely contribution to digital-literacy education. After a thoughtful rereading of Ellul's classic work, the book offers in a lucid exposition a wealth of original research and insights into the changing nature of propaganda in the twenty-first century. No student of media or reader who wants to better understand and defend themselves from the new generation of propaganda in the digital age can afford to ignore this extremely resourceful book."

—**Casey Man Kong Lum**, William Paterson University

"*Propaganda 2.1* is a brilliant contribution to our fragile planet and civilization. . . . The picture is bleak, but Fallon shows how the emergence of the worldwide web and various internet technologies can open up new possibilities—not just QAnon and Alex Jones, but WikiLeaks, Occupy Wall Street, and Black Lives Matter. Individuals and smaller movements can have a voice. Resistance, truth, justice, freedom, and community may not be likely—but they are possible with *Propaganda 2.1*."

—**David W. Gill**, International Jacques Ellul Society

D1732943

Propaganda 2.1

Propaganda 2.1

Understanding Propaganda in the Digital Age

Peter K. Fallon

CASCADE *Books* · Eugene, Oregon

PROPAGANDA 2.1
Understanding Propaganda in the Digital Age

Cascade Books
An Imprint of Wipf and Stock Publishers
199 W. 8th Ave., Suite 3
Eugene, OR 97401

www.wipfandstock.com

PAPERBACK ISBN: 978-1-6667-3134-7
HARDCOVER ISBN: 978-1-6667-2374-8
EBOOK ISBN: 978-1-6667-2375-5

Cataloguing-in-Publication data:

Names: Fallon, Peter K., author.

Title: Propaganda 2.1 : understanding propaganda in the digital age / by Peter K. Fallon.

Description: Eugene, OR: Cascade Books, 2022 | Includes bibliographical references and index.

Identifiers: ISBN 978-1-6667-3134-7 (paperback) | ISBN 978-1-6667-2374-8 (hardcover) | ISBN 978-1-6667-2375-5 (ebook)

Subjects: LCSH: Propaganda. | Computer networks—Political aspects.

Classification: HM263 F36 2022 (print) | HM263 (ebook)

09/02/22

To André Kehoe

"Níl ach na daoine ciúin ciontach . . ."

Contents

Acknowledgments

There are two people I wish to thank for encouraging me in my work; first, and always, my dear wife and best friend Dr. Mary Pat Fallon, who somehow manages to remain patient in my (mental, if not physical) absence, and is more supportive and loving than any human being I've ever known. Without her, her love, her patience, and her friendship, I could never have written a word. As always, whatever good comes of this work, I owe to her.

Second, in Dublin in 1990 while researching my first book, *Why the Irish Speak English*, I met an expatriate Irishman living in France named André Kehoe. We were staying in a Jesuit dormitory near St. Stephen's Green while we did our respective bits of research, and we shared a few meals, several pints, and many stories together. He was writing a book about capitalism, power, war, global geopolitics, justice, religion, and, not incidentally, propaganda. He was also a walking repository of knowledge about Irish history and culture, a deeply literate man in every sense of the word, and my understanding of Yeats, Joyce, and Becket, De Valera and Collins, Cuchullain and Finn MacCumhal, were all expanded as a result of my brief acquaintance with him.

What I did not know at the time was that André Kehoe had spent his career (he must have been well into his sixties when we met) as an administrator with the Office of Economic Cooperation and Development in Paris, the Food and Agriculture Organization of the United Nations in Rome, the United Nations Development Program in Africa, and consulting with UNESCO and the World Bank around the world. He knew the global establishment well.

His book *Christian Contradictions and the World Revolution: Letters to My Son* is encyclopedic in its grasp of indictable offenses against human civilization perpetrated by the forces behind mass culture. André was a sort of Irish Jacques Ellul, another lone voice of reason crying in the mass wilderness, and it is doubly a shame that he did not publish more in this vein, and that so few people have heard of him or have read his book.

He was also something of a raconteur. One evening, we walked through St. Stephen's Green on our way to Grogan's Castle Lounge for a couple of pints. As we walked through the park, he told me about the "activities" there during the 1916 uprising, rolled off a fairly comprehensive biography of Countess Constance Markievicz in front of her memorial, recited Yeats's "September 1913" to give me an idea of the social circumstances of Dublin leading up to the Great War and the uprising, then recited "Easter, 1916" to illustrate the impact of the uprising on the Irish people—all changed, changed utterly. Then, before exiting the park onto Grafton Street, we stopped at the monument to Jeremiah O'Donovan Rossa. He related O'Donovan Rossa's life, death, and return to Ireland for interment, and then declaimed from memory (performed might be a better word) Padraig Pearse's funeral oration over the old Fenian's grave in Glasnevin Cemetery. During our walk through the park, André had attracted a following of a dozen or so curious onlookers, and at the end of Pearse's oration—"They think that they have provided against everything; but the fools, the fools, the fools! They have left us our Fenian dead, and while Ireland holds these graves, Ireland unfree shall never be at peace!"—the dozen or more people who had fastened themselves to us and had become part of André's retinue, broke out in raucous, spontaneous applause. André turned to them, smiled shyly, nodded, and quietly said "Thank you." Only then did we go and have our Guinness.

A year later, in June of 1991, back home in New York, I was surprised by a large package that appeared at my door. I opened it to find a 507-page book, *Christian Contradictions and the World Revolution: Letters to my Son.* On the first page André had dedicated the book to "Jeanne-Françoise, Charles, Siún, Clotilde, Brigitte, Pierre" but he added, in his own hand, "and Peter, with the author's compliments, and hoping you will continue to struggle for sanity in America against the forces that are destroying it.—André. 14.5.91" There was a bookmark inserted at page 373. I thought nothing of it at the time. Later, when I began reading the book and finally reached the place where he had thoughtfully placed the bookmark, I was astounded to read the following:

> Part of the problem is that the media men have the masses by the throat, especially on television, but they are all part of the same pattern and you will find so-called serious journalists in

the written media writing what appear to be critical analyses of television personalities to provide them with publicity in a game of mutual backscratching . . . This bogus culture imposed hour after hour on the people by the media is a serious interference with free thinking and therefore free action. It is part of what Peter K. Fallon of New York University, in an admirable phrase, calls the Disneyization of society.[1]

Nearly three decades later, with *Propaganda 2.1: Understanding Propaganda in the Digital Age*, I hope to make my own contribution to the general understanding of "this bogus culture" that interferes with our "free thinking and therefore free action."

For André Kehoe's intelligence, his critical yet creative mind, his moral imagination, his passion for social justice, and his friendship and generosity to a young scholar researching his first book, I dedicate this present book to his memory.

Peter K. Fallon

Chicago
September 2021

---

1. Kehoe, *Christian Contradictions and the World Revolution*, 373.

Introduction

This book was written as an addendum to Jacques Ellul's masterful sociological study *Propaganda: The Formation of Men's Attitudes*. My purpose in writing it was to update and adjust the ideas found in that book for the twenty-first century. I labor under no delusion that I can improve on Ellul's work and in fact take the principles contained in his *Propaganda* as the foundation of all my investigations.

Ellul published the original French text *Propagandes* in 1962, and through its English translation Ellul was introduced to American readers back in 1965. Newspapers were still Americans' prime source of news. Television had only recently eclipsed radio and was well on its way to toppling the monopoly of knowledge established by newspapers centuries earlier. At the time of Ellul's death in 1994, the internet and World Wide Web were still in their infancy and their new technology spawns—smartphones, the mobile, cellular internet, social media, the cloud, etc.—were little more than techno-utopian fantasies. In the three decades since Ellul's death we've read about the inevitability of a "digital revolution" resulting from the decentralized information flow of digital technologies. The old-technology stranglehold on information would be broken and individuals would be free to share new and revolutionary ideas; democracy would be revitalized as individuals could begin to write the political narratives most recently monopolized by highly paid consultants; corporations would lose power as the marketplace was recolonized by small businesses, etc. In the same way that the fall of Soviet communism was supposed to mark "the end of history," the digital revolution should have marked "the end of propaganda."

Today, however, it would be easy to think that the "revolution" has been nothing more than another example of what Ellul called "the technological bluff." The primacy of technique in the digital age (and our internalization of the technological value system) has so far empowered the corporation as much as the individual; democracy, for a hopeful minority, appears revitalized, but the organized force of capital leaves true democracy in a virtual state of life support, rapidly approaching its demise; and the individual, for the most part, has approached digital technologies in exactly the same way he approached older technologies: with the fascination and enthusiasm of a passive receiver of mass-produced amusements and agonistic controversies du jour. Meet the new boss, same as the old boss . . .

Ellul lived to see none of this, of course, so his otherwise visionary *Propaganda* couldn't possibly anticipate the restructuring of the technical system and the redrawing of boundaries among our society's individuals, institutions, and centers of power. If my role in writing this book is not to improve Ellul's work (and it is not), then perhaps I can legitimately claim that its goal is to reinterpret it for a new century and to conform Ellul's analysis to the contours of our new digital landscape.

Propaganda affects everyone, every day, in just about every facet of our lives, and its effects are substantial and serious, whether we're aware of them or not. And most of us are not. The fact is that propaganda pervades our lives and the life of our society and it is inescapable. It suffuses every human social institution, from our politics, to our education systems, our religions and houses of worship, our economic affairs, and our interpersonal relationships—both actual and virtual. It permeates our conscious (and unconscious) minds, creating a "reality" that few will ever consider questioning publicly or privately, even though for many this "reality"— when seen objectively—seems utterly bereft of authentic human meaning. This is not entirely new. "The mass of men lead lives of quiet desperation," wrote Henry David Thoreau in 1854 about the burgeoning technological civilization. "What is called resignation is confirmed desperation . . . it appears as if men had deliberately chosen the common mode of living because they preferred it to any other. *Yet they honestly think there is no choice left.*"[1] (My emphasis.) This inability to recognize our own freedom and power that Thoreau wrote of more than a century and a half ago has only increased in the intervening years, and increased exponentially with the development and spread of technology.

But wait—you're probably thinking—that doesn't sound like propaganda to me. Propaganda doesn't happen all the time, and when it does, I'm completely aware of it *because* I'm free. Propaganda consists of lies and manipulation and attempts at subversion. Propaganda is an evil act perpetrated

---

1. Thoreau, *Walden*, 4–5.

by a cabal of sinister agents—usually acting on behalf of a foreign power or competing ideology—with the intent of demoralizing us, weakening our faith in our own government or system, undermining our society and institutions, and destroying our way of life. Propaganda is recognizable precisely because it doesn't accurately reflect the reality that I, with my intelligence and free will, experience on a daily basis. Propaganda is recognizable because it goes against all the shared values, attitudes, and assumptions of our culture. Propaganda is un-American—as are those who engage in it.

Some of this might, in fact, be true—to a point. The problem, however, is that none of it is *entirely* true, and much of it is completely false. Few people recognize that in a highly technologically developed society such as ours, propaganda is a constant: it is *always* happening, and it is *everywhere.* Propaganda may be based on lies (Ellul tells us, by the way, that such propaganda is destined to fail in the long term), but to be effective it must be based on "facts." Propaganda is most certainly a form of manipulation; but we probably don't feel as though we're being manipulated when we're merely being reminded of the things and ideas we grew up with from childhood and already believe in. Propaganda may at times be evil. I would argue, along with Ellul, that while it is both a necessity and an inevitability, it is never an objective good. But in a highly technologically developed mass culture, it is most certainly a necessity, and the vast majority of us experience it (without calling or thinking about it as propaganda) as a good. Propaganda does indeed come to us from agents and agencies beyond our borders motivated by bad intentions. But the vast bulk of the propaganda experienced by citizens of the United States is domestically produced and distributed, and while we willingly, even gleefully, turn to it day after day, it still might not be a bad idea to question the intentions of its creators. Propaganda is *not* un-American. Propaganda is *the American way of life itself* because it is the way of mass technologies.

More than just the way things are, propaganda presents itself to us as the way things *ought to be.* A mass-manufactured reality that defines human needs and then delivers all of the material goods it defines is not to be taken lightly. If no one believes he is susceptible to propaganda it is because dominant establishment sources of information give us nothing that would call the status quo into question. Indeed, for that very reason no one *wants to believe* he is susceptible to propaganda. And that is precisely the evidence necessary to show the seriousness of the problem—and why I believe everyone needs to know about it.

* * *

For millennia, philosophers, scholars, and researchers have examined *messages*; the messages flowing through our societal systems of mass communication. The general thought was that messages were the key to persuasion. In one specific school of thought (rhetoric), people were trained how to argue persuasively, even in the absence of evidence to support one's claim; in another it was believed that if the right message hit the right person at the right time (something that mass media made more likely than interpersonal communication alone could do), that person could be expected to pass that message on to others, thereby creating a chain of persuasion that would inevitably result in, if not a consensus view, then certainly a majority one; yet another school of thought was more blunt: viewers, readers, and hearers of mass-mediated messages passively internalize those messages and are equally passively affected by them. In this view, it is as though some medium directly injects ideas into our heads. We become what we consume.

I will refer to these theories in the coming chapters and it is my hope to highlight what they got right as well as to critique what they might have missed or gotten entirely wrong. But our very concern for propaganda, our perception of its actions as lies, deceit, and manipulation through the use of cunningly crafted messages, blinds us to the real danger that it poses for us. Undue focus on messages distracts us from the fact that we live in an environment of mass propaganda each and every day of our lives with no possibility of escape, and few of us are aware of this fact; and when made aware enter a mode of deep and disdainful denial. When we focus on messages, we get the misleadingly comforting feeling that we know right from wrong, truth from falsehood, straightforward exposition of facts from manipulative spin and we immediately tell ourselves "I know the difference between truth and propaganda."

We tend to think, for the same reason, that we are immune to propaganda. We tell ourselves "Propaganda is manipulation, and I'm too strong to be manipulated." "Propaganda is brainwashing, and I'm too intelligent and strong-willed to be brainwashed." "Propaganda is a conspiracy of the powerful over the weak, and as a citizen of a democracy I have the power to fight propaganda." "Propaganda is lies and I can tell a lie from the truth." And so on.

What we fail to see, by such thinking, is that while the messages of propaganda are not without their own power and effectiveness, the real power of propaganda lies in the material superstructure of mass information itself, in its ability to conform the beliefs, values, attitudes, and especially behaviors of millions of people at a time, in its capacity for engendering and supporting the conception of reality we wake up to and accept in our daily lives. Our global system of mass communication is really nothing more than an enormous and highly efficient (and profitable) "information pump," and its content—delivered to us through countless thousands of channels twenty-four hours each day, seven days a week, 365 days a year—is information, much of it organized into forms we call "messages," but a surprising proportion of it of questionable meaning or use. The point is that messages come, and messages go, and when we open the spigot to fill our cup with one message, there are more messages right behind. Our collective cup literally runneth over with messages. In an information environment like this, messages are essentially interchangeable, and no single message is that important or powerful. It is the *organization of the system*, and not the message, that holds the power. This is, for most people, however—and not just for the layman, but for scholars as well—a difficult concept to understand and even more difficult to accept. As Marshall McLuhan wrote in *Understanding Media*, "Political scientists have been quite unaware of the effects of media anywhere at any time, simply because nobody has been willing to study the personal and social effects of media apart from their 'content.'"[2] As a result of this culture-wide blind spot we tend to fall back on our understanding of propaganda as "messages we don't like."

So an unfortunate "natural" reaction to a book such as this is to say, simply, "It doesn't apply to me. I know propaganda when I see it. I don't need this book." Part of my task in writing it, then, is to persuade you that you do. I readily and willingly admit that this book is a straightforward work of *counterpropaganda*.

* * *

At its core, propaganda is about social control. It takes many forms, moves in many directions simultaneously, and is directed towards numerous ends. It may, for instance, be concerned with promoting and enforcing adherence to a particular set of values and standards of behavior, or it may be an attempt to subvert those values and standards and establish new social norms. It may be a celebration of unifying cultural myths, or it may present itself as an attempt to question the meaning of those myths, thereby diminishing their power. It may be a means of integrating new members of society (either immigrants or developing children) into the "legitimate" (i.e., dominant) culture, or it may be an attempt to delegitimize the dominant culture and to encourage the acceptance of "diversity"—diversity of language, customs, traditions, religions, etc., that have come to us from the outside. It may be focused on the control by a powerful elite of a weaker majority, or it may

2. McLuhan, *Understanding Media*, 281.

be concerned with weakening that control. And it may be concerned with spreading doubt, fear, and a sense of hopelessness in order to disengage the mass from the political process, or it may try to provide hope and a sense of·empowerment. Whatever the case, "good" or "bad," "white propaganda" or "Black propaganda," it is always in its essence an attempt to either establish and defend a certain order and uniformity in society, or destroy them and impose a new order, in the face of the natural diversity—of thought, of attitude, of behavior—of a mass of millions of *individual* human beings. Propaganda is a tool of social control, a technological extension of *the social contract,* and effective propaganda is power.

As Carl von Clausewitz once said, war is simply politics by other means. I maintain that if you look at the relationship between propaganda and politics, propaganda is simply war by other, nonviolent (or, perhaps, less physically violent) means. And it is a form of war that government uses not just on some foreign "enemy," but on its own civilian population as well. Abandoning rifles and mortars and bombs, the commanders and foot soldiers of propaganda wage a form of war on their own citizens. Their ultimate purpose is the (usually peaceful) subjugation of the populace, a bending of the people's will to the imperatives of government, society, or economics. There may be no physical violence involved, but a different kind of violence arguably occurs: the subsuming of the individual will into that of the mass, and the alienation of the person from the self. This is not necessarily new, at least in principle; but in a highly technologically developed mass society it occurs on a new and much larger scale: *the scale of the mass.*

Our world today is one of global digital connections, of a free and unrestricted multidirectional information flow, of the many directly connected to the many, the one to the one, the one to the many, and of the many to the one. The decentralized, distributed network, we were told, was meant to break down the oppressive centralized network with its maximum information control and empower us—individual people—by providing us with a wealth of diverse information; all the information we really need to make informed decisions in our lives. The internet, by its very nature, appeared to many as a democratic medium and democratic processes should have flourished under its reign. It was meant to allow us *to govern ourselves.* Its pioneers envisioned the internet itself as a new sort of social contract.

They may have been wrong. But they could still be right.

* * *

There's another circumstance I should mention regarding my reasons for writing this book, and I believe it is a testimony to the continuing incisiveness of Ellul's analysis of propaganda in the technological society. If Ellul's model is correct (as I believe it is), then the political upheaval we've been witnessing over the last few years—culminating, disturbingly, in the election of Donald J. Trump to the US presidency—is strikingly explicable by poring over the text of his *Propaganda*.

When independent US senator Bernie Sanders announced his candidacy for the presidency on April 29, 2015, a surprising number of Americans were flush with excitement. I was one of them. I had been paying attention to Bernie's career since the 1980s when he was the mayor of Burlington, Vermont—at the time, the only popularly elected Democratic Socialist public official in the United States. Like the millions of Americans who have since come to know him and hear him speak on issues of American social and economic justice, I admired him and what he was doing in Burlington. His tenure saw the rejuvenating and "greening" of a city that had suffered postindustrial blight. He encouraged the growth of "the commons," fought against the socially divisive effects of "gentrification," and demanded *not* that business should bear the cost of supporting a "socialist paradise," but that it should recognize its central role in the economic life of a *community* and act responsibly in that role.

So, yes, I was excited when Bernie announced his candidacy. But *never in a million years* did I expect that he might win. There was too much at stake in this highly technologically developed society for its owners and controllers to risk, and they were simply not going to let it happen. Still, I never expected that his candidacy would generate the kind of excitement—not only on the left, but even in significant portions of the populist right—that I observed as I watched the primary process over the next sixteen months. My politics has always been far to the left of the American center; but compared with the politics of many of the European nations I am little more than a solid centrist. Since the "Reagan revolution" of the 1980s, I had assumed I was alone in my political and economic views, and following the hostile takeover of the Democratic Party by the neoliberal Democratic Leadership Council and the subsequent election of Bill Clinton to the presidency, my assumption was bolstered. I began to think of myself as a radical, even though I didn't feel particularly radical. Bernie's candidacy opened my eyes to the fact that there are countless millions of people in the United States who have the same political, social, and economic ideas I have.

This is where Ellul comes into the picture, and this is one of the things that motivated me to write this book. I propose that the years between 1980 and 2008 marked a high point in the development and spread of Ellul's "technological society." Those (nearly) three decades saw the ascendancy of what Ellul calls "technique" to a position of unquestioned dominance. In the economic sphere, we witnessed the legitimation and spread of supply-side economic theory and the deregulation of business, first in the US, but soon globally. Government regulation of business, tampering as it does with the "invisible hand" of the free market, was inherently inefficient and had to stop. Markets govern themselves, and businesses must be allowed to succeed or fail on their own merit; this, of course, would have to include what we call "the labor market." Those who see free-market capitalism as a technique look at organized labor as an artificial, external, and alien attempt at regulation from outside the marketplace. This is an intolerable situation from the narrow perspective of capitalist technique. If you can work, you must work—for whatever wage your employer thinks appropriate. If you can't work, you're on your own. Welfare programs—another form of government interference in the market—are regressive, inefficient, discourage work, and create a "culture of dependency."

In the geopolitical sphere, we saw the collapse of Soviet Communism and the breakup of the Union of Soviet Socialist Republics into a "Commonwealth of Independent States." This had the dual effect of 1) "purifying," if you will, the technoculture by shifting the economy of nearly one-half billion people from a highly inefficient one (Communism) to an already efficient one, but one now rapidly increasing its efficiency (capitalism); and 2) freeing the technoculture from the last geopolitical impediment to expanding, unimpeded, to truly global proportions.

In the cultural sphere, we witnessed the rise of personal computing, the birth of the internet, the global proliferation of digital devices, the once unimaginable rapid movement of information—and capital—around the world, and the creation of an entirely new category of economic activity: e-commerce. We saw the beginning of "mash-up" culture, the weakening of copyright and intellectual property laws, personal, "on-demand" publishing, profit potential from viral videos, the rise of (or descent into) a "gig economy," and the growing dominance of "social media."

Following the fall of Communism, more or less simultaneous with the "digital revolution," we witnessed (once again in the economic sphere) the rise of a global "free market," nominally "regulated" by the World Trade Organization, the World Bank, and the International Monetary Fund; but regulated in a way that benefits the economic power of the technoculture rather than its people or the common good. We saw an increase in trade, an increase in global investment, but a decrease in any sort of barrier to efficiency in commerce that might exist in the form of national legislation; a global policy of deregulation enforced not by any democratically elected body, but by the owners and leaders of the technological society itself.

So, consequently, we also watched sweatshops exploit the developing world, where so many countries have little or no labor protections, environmental protections, worker safety protections, or minimum wage. We saw threats to labor as international free trade agreements allowed corporations to "outsource" jobs to the developing world. We watched the rise of income inequality as the incomes and net worth of the wealthiest 10 percent of most countries rose greatly, those of the upper 40 percent rose slightly, and those of the bottom half stayed the same—actually increasing poverty as the increased wealth at the top of the system drives commodity costs up for the entire population.

And we saw in those thirty years the proliferation of what is arguably the most potent response to—and natural consequence of—a mindset more focused on efficiency than on humanity: *terrorism.* On September 11, 2001, the entire world watched in breathless horror as three hijacked airliners destroyed the World Trade Center and damaged the Pentagon, and a fourth— likely heading toward the US Capitol—plummeted into a field in Shanksville, Pennsylvania. Americans, at that moment, were embraced by the global grief of six billion people, and the US government, in the abject misery of that same moment, had the opportunity to give a serious, reflective answer to the question on every American's lips: "Why do they hate us?"

We had a choice either to: 1) defend the integrity and efficiency of the technoculture, or 2) rethink the ends of economic activity, the role of government in the lives of its people, our relationship with the developing world, and then to change the way we do business. We chose technique, and that choice was authorized and endorsed by politicians of both of the major US parties, Republican *and* Democrat.

Our invasion of Afghanistan, misguided and ineffective as it was, and culminating in our recent abandonment of the country to the Taliban, was at least understandable given the circumstances of the moment. However, our invasion of Iraq, and its subsequent "reconstruction," was a cynical (and immoral) act of aggressive, violent economic opportunism. Even as an estimated 175,000[3] to 461,000[4] innocent Iraqi civilians died as a direct result of our invasion, the technoculture looked upon the Iraq War as an extraordinary opportunity for further expansion. All the inefficiencies of recent wars would be avoided, either secretly or through canny public relations: costly armor on troop carriers, military engineers and

3. "Iraq Body Count."
4. Hagopian et al., "Mortality In Iraq."

builders, logistical support for combat, detention of prisoners ("enemy combatants"), abiding by international law and treaties—all could be dealt with by outsourcing services to the private sector. All the inefficiencies of Ba'athist socialism and tight government control over resources would be wiped out in a matter of days, and the technoculture would be ready to declare Iraq "free"—and open for business.

The Bush administration stretched the US Constitution beyond its limits, virtually shredding it. No prisoner of war status for either combatants or noncombatants; no habeas corpus or due process; the outsourcing of transportation, engineering, and construction to private companies (Halliburton); the historically unprecedented use of private, corporate armies (Blackwater, Triple Canopy) in time of war, private interrogators and torturers (CACI and Titan), third-state "black site" detention centers, kidnapping (euphemistically called "extraordinary rendition"); all this and more, and more, and more, ad nauseam. And then the public spectacle of Abu Ghraib.

Support for the war dropped, President Bush's job approval rating plummeted from 90 percent immediately after 9/11 to the high 20–low 30 percent range in 2008, and there was no end to the war in sight, despite a rosy and much publicized pre-war "exit strategy" that had us leaving a functioning democracy behind us, and Iraqi civilians showering us with flowers as we boarded the plane.

Meanwhile at home, the deregulation of the financial industries under the neoliberal Clinton administration had set the stage for the biggest economic collapse in eighty years. A candidate for the presidency with the unlikely name (for American politics) of Barack Hussein Obama promised Americans "hope" and "change" and they believed him, perhaps out of desperation since millions of them lost their jobs, twenty million lost their homes, and thirty million Americans' homes were "underwater"—with a market value less than what was owed on their mortgage. This is the tableau upon which both Bernie Sanders's improbable candidacy and Donald Trump's even less probable—and tragically dangerous—presidency must be viewed in order to make sense.

Ellul's model of *effective* systematic total propaganda includes some necessary prerequisite conditions, of which, right now, I'll mention only three: 1) the need for an average standard of living, 2) the need for an average culture, and 3) the need for shared information.

One of the effects of the technological society's spectacular success and dominance over the last thirty years has been, ironically, to undo some of the conditions that ensure the effectiveness of propaganda. The average standard of living embodied in the American middle class has suffered in the last four decades. The median household income (adjusted for inflation) has effectively flatlined, even as more households have shifted from one- to two-paycheck families. Real unemployment (measuring those not reflected in the "official" rate—people who have still not found work when compensation ends) has risen, even in times of economic growth. Of those who are able to find work, more people are working two or more jobs than ever before just to make ends meet. Following the collapse of the investment and financial industries in 2008–2009, the official poverty rate was nearly 20 percent—as high as it had been since Lyndon Baines Johnson announced his "war on poverty" in 1964[5]—the very moment Ellul's *Propaganda* was published in English and introduced to an American audience.

As for the "average culture," Ellul notes that propaganda—particularly propaganda of integration—cannot work on those who are ignorant of the shared knowledge of the culture. Education is a fundamental necessity to effective propaganda. But look at our education system! It is a case study in ineffectiveness and failure. A far-too-large segment of the American population believe that both science and religion are equivalent and interchangeable worldviews. Only one in five Americans can enumerate all five rights protected by the first amendment—but more than 80 percent can name all five members of the Simpson cartoon family. The 2012 Texas GOP platform included a plank against the teaching of critical thinking in public schools! And those Americans who make it to college will most likely be attending a four-year, $120,000 vocational school, training for the workplace rather than expanding their understanding of the world. Most will live with that student loan debt for the rest of their lives.

And in the forty-some-odd years since Ronald Reagan took office, many Americans lost all respect for meaningful information and escaped into trivia. In fairness, the rise of the internet and social media illustrate the extent to which many Americans view information as a very subjective phenomenon. The web can be a solipsistic universe where we feel free to surround ourselves with only the bits of information that affirm our sense of self and support our worldview. It is fair even to ask precisely what we mean by information today, since one person's "fact" is another's "alternative fact," and one person's "news" is another's "fake news." Many blame "the media" for this loss of faith in the integrity of information; a 2016 Gallup poll showed that only 32 percent of Americans combined have either "a

---

5. Except that in 1965, 19 percent of the US population of 194 million people was nearly thirty-seven million, and 19 percent of our current population of 321 million people is nearly sixty-three million—a 60 percent increase in the *number* of Americans living in poverty.

great deal" or "a fair amount" of trust and confidence in the mass media that deliver information to them.[6]

The very fabric of American society appears to be in tatters. Not only in the alternative media, but a spate of articles and stories in mainstream media outlets like CNN, PBS, *USA Today*, *The Atlantic*, *The Washington Post*, *Fortune*, and many others have recently asked "Is the American Dream Dead?" (As one might expect, Rupert Murdoch's *New York Post* answered "Yeah, pretty much so.")[7] A study by researchers from Princeton University and Northwestern University concluded that the United States may no longer be a democracy and has taken on the characteristics of an oligarchy.[8] The American people are losing faith in the system and no longer trust its institutions. The propaganda that once held us all together is failing.

Seen in this light, and through the lens of Jacques Ellul's *Propaganda*, our current political situation appears far more understandable, and even predictable. Which makes one wonder whether someone, somewhere didn't see this all coming long before it happened. But to suggest that our current situation may not only have been anticipated, but perhaps even *planned*, is to mark yourself as a "conspiracy theorist." And our mainstream mass media are more than happy to do so if you think dangerous thoughts like that.

* * *

This book is organized in the following manner: we'll begin with the popular conception of propaganda and see how it differs from other persuasive techniques (e.g., rhetoric, coercion, etc.). We'll survey important moments in the history of propaganda and important thinkers who either excelled at the technique or thought deeply about it and shared those thoughts with the public. We'll begin as far back as the fourth century BC to understand why Aristotle's *Rhetoric* set the stage for two millennia of rhetorical criticism focusing on messages (and how they're delivered). This roughly two-thousand-year period is what I'll be referring to as propaganda 1.0.

We'll then look at what I call propaganda 2.0, the era of an uncontrolled explosion of information that followed the development of moveable-type printing and culminated in (among many other things) the Protestant Reformation and the Catholic Counter-Reformation. It is here, in the Vatican's establishment, in 1622, of the *Sacra Congregatio de Propaganda Fide* (Sacred Congregation for the Propagation of the Faith) that we find the roots

6. Gallup, "Americans' Trust in Mass Media Sinks to New Low."

7. Perez, "'American Dream' Is Pretty Much Dead."

8. Gilens and Page, "Testing Theories of American Politics."

of modern propaganda, where we need to look in order to understand how propaganda got the bad name it deservedly bears, and why, for nearly half a millennium, we rarely recognized propaganda except when associated with religious controversy. And we'll also take note of the fact that in this early era of actual, unquestionable propaganda, the primary analytical tool for understanding its impact remained rhetorical criticism.

In the second part of the book we'll move on to the twentieth century to observe the first changes in systematic thinking about propaganda prompted by the First World War. We'll survey the ideas of a number of propaganda theorists and practitioners, including George Creel, Harold Laswell, Edward Bernays, Walter Lippmann, Edward Filene, and others. In the middle of that century the focus in propaganda studies began to shift from messages to *control of information movement*. We'll also take a simultaneous and I believe significant look at one of the schools of thought in the ascendance at the same moment in order to consider what effect it might have had on the focal shift from message to information movement: systems theories. Systems theory is an interdisciplinary field concerned with the structure and function of complex systems, whether biological (e.g., the human body, the environment), mechanical (machines, computers), human (human societies, governments, markets, etc.), or cybernetic (human/machine systems). All properly functioning systems, no matter what their origin, share a number of characteristics including a purpose or goal, internal interdependence, self-regulation, and an internal tendency to both resist change (homeostasis) and to adapt to external demands in order to pursue its goals (adaptation). We'll examine the ideas of several thinkers who, whether they went by the label or not, I consider to be examples of systems thinkers, including Norbert Weiner, Claude Shannon, and Warren Weaver. It is in this era, and arguably under the influence of the rise of systems thinking, that we begin to recognize propaganda 2.0, of which Ellul's model is the most elaborately and meticulously articulated. It is Ellul's model that demands we rethink the popular conception of what constitutes propaganda.

Having established the foundations of propaganda 2.0, we will then briefly review Ellul's thoughts on propaganda, applying his ideas to contemporary cases, and making judgments about the continuing validity of his thoughts and theoretical model.

In the third section we'll proceed to a place Ellul only approached and never entered: propaganda 2.1—the world of freely flowing, multidirectional digital information and digital propaganda—where we're not only passive receivers of information, but we're (potential) creators and distributors as well; where we're all not only the objects of propaganda, but also its subjects—and see whether his thoughts on propaganda remain well-founded and credible. Propaganda 2.1 is the "post-truth" world in its fullness, with alternative facts being churned out on a second-by-second basis across the globe and dumped into the info pump for *everyone's* consumption. But it is also a world of infinite potential for learning new information unavailable within the confines of the mass culture of propaganda 2.0—if one only has the courage to confront and criticize it.

Chapter 1

Propaganda 1.0

————————————— Rhetoric, Persuasion, and Propaganda

What, exactly, is propaganda, and how does it differ from—and relate to—what we might think of as "ordinary" persuasion? This should not be as difficult a question to answer as it actually is. How we answer the question is, perhaps, more an indication of our own assumptions about the phenomenon of propaganda than of its actual characteristics. The difficulty comes from a certain conceptual clouding brought on by the historical circumstances of propaganda and its relationship with persuasion. It is a word fraught with emotional consequence.

The average person, when thinking about the relationship between persuasion and propaganda, usually comes up with a checklist of more or less reliable distinguishing features based on perception and common sense:

- We generally think of persuasion in a neutral, nonthreatening way. We might easily be persuaded by friends, for instance, about certain ideas and reserve the right to persuade others about our own ideas.

- We tend to think of propaganda in a more threatening way, as a form of manipulation or "brainwashing."

- We think of persuasion as an interpersonal activity that takes place within a context of human relationships.

- We think of propaganda as an anonymous activity, set apart from interpersonal interactions, by some sort of a conspiracy of the powerful over the weak.

- We think of persuasion as being based on trust—you can be persuaded by a friend because you know them and their character; you trust their word.

- We tend to think of propaganda, however, in terms of lies; propaganda is lies and the propagandist is a liar, a manipulator, and not to be trusted.

- We think of persuasion as being moderated by reason; even a friend can't persuade us of something if we believe truly that it is wrong.

- But we think of propaganda as a fundamentally irrational phenomenon, and our ability to reason and discern truth from falsehood protects us from vulnerability.

In short, we tend to see persuasion as good (or at worst neutral), and propaganda as bad. There appears to be a mutuality to persuasion that propaganda seems to lack. The person subjected to propaganda is considered a victim rather than a participant (in today's parlance, a "tool"); or if he is, in fact, participating, then he or she must certainly also be a dupe (or a "bot"). In each case, we are wrong—at least partially. Both persuasion and propaganda can be based on either truth or falsehood. The mutuality that exists in persuasion actually has a counterpoint in propaganda; we need propaganda and often seek it out, because propaganda helps us to make sense of the world in which we live. We also need it and seek it out because it rationalizes our own sense of reality. In each case, however, we simply fail to recognize it or categorize it as propaganda.

Moreover, while there is certainly an element of rhetoric involved in propaganda (because there are elements of both language and persuasion), rhetoric, properly understood, can never be propaganda. There is a final structural, categorical difference between the two that very few people recognize, which makes it all the more important that we acknowledge: rhetoric is always an interpersonal or group phenomenon; propaganda—in order to *be* propaganda at all—is always found on the level of the *mass*. Propaganda is *mass persuasion*.

From the moment that Gutenberg retooled his wine press to print letters on paper, we've been living in an environment of propaganda. It didn't matter whether you were printing Bibles or devotional works, or tracts criticizing the Pope and the Church's sale of indulgences; it was propaganda, because the mass-produced printed text could move more quickly and spread more widely than either the spoken or the handwritten word. Print delivered messages to hundreds of people in a single day, thousands in a week, and millions in a matter of months. And the precise content of the messages was of very little importance; once you find yourself in an environment of millions of people, all repeating the same message, the enormous power of that experience can certainly have a profoundly persuasive effect on you.

And so our misunderstanding of rhetoric and persuasion, and our commonplace attitudes about propaganda—especially our belief in our own power to resist it—can be very dangerous and can actually increase both our susceptibility to propaganda and its effectiveness as a tool for social control. Let's look a bit closer at the relationships between rhetoric, persuasion, and propaganda to place them in their proper historical contexts in an attempt to see more closely both their similarities and their differences.

Persuasion and Rhetoric

Persuasion is virtually as old as our species. It was a necessary art to develop for human beings interacting peacefully in cooperative social, economic, and political environments. It is, in a sense, an implicit part of any social contract, a constant negotiation over, and compromise of, individual rights for the benefit of the common good. In the absence of such a social contract ensuring cooperative social structures and peaceful methods of persuasion, human beings will fall back into the default "state of nature" and focus on self-interest and, perhaps, resort to violence.

However, not all social contracts are equal: some may apportion more power to the mass of the populace than to whatever governmental or regulatory structures arise as a result of the contract; others may assume that power must be apportioned to those in the society who have shown the qualities of leadership. Persuasion, then, is simply implicit in the social contract of any society. The explicit social contract, however, will likely have a profound influence on the types of persuasive measures used and how they are used.

The state, to the extent that such a construct exists in any given society, needs to maintain its social order, and so will always be walking a tightrope between gentle persuasion and violent coercion. With the rise of democratic forms of government in fifth century (BC) Greece, rhetoric, the art of per-suasive language, became central to the social processes of law and politics. Citizens needed to become public speakers who understood the demands of self-government, so that they might formulate proposals to persuade their fellow citizens—and their ruler. The art of speaking persuasively was imperative to citizenship, as well as to grasping onto opportunities to rise to positions of leadership in government and the law.

Some of the earliest practitioners of rhetoric were the Sophists. Soph-ism arose more or less simultaneously with philosophy in general. The Soph-ists were itinerant teachers of young gentry, the children of political and business leaders, who took payment for their services. They taught many subjects including mathematics, grammar, music, and rhetoric. Their main goal was the development of excellence or virtue (*arete*) in their students.

It was in the nature of sophism to be more concerned with appearance than with reality; eloquence and force of personality outweighed facts and logical consistency. Sophists tended to be relativistic in their thinking and taught their students to be skeptical about universal truths. But some were more nihilist than relativist, more cynical than skeptical.

The Sophist Gorgias (c. 483–375 BC) was an early practitioner and teacher of rhetoric. Gorgias considered rhetoric to be a means to an end desirable to the speaker—nothing more than a technique of persuasion. He saw his job as a rhetor as limited to persuading an audience on behalf of his cause, or that of his patrons or benefactors; and as a teacher to making his pupils skillful in the arts of persuasion without regard to the truth or falsehood of their arguments. His students should be prepared, he believed, to speak on any proposition, arguing either for or against it. The rhetor's goal, Gorgias insisted, was always to provoke a particular belief in an audience, not to find, promote, or spread truth. As a consequence, he was more concerned with style than substance, with efficiency rather than principle, with means rather than ends.

In the Platonic dialogue *The Gorgias*, Socrates questions Gorgias and Polus on the nature of rhetoric. In due course, he paints Gorgias into a corner, suggesting that there is no need for rhetoricians to have any real knowledge of the things of which they speak, "but it is enough for them to have discovered some instrument of persuasion which may enable them to present the appearance to the ignorant of knowing better than the well informed."[1] To which Gorgias replies, "Well and isn't it a great comfort, Socrates, without learning any of the other arts, but with this one alone, to be at no disadvantage in comparison with the professional people?"[2]

After voicing some aggravation with Socrates's annoying questioning, they press him in return for his opinion. "It seems to me then, Gorgias," Socrates responds, subtly but clearly damning the "art" of rhetoric, "to be a sort of pursuit not scientific at all, but of a shrewd and bold spirit, quick and clever in its dealings with the world. And the sum and substance of it I call flattery,"[3] an unctuous appeal to the vanities and emotions of the listener. Furthermore, he bemoans the use of such flattery "whether it be applied to body or soul or anything else, when the pleasure alone is studied without any

---

1. Plato, *Plato's Gorgias*, 20.

2. Plato, *Plato's Gorgias*, 20.

3. Plato, *Plato's Gorgias*, 27.

regard to the better and the worse,"[4] in other words, when one's goal is persuasion for its own sake without regard to moral or ethical judgments.

To be sure, not all rhetoric is *sophistry*, the type of rhetoric that Socrates refers to as flattery. Some rhetoric genuinely informs; that is to say it provides a foundation of knowledge based on demonstrable fact. Some rhetoric, however, appeals to prejudged belief, which itself may be either true or false. Early rhetoricians understood that if there was a "science" of rhetoric, it must consist of persuasive speech on many subjects, in not all of which the rhetor can claim expertise. Plato was, perhaps, being too harsh on rhetoric in general, and on the Sophists in particular, but there is no question that many Sophists were irresponsible in their use of persuasive speech.

The first systematic guide to the art of rhetoric was Aristotle's (384–322 BC). It categorized the distinct types of rhetoric that existed in the increasingly self-governed Greek life: *forensic rhetoric*, which dominated the courts of law; *deliberative rhetoric*, the oratory of the public assembly and lawmaking; and *epideictic rhetoric*, the oratory of praise and blame derided by Socrates as flattery. The systematic nature of Aristotle's *Rhetoric* is also evident in the analysis of *proofs* earlier rhetoricians had overlooked.

Aristotle defined rhetoric as "the faculty of discovering the possible means of persuasion in reference to any subject whatever."[5] It is the counterpart of dialectic, the art of logical discussion so valued by Socrates. Like Plato's, Aristotle's concern with rhetoric was psychological; it was a study of the many ways of influencing thought. It would be nice to think that Aristotle wished to provide a guide to influencing thought through the use of reason, which is at least partly true; but in the final analysis *The Rhetoric* provides instructions not only for reasoned argument, but for the manipulation of emotions as well.

The core of Aristotle's theory of rhetoric is syllogistic logic. The *enthymeme* is a sort of syllogism that omits at least one of the premises we would expect to find in a formal syllogism. The enthymeme is useful for at least two reasons: its terseness and its resemblance to informal, idiomatic speech. But there may be a third reason for the effectiveness of an enthymeme: in omitting one of the premises, a statement can easily be overgeneralized, giving the impression that it applies to a case for which it is not genuinely appropriate; it can function as innuendo. A speaker well-versed in syllogistic logic ought to easily gain skill in the use of enthymemes.

Along with exemplification, the enthymeme is the heart of what Aristotle called the proofs of a rhetorical argument, of which there are two

---

4. Plato, *Plato's Gorgias*, 93.

5. Aristotle, *"Art" of Rhetoric*, 15.

types: the *artificial* proof and the *inartificial* proof. Inartificial proofs are "all those which have not been furnished by ourselves but were already in existence, such as witnesses, tortures, contracts, and the like"[6]—in other words, what we might consider today to be documentary evidence—*facts.* By contrast, artificial proofs are the speaker's inventions, "all that can be constructed by system and by our own efforts."[7]

Aristotle described two major categories of artificial proofs: 1) the *enthymeme* (already discussed), and 2) the *example.* While enthymemes, being a type of syllogism, start from universal principles to deduce particular inferences, examples move in the opposite direction: they begin with specific facts or data in order to induce broad inferences. For example, in the classical syllogism, a) all men are mortal, b) Socrates is a man; therefore, c) Socrates is mortal, we move from the universal principle to the particular premise to deduce that Socrates will someday die. By contrast, the example would move in this direction: a) John was a heavy smoker, b) John died very young, therefore, c) Bill, who smokes heavily, is likely to die young; a conclusion which is of course possible but by no means certain. Not every heavy smoker dies at an early age even if his eventual death is smoking-related. The logical flow—and the logical flaw—is the movement from the particular example to an induced universal principle.

Aristotle presumed the enthymeme to possess the greater persuasive power of the two categories of inartificial proofs, as it is more likely to deduce reasonable and convincing conclusions from widely shared and accepted facts. But in moving from individual examples to broad generalizations there is a greater possibility that the speaker will make an unpersuasive case, or that the audience will resist coming to the specific conclusion the speaker desires. So while Aristotle, sharing Plato's disdain of sophistry, continued to insist that reason reign in persuasive speech, he conceded that there was a particular power to the *performance* of rhetoric and that this, in fact, had to be taken into account in any systematic model of rhetoric.

> [S]ince the whole business of Rhetoric is to influence opinion, we must pay attention to [performance], not as being right, but necessary; for . . . as we have just said, it is of great importance owing to the corruption of the hearer.[8]

Aristotle then identified and explained what he saw to be three dimensions of performance: the *logos,* the *ethos,* and the *pathos.* The logos is

6. Aristotle, *"Art" of Rhetoric,* 15.

7. Aristotle, *"Art" of Rhetoric,* 15.

8. Aristotle, *"Art" of Rhetoric,* 347.

the logical appeal of a rhetorical argument as judged by the quality of its reasoning, its evidentiary support, and its formal consistency. A speaker appeals to the logos when there is, simply speaking, a good, cogent, and logical argument to be made, and when the speaker can depend on the reasoning capabilities of the audience thereby making such an appeal useful. But, as Aristotle suggested, the rhetor can't always depend on the reasoning capabilities of the audience, owing to their weaknesses.

But the speaker can appeal to the *ethos* of the audience—the shared values, beliefs, attitudes, and assumptions of a group. These values, beliefs, attitudes, etc., may be noble or vulgar; the speaker must embrace them, either way. The point is to make the audience believe that the speaker shares their values, that they see the speaker as sympathetic and trustworthy. And since the goal of the speaker is to persuade (and not to be noble or to affirm the truth) this is not necessarily an obstacle to achieving the desired end.

If an appeal to either the logos or the ethos appears to be unproductive, the speaker has at least one more option, and can always make an appeal to the *pathos* of the audience, exploiting the audience's emotions. The choice of words, the tone of voice, the wringing of hands, the gestures, the postures, the facial expressions—all of these can have a powerful impact on an audience and can make the difference between a successful appeal and a failure.

In the final analysis the point of rhetoric is to persuade an audience. And here we must recognize one more factor that Aristotle makes note of to which persuasive speakers can avail themselves: the *kairos*. The Greeks had two conceptions of time; one was *chronos*, which is more or less how we think about the linear, progressive movement of time today. The other, however, was *kairos*, which essentially focuses on the idea of time as a fickle friend or unpredictable foe, as a door opening or closing. Time is in constant motion, as the ocean tides ebb and flow and waves either crash upon the shore or roll in gently. One person wishing to collect shellfish washed upon the shore will surely wait for low tide to do so; another wishing to surf will wait for a higher tide and a rougher sea. *Kairos* is the conception of time as movement and the goal-oriented person will pay attention to "the signs of the times" to know when to act; what we might today think of as "the opportune moment." The skilled rhetor knows when to moderate a message and when to cast off restraints and stroke, charm, or even cajole and incite an audience.

Aristotle's *Rhetoric* laid the groundwork for all our thinking about persuasion for the next two thousand years and, indeed, his model remains an important foundation for the analysis and criticism of persuasive messages even today. Yet rhetorical criticism, as applicable to understanding persuasion as it remains, is limited and insufficient in dealing with propaganda, because propaganda consists of more than mere messages. Two millennia after Aristotle, an event took place that would usher in a different form of persuasion and persuasive techniques and function as the foundation of a new social phenomenon that we call *propaganda*. The invention of printing in the middle of the fifteenth century made it possible to deliver messages to a *mass audience* of thousands or tens of thousands (and eventually many millions), a fact which would inevitably come to be recognized as of singular importance, effectively outweighing the power of logos, ethos, pathos, and persuasive speech. With the invention of moveable-type printing the *mass medium* was born and, although it would take another half millennium for students of communication to recognize and then to understand it, the still-hazy boundaries of propaganda 2.0 were coming into view.

The Printing Press and the Rise of Propaganda

Johannes Gutenberg (c. 1399–1468) actually had no idea what he was doing when he established his printing shop in Mainz, Germany, somewhere in the middle of the fifteenth century. His system of reusable, moveable types was certainly innovative and even genius—even though others across Europe seem to have been engaged in similar experiments with "artificial script." Saul Steinberg notes that "Avignon, Bruges, and Bologna are mentioned as places where such experiments were carried out," and that the "general climate of the age was undoubtedly propitious for Gutenberg's achievement."[9] But if Gutenberg was the first person to successfully cast durable and reusable types out of lead, antimony, and tin, the first to develop and use an oil-based ink, and the first to use the "piston and platen" techniques to press fonts to paper, it is still fair to say that he was not a natural businessman and lacked the vision to recognize the significance and potential of his invention.

In the first place, he seemed to think about the printing press as a sort of "mechanical scribe" that would replicate the work of the monastic clerics, making them redundant and, ultimately, obsolete. It is not merely coincidental that the first dated printed product traceable to Gutenberg's workshop was an indulgence printed for the Church,[10] or that his best-known work is the forty-two-line Bible—the so-called Gutenberg Bible. In fact, there is little evidence that he did any work of a private or public nature, and up until the time of Gutenberg the Roman Catholic Church, its monasteries, and scribes controlled a virtual monopoly over the very limited production and even more limited distribution of information in Europe.

9. Steinberg and Trevitt, *Five Hundred Years of Printing*, 4.

10. Eisenstein, *Printing Press as an Agent of Change*, 375.

Gutenberg was simply unable to anticipate the threat to that monopoly—or the opportunity to make money—his press represented.

Gutenberg was unable to see that he was not only a printer, but an *entrepreneur*; the first of a new breed of businessmen, one engaged in the mass production and distribution of information. He was unable to think as an entrepreneur would think and unnecessarily limited the types of information he would produce and sell. In 1455 his partner and financier Johannes Fust foreclosed on the loan of 1,600 guilders he had given to Gutenberg some years earlier, effectively bankrupting him and taking control of the press and half of all the forty-two-line Bibles he had produced. Gutenberg died nearly penniless, living on a pension provided to him by the Archbishop of Mainz.

Peter Schoeffer, Gutenberg's erstwhile assistant, gained control over Gutenberg's shop, press, and business. He did not fail as a businessman, nor did the thousands of other printers who set up shop across Europe in Gutenberg's wake. Like any other manufacturing business, the burgeoning printing industry faced market-based obstacles that needed to be surmounted in order to achieve success. First, the printer needed to find capital to set up shop. Second, he needed to be attuned to the needs and desires of the market; there had to be a demand for the product. Third, he needed to manufacture his product as inexpensively as possible. Fourth, the printer needed to be flexible; in a market glutted with a particular commodity, he needed to constantly produce new products.

But the printing industry differed from other manufacturing businesses in significant and advantageous ways. In one sense, a book is the product of the printing industry. In its physical form, every book is similar to every other book—it has pages, it has a binding, the pages are imprinted with ink, etc. But in another sense, it is not the book that is the commodity, it is *the content*. Information was now a saleable commodity. For the printer, the process of retooling so necessary in industry when switching from the manufacture of one product to that of another consisted not of redesigning machines, cutting new jigs, dismantling and rebuilding block, tackle, pulley, and crane, but simply of resetting the type for one book in order to print another. This was both a powerful facilitator and a motivation for the printer not only to be looking constantly for new material to publish, but looking for content that an audience *would want to buy and read*. In the early era of print this was an easy task; a growing market of readers was hungry for anything new. Lewis Mumford tells us that by the end of the fifteenth century "there were over a thousand public printing presses in Germany alone, to say nothing of those in monasteries and castles; and the art had spread rapidly, despite all attempts at secrecy and monopoly, to

Venice, Florence, Paris, London, Lyons, Leipzig, and Frankfort-am-Main"[11] and "in Nurnberg a large printing business with twenty-four presses and a hundred employees—typesetters, printers, correctors, binders"[12]—had been established. The fifteenth century ushered in an "information revolution" unlike any seen in earlier human history.

The changes wrought on Europe by this new medium were profound. During the *incunabula* (the first fifty years of the era of print) the vast majority of books were printed in Latin. Almost all early printed books resembled the manuscripts they were replacing; fonts were forged to look like the Carolingian or Gothic calligraphy of the clerical scribes. The vast majority were religious books—Bibles, devotional works, the writings of Augustine, the mystical writings of Thomas á Kempis, of Francis of Assisi, of Catherine of Siena, and others. And the vast majority of *readers* were those who were literate before the development of print—the clergy, the government (monarch, nobility, and their bureaucracy), the wealthy courtiers with disposable income and time on their hands.

By the sixteenth century, however, this began to change, and change dramatically. The steady spread of printing in the vernacular weakened the position of Latin as the language of the educated, and encouraged the growth of national literatures.[13] New fonts were designed and forged that were easier to read. The classics were rediscovered—the philosophy, poetry, fables, and drama of the Greeks; Virgil, Ovid, Juvenal, and Cicero from ancient Rome. New genres of literature were created: the chivalric romances, the *chansons de geste*, scientific or other scholarly treatises, reference books, works of political and moral philosophy, and, eventually, the novel. And a readership grew among that part of the "peasantry" that was, at the same moment, emerging from the ashes of feudal subsistence and poverty, engaged not in agriculture or husbandry, but in providing services to the wealthy in pottery, coopering, blacksmithing, carpentry, and merchandizing. This growth in reading was aided by both the rise of itinerant teachers and the explosive abundance of reading material made possible by the press.

Other, more subtle changes, barely (if at all) visible to even the most astute observer, but profound in their social and cultural implications, accompanied the swift rise of printing and the growth of literacy, changes critical in understanding the role of printing in the rise of propaganda. Literacy, for example, displaced orality as the dominant epistemology, weakening the power of rhetoric and encouraging more critical thought about messages.

11. Mumford, *Technics and Civilization*, 135.

12. Mumford, *Technics and Civilization*, 136.

13. Febvre et al., *Coming of the Book*, 262.

Mumford noted that print "frees communication from the restrictions of time and space and makes discourse wait on the convenience of the reader—who can interrupt the flow of thought or repeat it or concentrate on isolated parts of it."[14] The printed word, he continued, "furthered that process of analysis and isolation which became the leading achievement"[15] of the modern age. The rise of literacy, Walter Ong taught us, restructured consciousness, weakening the hold of speech by aiding our rejection of "the old oral, mobile, warm, personally interactive lifeworld of oral culture";[16] by shifting our dependence on memory to written records in preserving the past;[17] by putting an objective distance between the knower and the thing known;[18] by changing the human sensory balance from ear dominance to eye dominance;[19] and by bringing on an expanded interior life impossible without the act of reading. The printing press, Ong wrote, "is important in the history of the word not merely exteriorly, as a kind of circulator of pre-existing materials, but interiorly, for it transforms what can be said and what is said. Since writing came into existence, the evolution of the word and the evolution of consciousness have been intimately tied in with technologies and technological development. Indeed, all major advances in consciousness depend on technological transformations and implementations of the word."[20] Neil Postman further explained that "[a] new technology does not add or subtract something. It changes everything. In the year 1500, fifty years after the printing press was invented, we did not have old Europe plus the printing press. We had a different Europe."[21]

To say that printing amplified the flow of information, however, as true as it may be, is to miss the crucial point that not all information is equal. For one thing, the fundamental human conception of what constituted information changed. The rapid movement of new, commodified information created an appetite for the constantly changing and novel; old forms of information—Scripture, tradition, folk wisdom, proverbial knowledge—began to recede into the shadows of the new. European culture became more and more dynamic and open to new (some thought dangerous) ideas and change. For another thing, information was no longer

---

14. Mumford, *Technics and Civilization*, 136.

15. Mumford, *Technics and Civilization*, 136.

16. Ong, *Orality and Literacy*, 80.

17. Ong, *Orality and Literacy*, 96.

18. Ong, *Orality and Literacy*, 105.

19. Ong, *Orality and Literacy*, 117.

20. Ong, *Orality and Literacy*, 42.

21. Postman, *Technopoly*, 18.

being controlled by powerful authority figures (like the Church), but by a free market. There soon arose a stigma which attached itself to the printed book as well as to the printer, who was seen by some as an avaricious businessman desperate to put anything into print that might make a profit. "It was already apparent," Elizabeth Eisenstein wrote, "that printers would be more likely to profit from the popular appetite for sexually titillating stuff than from serving the needs of austere scholars and ascetic monks."[22] She added that "there was not only a discourse of praise for Gutenberg's invention but also a discourse of resistance" welling up from "aristocrats, scholars, the erudite" who "believed that print culture was commercial" and that "the printing process was corruptive."[23]

Martin Luther and Reformation

On November 10, 1483, in the town of Eisleben in that part of the Holy Roman Empire we now call Germany, Martin Luther was born to Hans and Margarethe (Lindemann) Luder. Luther was part of a new generation of Europeans, one nurtured and intellectually sustained by printed words. His education brought him into contact with the Latin language, the writings of the Scholastics, of Aristotle (whose emphatic defense of reason he came to detest), and of William of Occam. His teachers taught him to be skeptical of authority, of men "who might give the impression of being certain about assertions and claims when they were not or had no reason to be."[24] In 1501 he entered the University of Erfurt and received the baccalaureate degree the next year. He then continued at Erfurt in pursuit of a doctorate in law. In July of 1505, Luther temporarily abandoned his studies and entered the Augustinian monastery in Erfurt. He was ordained in 1507.

When Luther returned later that year to the university, it was to pursue a doctorate not in law (as his father insisted), but in theology. He transferred to the Augustinian community at Wittenberg in 1508, and continued his work at the university there, finishing his baccalaureate in Scripture in just a year. His further scholarly activities were interrupted by an assignment to Rome, but on returning to Wittenberg he resumed his studies and received his doctorate in theology in 1512, finally assuming the professorship in biblical studies at the University of Wittenberg, a position he held for the rest of his career.

22. Eisenstein, *Divine Art, Infernal Machine*, 28.

23. Eisenstein, *Divine Art, Infernal Machine*, 32.

24. Marty, *Martin Luther*, 4.

Luther was a difficult person, a headstrong man in vain pursuit of certainty. His was a theology of paradox; the Christian was, simultaneously, saint and sinner. Christianity was at the same time a religion of glory and of suffering. And Luther himself, a profoundly rational thinker, felt forced to turn his back on reason as an enemy of faith. As Karl Jaspers has told us, "To study [Luther] is indispensable."

> He is a theological thinker who despises philosophy, speaks of the whore reason, yet he himself thought out the basic existential ideas without which present philosophy would scarcely be possible. The combination of passionate seriousness of faith and of opportunistic shrewdness, of depth and hatred, of brilliant penetration and coarse bluster make it a duty, almost a torment to study him. This man gives forth a profoundly antiphilosophical atmosphere.[25]

In October 1517 Luther nailed his Ninety-Five Theses to the door of the Castle Church in Wittenberg. This was a list of propositions for debate over the issue of the Catholic Church's selling of indulgences. This was no revolutionary act; Luther had the right as a doctor of theology to invite other theologians to debate controversial issues. What made this event singular not only in the history of the Church, but in the history of European culture, was the fact that somehow a copy of the Ninety-Five Theses was printed and distributed. Copies spread rapidly and were multiplied in other cities that had presses. Luther claimed to have no idea how this happened, but historians suspect he at least knew about the possibility of its being printed and tacitly agreed to it. If that is the case, then Luther not only sparked a reformation in the church, but may also have engaged in the first act of press agentry in history.

Copies of Luther's theses spread like shrapnel from an explosive shell across the face of Christendom. Few other individual statements, messages, or pieces of information in human history had ever before spread as widely and as quickly as did Luther's theses. In December 1517 "three separate editions were printed almost simultaneously in three separate towns."[26] As medievalist and ecclesiastical historian Margaret Aston wrote,

> The theses . . . were said to be known throughout Germany in a fortnight and throughout Europe in a month . . . Printing was recognized as a new power and publicity came into its own. In doing for Luther what the copyists had done for Wycliffe, the

---

25. Jaspers, *Way to Wisdom*, 182–83.
26. Eisenstein, *Printing Press as an Agent of Change*, 307.

printing presses transformed the field of communications and fathered an international revolt. It was a revolution.[27]

The Lutheran controversy became fodder for a hungry audience. When Holy Roman Emperor Charles V issued an edict banning Luther's writings and calling for his books to be burned, it only increased the public's desire to buy and read them.[28] "[Luther] became at one stroke a figure of national fame," Steinberg tells us, "and the small Wittenberg press of Hans Lufft suddenly gained a place among the biggest firms. Thirty editions of Luther's *Sermon on Indulgences* and 21 editions of his *Sermon on the Right Preparation of the Heart*—authorized and pirated—poured from the presses within two years (1518–1520). Over 4,000 copies of his address *To the Christian Nobility* were sold within five days in 1520."[29] "Between 1517 and 1520, Luther's thirty publications probably sold well over 300,000 copies . . . Lutheranism was from the first the child of the printed book, and through this vehicle Luther was able to make exact, standardized, and ineradicable impressions on the mind of Europe."[30] Before the printing press, the very idea of a uniform and measurable public opinion was unthinkable and irrelevant. Now, with the rapid and widespread dissemination of information in the vernacular of the people, the idea of "the public" began to develop in earnest.

The Protestant movement represented a grave threat to the Church's claim to universal apostolic legitimacy. The Church was quick to respond, but did so at first clumsily and in small, ineffectual increments. Pope Leo X issued a papal bull, *Exsurge Domine* ("Arise, O Lord"), in 1520, condemning the Ninety-Five Theses and other writings and calling on Luther to recant them at threat of excommunication. Luther refused and instead published a series of anti-papal polemical tracts. In 1521 Holy Roman Emperor Charles V convened the Diet of Worms, essentially trying Luther for heresy, and culminating in the Edict of Worms, which declared him a heretic and ordered his arrest. Luther then spent several years in the protection of his supporter Prince Frederick at Wartburg Castle, where he continued to flout Church authority by translating the Bible into German for publication.

Later responses were, perhaps, more sweeping but ultimately powerless to arrest the progressive spread of new and "dangerous" ideas flowing through Europe. Pope Paul IV instituted the *Index Librorum Prohibitorum* in 1559, which forbade Catholics from reading books on the list. And, of course, in the seventeenth century the Church finally established its "Sacred

27. Aston, *Fifteenth Century*, 76.

28. Febvre et al., *Coming of the Book*, 290.

29. Steinberg and Trevitt, *Five Hundred Years of Printing*, 64–65.

30. Dickens, *Reformation and Society*, 51.

Congregation" for propaganda with its own printing office "well armed with fonts in a vast variety of exotic languages"[31] that produced counterpropaganda in the form of books and pamphlets meant not only to defend the Church and reinforce Catholic doctrine, but equally importantly, to check the spread of Protestantism. These measures, both early and later, were originally intended as a response to Protestant heresy and schism, but as the printed book embedded itself more and more deeply into the newly literate European mind, they were also directed against scientists like Galileo, Francis Bacon, and Nicholas Copernicus; jurists like Hugo Grotius; philosophers like Rene Descartes and Thomas Hobbes; and poets like John Milton.

The Phenomenon of Propaganda

The Sacred Congregation for the Propagation of the Faith developed during two distinct periods, the first between 1572 and 1622 before it became a distinct pontifical office; the second after 1622 when the *Sacra Congregatio de Propaganda Fide* was formally instituted. It is directly from the name of this office that we derive our word *propaganda*. However, the phenomenon of propaganda began with *the establishment of printing itself* and not with the creation of a pontifical office. Propaganda is the mass publication of *any information* without regard to its truth or its falsehood, its provenance, or its intrinsic value. The publication of Luther's Ninety-Five Theses and his later works were all acts of propaganda, and the Church's eventual response—to print its own polemical literature countering Luther's "heresies"—were acts of counterpropaganda.

Luther's Protestant Reformation was the first social movement to capitalize fully on the printing press's power as a mass medium. And, as Eisenstein noted, the Reformation also constituted "the first movement of any kind, religious or secular, to use the new presses for overt propaganda and agitation against an established institution."[32] Over the next century, not only the Church but civil governments as well would come to understand the power of, in Eisenstein's phrase, "the printing press as an agent of change." They feared the messages the press might deliver, but they also understood—at least intuitively—that the instrument itself had power, without regard to whatever information might be flowing through it. It was better to control it and use it than to let others control it and remain helpless against it.

The inherent power of the printing press to dramatically increase both the amount of information available to a public and the speed at which that public receives it represents the seismic shift from propaganda 1.0 to

31. Eisenstein, *Divine Art, Infernal Machine*, 48.
32. Eisenstein, *Printing Press as an Agent of Change*, 304.

propaganda 2.0. Propaganda 2.0 occurs through the sheer power of a mass medium to make an argument (or a message, or a simple idea, or an image) appear ubiquitous and timely. The ubiquity of an idea gives it the status of a shared reality; its timeliness gives it the urgency of a perishable commodity, available for use today, possibly gone tomorrow—a powerful motivating factor in a society transitioning from a long tradition of feudalism to burgeoning capitalism. But even with an undeveloped and intuitive understanding of a mass medium's power, the focus of attention remained on the message, and the word *propaganda* remained associated with religious controversy and proselytization. And so it would remain for the next five hundred years.

It's not until the twentieth century and the rise of electronic mass media of communication, especially radio and television, that scholars, theorists, and researchers from a number of diverse fields begin to take note of the mass media themselves and their intrinsic power as agents in the "social construction of reality." Despite the half millennium *de facto* presence of propaganda 2.0 in human affairs, it is only the twentieth century that reveals this to be the moment of its florescent maturity, as we begin to live lives of virtually total mediation in an environment where the avoidance of contact with mass information—even for a moment—becomes virtually impossible.

Marshall McLuhan famously coined the well-known aphorism "the medium is the message." "This is merely to say," he explained, "that the personal and social consequences of any medium—that is, of any extension of ourselves—result from the new scale that is introduced into our affairs by each extension of ourselves, or by any new technology."[33] By this he meant that messages, per sé, are not unimportant, but should not be the focus of our attention when dealing with the interplay of technologies and the cultures that assimilate them. Persuasion is always an interpersonal phenomenon, and rhetoric—persuasive speech—is rooted in the communication patterns of relatively small groups. But propaganda is a mass phenomenon, a direct and inevitable consequence of *mass communication*, and we can no longer depend on mere rhetorical criticism to understand its power and effectiveness. The power not only to share information among enormous masses of people, but to *control* that information, is the message of mass media, and the message of propaganda 2.0. It is not at all hyperbolic to claim that the culmination of the twentieth century's scholarship on the subject, and the clearest, most precise description of propaganda 2.0, can be found in Jacques Ellul's *Propaganda*.

33. McLuhan, *Understanding Media*, 23.

Chapter 2 ───

Propaganda 2.0

──────────────── New Ways of Thinking about Propaganda

A t the beginning of the twentieth century, our view of propaganda remained deeply rooted in the propaganda 1.0 mindset. Even as newspapers had established themselves as important providers of information in
eighteenth-century Europe and nineteenth-century North America, aided
by the telegraph and telephone, and even as radio was emerging as a powerful rival, even as all the apparatus and mechanisms of mass culture were
solidifying the role and functions of propaganda 2.0, Aristotle's rhetoric still
stood as a touchstone for evaluating messages. It remains so even today, a fact
for which the reasons should be obvious. To the extent that we are moved by
words, moved by the people who speak them, moved by their logic, moved
by the passion with which they are delivered, rhetorical criticism will always
be a useful instrument in the propagandist's tool kit.

But somewhere approaching the middle of the twentieth century different points of view emerged. We began to notice—first intuitively and later directly—that not all messages that sought to be persuasive were successful in
that pursuit in each and every medium. We began to notice that one medium
might be suitable for *message A* (let's say, for instance, a message supported
by facts, figures, evidence, etc., a message structured around the *logos*), but
ill-suited for *message B*. Another medium might be suitable for *message B* (a
deeply emotional appeal, perhaps, to take some sort of drastic—and controversial—action), but poorly suited to logical, rather than emotional, appeals.
We began to notice that, beyond the mere persuasive power of rhetoric, the
medium itself, and particularly the question of *who owned and controlled* the
means of production and distribution of information, was equally crucial.
These observations eventually launched new fields of research we know today under the general name of *social sciences*, and it is in the development of

this field of inquiry that we were first able to discern, and eventually define, the boundaries of propaganda 2.0.

When you consider the fact that propaganda 1.0, the rhetorical tradition, dominated our thinking for two and a half millennia, persisting five hundred years into the era of mass communication and propaganda 2.0, this roughly fifty-year transition from old to new ways of thinking is manifestly significant. We will look more closely at the years approaching the middle of the twentieth century and the emergence of ideas that changed our perceptions in a later chapter. But first we must investigate some of the preliminary events that prepared us for those changes.

The Emergence of Mass Culture

The printing press, as we have noted, helped to create the phenomenon of *the public*. The early printing shops that shot up all across the map of Europe in the century after Gutenberg, however, also functioned as a conceptual template for the burgeoning phenomenon of *mass production*. In a sense, the hand production of manuscripts, while it lingered on for some centuries after the development of movable type, was obsolete the minute Gutenberg printed his first Bible. Handicraft and handmade items would survive, of course, but they would be in the form of higher-priced luxury items produced for the connoisseur, for mechanization not only increased production, it allowed for the lowering of prices to consumers, thereby pushing handicraft aside. As Sigfried Giedion states, "The narrow circle of home production is broken as soon as mechanization sets in."[1] By the 1820s, the mass production of bread was achieved.[2] Agriculture was mechanized by 1858 with the development and spread of McCormick's reaper.[3] In the 1870s mechanized mills ground and processed flour in enormous quantities.[4] Farmers and bakers no longer produced according to the demands of subsistence, but of surplus, and sold that growing surplus on an open market. This spurred the move toward specialization; a market flooded with a particular commodity creates an incentive to produce a different product. "In America this trend to specialization set in [in the middle of the nineteenth century], when cheaper wheat from the middle west appeared in the Eastern states, and converted tilled land into pasture."[5]

1. Giedion, *Mechanization Takes Command*, 131.
2. Giedion, *Mechanization Takes Command*, 170.
3. Giedion, *Mechanization Takes Command*, 131.
4. Giedion, *Mechanization Takes Command*, 188.
5. Giedion, *Mechanization Takes Command*, 131.

The mass production of furniture, clothing, tools, appliances, and so many other commodities followed quickly, so that toward the end of the nineteenth century the need became pressingly apparent for the development of a new mass-mediated phenomenon, advertising. In 1840 Volney B. Palmer established the first advertising agency in Philadelphia,[6] which was bought by N. W. Ayer & Son in 1877 and resettled in New York. James Walter Thompson established the J. Walter Thompson agency in New York in 1896, and by 1899 had a second office in London, making it the first international advertising agency. In 1897, General Electric established the first in-house corporate advertising department.[7] By 1900, the effects of mass production, mass marketing, and advertising could be seen clearly; Americans owned more than a million telephones, eight thousand had registered automobiles, and had purchased 24 million electric lightbulbs. In 1899, American economist and sociologist Thorstein Veblen, in his *Theory of the Leisure Class*, identified and described a new and growing phenomenon: *conspicuous consumption*, or the consumption of goods not to fulfill fundamental human needs, but as a public symbol of status.

At the same time, the "massification" of time and space occurred with the development of the transcontinental railroad and the telegraph. The railroad was essential in the movement of mass-produced products from their point of origin to the market—often hundreds of miles away. Mass production demanded centralization and the railroads facilitated the movement of goods into the factories or plants and out to the far-flung corners of the continent. Beef cattle and other livestock from the West and Midwest were shipped by train to Chicago to be killed, processed, skinned, scraped, cut—all by machine—then sold and shipped again, in new refrigerated railroad cars, all over the country.

The telegraph, running for the most part directly parallel (both historically and geographically) to the railroads, radically accelerated the movement of information and increased its magnitude (and salability) dramatically. Information now moved from one end of the continent to the other—from Pasadena to Boston, from New York to San Francisco—at virtually the speed of light. This provided a profit motivation for those who collect and sell information to newspapers. Five New York newspapers banded together in 1848 to form the Associated Press; following suit, Paul Julius Reuter established the news wire service in London in 1851 that still bears his name. Information that was once regional or localized now took on national and even international prominence.

6. Fallon, *Metaphysics of Media*, 185.
7. Fallon, *Metaphysics of Media*, 186.

Information, of course, has always been a commodity as well as a medium of exchange. But the printing press, because it was the first *mass medium*, made information a saleable commodity in a *mass market*. However, in the speed-of-light movement of information brought on by the telegraph, and the mass distribution of that information by the local newspaper press, the buying and selling of information—like the buying and selling of other commodities—took on a new dimension, and the marketplace began to value newness and the satisfaction of curiosity that information could provide—even information of the most trivial nature. Henry David Thoreau, writing in 1854, captured the essence of the cultural change leading us toward that peculiar understanding of propaganda that I'm calling propaganda 2.0. In *Walden*, Thoreau wrote that "[o]ur inventions are wont to be pretty toys, which distract our attention from serious things. They are but improved means to an unimproved end . . . We are in great haste to construct a magnetic telegraph from Maine to Texas; but Maine and Texas, it may be, have nothing important to communicate."[8]

The mass culture—a consumer culture—was established. No such culture had ever before existed on Earth. It was a culture that needed to adapt itself—and did so willingly—to the dictates of the machine. It adapted itself to the monotony of specialization and repetitive stress in the workplace, to the homogenization of tastes in mass-produced foods, to a diminution of quality in the mechanized manufacture of products where once individual pride in craftsmanship reigned. Add to this the homogenization of information; everyone was beginning to share the same information with every other person, newspapers a thousand miles distant from each other printed the same stories. Information became a commodity to be bought and sold, valued more for its timeliness and titillation than for its inherent usefulness.

As a social system, human beings adapted to the demands of mechanization and massification. But as individual human beings, the process of adaptation—to stationary and often meaningless work, to the loss of pride in personal achievement, to the alienation from nature, to the "new normal"—was painful, partial, continuous, and incomplete. And adapt we did. But not without consequences.

The Emergence of the Social Sciences

Every society undergoes change; there is nothing startling in this observation. But society seemed to be changing more rapidly in the nineteenth century than ever before, and in ways never seen before the existence of

8. Thoreau, *Walden*, 33–34.

mass media and widespread mechanization. In 1838 Auguste Comte (1798–1857) coined the term *sociology* to denote a new way of looking at and understanding human societies, social relationships, interactions, institutions, and change. Since the very idea of society as we understand it today emerged only during that era we call the Enlightenment, then sociology must, by necessity, have awaited that emergence, which would make itself known only after the fruits of other fertile intellectual fields ripened and were ready for harvest. With the spread of printing and literacy in the centuries after Gutenberg and the proliferation not only of books, but of new genres of literature, political and moral philosophers published their theories about the relationship between government, citizens, and the state as a whole. The public became *the public* only because they were a *reading public*; no longer a peasantry mired in ignorance, they wanted a say in choosing the direction of their lives, and some element of control in directing their own societies' changes. Sociology, its growing band of practitioners hoped, would be a scholarly field that would play a role in understanding these needs, and anticipating social upheaval when they weren't met.

Comte believed that social change must be *progressive*, that is to say developing from simpler to more complex forms, and from inferior to superior ones. Societies evolve in stages, he said; first a religious stage, where gods and spirits are responsible for people's lives, then a metaphysical stage, where unseen forces are at work, and finally a positivist stage, where responsibility for the events of the world is given only to what can be observed and verified. Such a view could give one hope that, despite momentary discomfort with the immediate effects of mechanized culture, it was all part of a natural progression to a society and world built on facts and science.

Others had somewhat different views on social dynamics and the progressive nature of social evolution. Karl Marx (1818–1883) saw all of human history as a struggle between classes, with one class (capitalists) controlling the means of the production and distribution of goods, a second class (proletariat) suffering exploitation of their labor, and a third class, a middle class (bourgeoisie), composed largely of bureaucrats, merchants, and others who facilitate the smooth operation of the economy and who, by and large, are the dominant consumers of the commodities produced. Peripheral to his theory, but important to any discussion of propaganda, was what Marx called false consciousness, the ideology of the dominant class accepted unquestioningly by the exploited class. He expected the exploited worker to eventually achieve a new consciousness, a class consciousness, and overthrow the old order, bringing on socialism.

By contrast, Emile Durkheim (1858–1917) looked at the dynamic interrelationship of individuals and their collective institutions, particularly that institution we call *society*. Society, Durkheim said, is a complex phenomenon, more than merely the sum of its individual parts. In order to understand individuals' behaviors, Durkheim believed, those behaviors must always be investigated within the context of the societal norms and mores that motivate them. The individual and the mass of individuals we call society must be thought of as distinct entities. What is true and characteristic of an individual will not necessarily be true of a *mass of individuals*.

While some social scientists were busy devising theories about social thought and interaction, however, with the aim of understanding social relations, others were busy constructing models that provided a rationale for greater social control. The very *massness* of mass culture appeared to them as both challenge to authority and an opportunity to extend social control.

Precursors to the Study of Propaganda

In 1895 Gustave Le Bon (1841–1931) published *The Crowd: A Study of the Popular Mind*. Le Bon was a French sociologist sensitive to the transformation of individuals into crowds, or mobs, or a "public." He believed that when enough individuals were gathered together as a single entity, new psychological characteristics emerged that are not present (or, perhaps, latent but not evident) in the individuals themselves. The psychological characteristics evident in crowd behavior, Le Bon believed, are inferior to those of the individual.

Le Bon cast a cold and cynical eye on democratic principles and institutions (without actually calling for their abandonment). He looked back a century to a time when "the traditional policy of European states and the rivalries of sovereigns were the principal factors that shaped events. The opinion of the masses scarcely counted and most frequently indeed did not count at all."[9] But now, he noted ruefully, "the voice of the masses has become preponderant. It is this voice that dictates their conduct to kings, whose endeavor is to take note of its utterances."[10] Moreover, "it is possible that the advent to power of the masses marks one of the last stages of Western civilization,"[11] because civilization has ever only been "created and directed by a small intellectual aristocracy, never by crowds. Crowds are only powerful for destruction."[12]

9. Le Bon, *Crowd*, x.
10. Le Bon, *Crowd*, x.
11. Le Bon, *Crowd*, xii.
12. Le Bon, *Crowd*, xiii.

The behavior of crowds, Le Bon wrote, is predictable. They are moved not by reality, but by *impressions* of reality. They are gullible and susceptible to the power of suggestion. The behavior of one individual, motivated by his own subjective impression, can influence the behavior of the rest. "Before St. George appeared on the walls of Jerusalem to all the Crusaders he was certainly perceived in the first instance by one of those present. By dint of suggestion and contagion the miracle signalized by a single person was immediately accepted by all."[13]

Anticipating techniques that would be used—to sometimes horrifying effect—in twentieth-century propaganda, Le Bon observed that "a crowd thinks in images,"[14] and they respond only to images. "It is not by reason, but most often in spite of it, that are created those sentiments that are the mainsprings of all civilization—sentiments such as honour, self-sacrifice, religious faith, patriotism, and the love of glory."[15]

He took note of the fundamental irrationality and malleability of the crowd's opinions. One of the reasons for this volatility, he claimed, was "the recent development of the newspaper press, by whose agency the most contrary opinions are being continually brought before the attention of crowds . . . Become a mere agency for the supply of information, the press has renounced all endeavor to enforce an idea or a doctrine."[16]

Imperfectly brilliant, written with an elitist (and sometimes racist) bias, antidemocratic at its core, and probably thirty to forty years premature, Le Bon's *The Crowd* still marks a turning point in thinking about propaganda—not only mere mass persuasion in a mass culture, but the effective control of the mass of people by a small, powerful elite. It helped lay the foundation for a necessary conceptual pivot from propaganda 1.0 to propaganda 2.0. And it was influential in its own right, helping to form the basis of the study of mass psychology; *The Crowd* played a significant role in shaping the works of both Sigmund Freud and his nephew Edward Bernays (whom we will discuss shortly).

While Le Bon never clearly explained what a "crowd" is and how it differs from this curious phenomenon we call "the public," another French sociologist took pains to make that distinction and to make clear the connection of the public to the presence of mass media. "[T]he invention of printing," Gabriel Tarde wrote in 1901, "has caused a very different type of public to

13. Le Bon, *Crowd*, 15.

14. Le Bon, *Crowd*, 15.

15. Le Bon, *Crowd*, 71.

16. Le Bon, *Crowd*, 96–97.

appear, one which never ceases to grow and whose indefinite extension is one of the most clearly marked traits of our period."[17]

Tarde (1843–1904) was a sociologist concerned with psychological factors in human interaction, on both the individual and mass levels. He wrote his essay *The Public and the Crowd* in order to investigate "[w]here the public comes from, how it arises and develops; its varieties and relationships to the crowd, to corporations, to states; its strength for good or evil, and its ways of acting and feeling."[18] In his investigation he gives much credit to mass media—particularly newspapers—for both the creation of a public and its actions. The majority of humans were once (or certainly saw themselves to be) powerless to change the tide of history, swept along, as they were (or felt themselves to be), in the tide of historical circumstance. With the exception of those dangerous moments when people gather together as a crowd and inflict violence on those in positions of power, there had been a time when only an elite few in society possessed the political or economic power to influence events; but now powerless human beings, via a public opinion gauged and reported by newspapers, *felt* empowered, as though their wishes and needs were being directly addressed. Such people "do not come in contact, do not meet or hear each other; they are all sitting in their own homes scattered over a vast territory, reading the same newspaper."[19]

The work of both Le Bon and Tarde argued a need for powerful elites to use mass media to provide the public with appropriate symbols that would *keep them a public* and inhibit their devolution into a *crowd* or *mob*. The need for such mass-produced symbols suggested a parallel need for their creators and distributors.

The rise and growth of sociology and the social sciences in the nineteenth century provided a solid foundation for both the formal study and the formal practice of propaganda. And it is in the twentieth century that we witness the flowering of that study, and the aggressive advance of its practice.

By the late nineteenth century the idea of propaganda had taken on serious negative connotations having nothing to do with religion. In 1875 the entry for *propaganda* found in *A Dictionary of Science, Literature and Art* noted that "the name *propaganda* is applied in modern political language as a term of reproach to secret associations for the spread of opinions and principles which are viewed by most governments with horror

17. Tarde, *On Communication and Social Influence*, 277.

18. Tarde, *On Communication and Social Influence*, 277.

19. Tarde, *On Communication and Social Influence*, 278.

and aversion."[20] Propaganda was beginning to appear that threatened the balance—and control—of power in many countries. The portrait Matthew Brady made of Abraham Lincoln following the future president's speech at Cooper Union in New York City compelled Lincoln to acknowledge, "Brady and the Cooper Union speech made me President of the United States."[21] Harriet Beecher Stowe's *Uncle Tom's Cabin* was widely regarded as abolitionist propaganda. Lincoln, on meeting Stowe at the White House, is said to have remarked, "So you're the little woman who wrote the book that made this great war."[22] The cartoons of Thomas Nast (1840–1902) shook the very foundations of William Magear "Boss" Tweed's Tammany Hall. Suddenly people were beginning to see forms of information as having the power, perhaps, to make and to break; it certainly had the power to shape and mobilize public opinion. By the early decades of the twentieth century that power to shape people's thoughts and behaviors would become associated with treachery, bloodshed, lies, and war.

Propaganda in "The Great War"

World War I represented a proving ground for modern propaganda. It was the first war in which thirty-two countries were belligerents; it was also the first war in which mass media played so central a role in its execution—not only in bringing information from the front home daily to the citizens of the nations who were fighting, but in the use of the *full panoply of media available*—newspapers, magazines, posters, motion pictures, and the new electronic medium of radio—to build morale, motivate citizens to sacrifice, and demonize "the enemy."

Before the outbreak of the war, mass media were already engaged in the "softer" sociological forms of propaganda such as entertainment, news, marketing, and advertising; no national governments had ever established explicit propaganda offices. But the mere presence of those same mass media in a time of global war, and the recognition of their power in the speedy delivery of information across great distances, made it clear that, at least for the duration of the war, propaganda created and distributed by central governments was going to be a necessity. There was going to be a "fight for the minds of men, for the 'conquest of their convictions,'" with the battle line running "through every home in every country."[23]

20. Brande et al., *Dictionary of Science, Literature, and Art*, 114.
21. MOMALearning, "President Lincoln."
22. Vollaro, "Lincoln, Stowe, and the 'Little Woman/Great War' Story."
23. Creel, *How We Advertised America*, 3.

On April 13, 1917, seven days after the United States' entry into the war, President Woodrow Wilson established the Committee on Public Information (CPI). The CPI was the first state propaganda bureau in US history. Its purpose was to promote the war at home, to weaken the ardor (and the arguments) of the anti-war factions, and to reassure the world of America's righteousness and determination in fighting the war. Led by journalist George Creel, along with the Secretaries of State, War, and the Navy, the CPI had sweeping powers and responsibilities for the control of information affecting the US conduct of the war, and for all intents and purposes functioned as a distinct cabinet-level department, with Creel as its secretary.

Americans from many diverse backgrounds—business, journalism, film, academia, art—took part in CPI programs, either planning, designing, writing, administering, or executing them. The CPI used modern advertising techniques fused with a sometimes blatant appeal to emotions, and its efforts represent the first time that such techniques were employed by a modern government on its own people on such a large scale. As Stuart Ewen noted, "the CPI constituted a more audacious approach to publicity than had previously existed."[24] Creel knew that in order to sell this war to the American people, more than newspapers would be necessary. "How could the national emergency be met without national unity?" he asked, and how could unity be achieved without reaching all the people? "The printed word, the spoken word, motion pictures, the telegraph, the wireless, posters, signboards, and every possible media [sic] should be used to drive home the justice of America's cause."[25]

The CPI's Division of Films—the first use of the growing motion picture industry in the cause of organized national propaganda—supervised the production of such films as *Pershing's Crusaders*, *America's Answer*, and *Under Four Flags* to be shown in theaters across the country—and around the world—along with more typical Hollywood fare.[26]

The CPI pursued and recruited about 75,000 "Four Minute Men," volunteers who spoke about the war to 314 million people in more than 5,000 communities during the eighteen-month duration of US involvement. They spoke for no longer than a well-scripted four minutes at local civic events, movies, town meetings, churches and synagogues, and workplaces on topics such as why the US was fighting, the need for a draft, unmasking German

24. Ewen, *PR!*, 112.

25. Ewen, *PR!*, 112.

26. Ewen, *PR!*, 115.

propaganda, the danger to democracy, the value of sacrifice, the patriotism of buying bonds, and the meaning of America.[27]

A secondary function of the Four Minute Men was the policing—and suppressing—of thought that was "subversive" of the war effort. "Audiences were encouraged to identify, interrogate, and even report people in their communities who expressed antiwar sentiments."[28]

Such a program as the Four Minute Men had never been undertaken in history and in that sense can be seen as a stunning achievement. Modernizing the art of Aristotelian rhetoric, CPI took what was once an act of interpersonal or small-group communication and amplified it to mass proportions, delivering the same speech 150,000 times each week all across the nation.[29]

The CPI's relations with the Republican-controlled Congress were uncomfortable at best, with many legislators uneasy about the formal establishment of a propaganda bureau; they feared censorship and the temptation of an administration to use propaganda for political purposes as well as for generating and strengthening support for the war. The CPI had, in fact, tried to ban some newspapers, for example the Socialist papers *The Call* and *The Jewish Daily Forward*, on the grounds that they were somehow impeding the war effort.[30] Creel resisted the notion that the CPI was engaging in thought suppression and insisted that he was not leading a censorship bureau; he proposed instead "a voluntary agreement that would make every paper in the land its own censor, putting it up to the patriotism and common sense of the individual editor to protect purely military information of tangible value to the enemy."[31] In fact, however, CPI maintained such tight control on all war-related information (and during the war that meant virtually all information) and the pressure they were able to exert on journalists and newspaper owners so extensive, that the average American learned nothing of the war that had not passed through CPI hands for approval.

> Every item of war news they saw—in the country weekly, in magazines, or in the city daily picked up occasionally in the general store—was not merely officially approved information but precisely the same kind that millions of their fellow citizens were getting at the same moment. Every war story had been censored somewhere along the line—at the source, in transit, or

27. Ewen, *PR!*, 117.

28. Ewen, *PR!*, 118.

29. Ewen, *PR!*, 104.

30. Steel, *Walter Lippmann and the American Century*, 125.

31. Creel, *How We Advertised America*, 18.

in the newspaper offices in accordance with "voluntary" rules established by the CPI.[32]

"We did not call it propaganda," Creel wrote after the war, "for that word, in German hands, had come to be associated with deceit and corruption. Our effort was educational and informative throughout, for we had such confidence in our case as to feel that no other argument was needed than the simple, straightforward presentation of facts."[33]

Harold Lasswell (1902–1978), however, writing in 1927, catalogued the emotional and psychological techniques of propaganda used during the war, and it is difficult, on the basis of the evidence, to justify Creel's pleas of innocence. One prominent CPI technique was the ascribing of guilt. "If the propagandist is to mobilize the hate of the people, he must see to it that everything is circulated which establishes the sole responsibility of the enemy."[34] Another was the demonizing of the enemy, the overall theme of this technique easily summarized as "Any nation who began the War and blocks the peace is incorrigible, wicked and perverse . . . the guilty is the satanic and the satanic is guilty."[35]

Along with the demonization of the enemy came the notion that whatever messages we receive from him will be "lying propaganda."

> This theme is of particular importance. Unfavourable reports about allies, the heads of the army, the conditions at the front, and the bureaucracy are certain to leak past the censorship, or to spring full-blown inside the ramparts. Psychological barriers must be interposed between dangerous news and subversive responses. This psychological barrier consists in the suspicion that unfavourable news is likely to be a cunning specimen of enemy propaganda.[36]

Hatred was another technique, Lasswell suggests, much employed in World War I, as it has been in the past, and as it will be in the future. "A handy rule for arousing hate is, if at first they do not enrage, use an atrocity."[37] Such atrocity stories become almost mythic and the most effective ones have certain archetypal elements: "Stress can be laid upon the wounding of women, children, old people, priests and nuns, and upon sexual enormities,

32. Sweeney, *Secrets of Victory*, 15–16.
33. Creel, *How We Advertised America*, 4.
34. Lasswell, *Propaganda Technique in the World War*, 47.
35. Lasswell, *Propaganda Technique in the World War*, 77.
36. Lasswell, *Propaganda Technique in the World War*, 79–80.
37. Lasswell, *Propaganda Technique in the World War*, 81.

mutilated prisoners and mutilated non-combatants . . . A young woman, ravished by the enemy, yields secret satisfaction to a host of vicarious ravishers on the other side of the border."[38]

Noting that it is difficult for human beings by nature to imagine such satanic power embodied uniformly across an entire population, Lasswell cited another technique in support of demonization, one still very much in use in today's political propaganda. The noncombatant citizens at home "need to have some individual on whom to pin their hate. It is, therefore, important to single out a handful of enemy leaders and load them down with the whole decalogue of sins."[39]

But Lasswell ultimately approved of propaganda; indeed, he remained a vocal and very public champion of the use of "scientific" propaganda:

> [T]he fact remains that propaganda is one of the most powerful instrumentalities in the modern world. It has arisen to its present eminence in response to a complex of changed circumstances which have altered the nature of society . . . A newer and subtler instrument must weld thousands and even millions of human beings into one amalgamated mass of hate and will and hope. A new flame must burn out the canker of dissent and temper the steel of bellicose enthusiasm. The name of this new hammer and anvil of social solidarity is propaganda.[40]

Not only an academic affair, criticism of wartime propaganda came also from some unlikely quarters. At the time of his death the most decorated military officer in the United States, in 1935 Brigadier General Smedley D. Butler wrote a pamphlet titled *War Is a Racket*. It is a highly contentious text coming from a career Marine officer, an indictment of war profiteering, imperialism, and propaganda. With the clouds of war once again amassing over Europe, Butler's recollections of the Great War stripped George Creel's and the Committee on Public Information's propaganda campaign of all its grandiloquent symbolism, bombastic patriotism, and exaggerated national self-righteousness, and put the war—and its costs—in a more human perspective.

> The normal profits of a business concern in the United States are six, eight, ten, and sometimes twelve percent. But war-time profits—ah! That is another matter—twenty, sixty, one hundred, three hundred, and even eighteen hundred percent. All that the traffic will bear. Uncle Sam has the money. Let's get it.

38. Lasswell, *Propaganda Technique in the World War*, 87.
39. Lasswell, *Propaganda Technique in the World War*, 89.
40. Lasswell, *Propaganda Technique in the World War*, 220–21.

Of course, it isn't put that crudely in war time. It is dressed into speeches about patriotism, love of country, and "we must all put our shoulders to the wheel" . . . [41]

In the World War, we used propaganda to make the boys accept conscription. They were made to feel ashamed if they didn't join the army.

So vicious was this war propaganda that even God was brought into it. With few exceptions our clergymen joined in the clamor to kill, kill, kill. To kill the Germans. God is on our side.[42]

Beautiful ideals were painted for our boys who were sent out to die. This was the "war to end all wars." This was the "war to make the world safe for democracy." No one mentioned to them, as they marched away, that their going and their dying would mean huge war profits.

No one told these American soldiers that they might be shot down by bullets made by their own brothers here. No one told them that the ships on which they were going to cross might be torpedoed by submarines built with United States patents. They were just told it was going to be a "glorious adventure."[43]

Postwar Propaganda and Criticism

Walter Lippmann

Five years after the end of the war, Walter Lippmann (1889–1974) wrote *Public Opinion*, his influential study of democracy in an age of mass communication. During the war Lippmann, a Pulitzer Prize-winning journalist, essayist, and author, had advised President Wilson on the establishment of the Committee on Public Information. A sharp critic of George Creel's leadership there, in October of 1917 Lippmann wrote a memo to Wilson suggesting that the best administration policy regarding Socialist anti-war criticism was to be "contemptuously disinterested" but respectful of free speech. Censorship, he told Wilson, should "never be entrusted to who is not himself tolerant, nor to anyone who is unacquainted with the long record of folly which is the history of suppression."[44]

---

41. Butler, *War Is a Racket*, 15–16.
42. Butler, *War Is a Racket*, 38.
43. Butler, *War Is a Racket*, 38–39.
44. Steel, *Walter Lippmann and the American Century*, 125.

A democratic idealist at heart, Lippmann nonetheless understood the role, if not of censorship, then at least of the control and perhaps, even if only implicitly, the manipulation of information. In *Public Opinion* Lippmann argued that democracy as an ideal and democracy as it actually functions in a mass society were two phenomena steadily drifting further and further apart. The average person, Lippmann argued, does not know or understand the world in which we live; we know only the *pseudo-environment* presented to us on a daily basis by our media.[45] We are cut off from reality by

> the artificial censorships, the limitations of social contact, the comparatively meager time available in each day for paying attention to public affairs, the distortion arising because events have to be compressed into very short messages, the difficulty of making a small vocabulary express a complicated world, and finally the fear of facing those facts which would seem to threaten the established routine of men's lives.[46]

Propaganda—"the effort to alter the picture to which men respond, to substitute one social pattern for another"[47]—is necessary in a democracy in order to free us from "the intolerable and unworkable fiction that each of us must acquire a competent opinion about all public affairs."[48]

Not all people, Lippmann argued, are able, through no fault of their own, to be knowledgeable about their world. The prosperous person who has leisure time to read widely, for instance, and sufficient income to travel is more likely to be well informed than the poor person. And regardless of income level or class, not everyone is inclined to learn about the world, and many remain satisfied with their pseudo-environment as delivered to them. Yet of those who are inclined to know reality and have the resources to explore and observe it firsthand, only a fraction will come away from the experience with a clear picture. Our preconceived notions about the nature of reality coupled with our familiarity and comfort with the pseudo-environment get in the way of objective clarity. "For the most part we do not first see, and then define, we define first and then see."[49] This made journalism a less than ideal servant of a democratic body politic.

What was needed, Lippmann concluded, was a new governing class of experts, analysts, and bureaucrats who can advise the government about the "unseen facts" of the world that journalism fails to uncover, and

---

45. Lippmann, *Public Opinion*, 13.

46. Lippmann, *Public Opinion*, 21.

47. Lippmann, *Public Opinion*, 19.

48. Lippmann, *Public Opinion*, 22.

49. Lippmann, *Public Opinion*, 48.

then shape a message about those facts that will contribute to a greater public awareness of the objective reality in which they live. Thus both the governors and the governed may be in agreement with the facts of the world, and perhaps nearer to agreement on the meaning of those facts and the government's range of acceptable response to them. It was a very rational and linear process: the finding and analysis of facts by reliable "experts," their consultations with government, and the mass delivery of the government's proposed actions to the people. Lippmann called this process "the manufacture of consent."[50]

Lippmann's argument begs the question—several questions, in fact—of the reliability of data, the bona fides of experts, the integrity of analysis, and the incorruptibility of all persons involved in this new governing class. It also ignores the question of whether, in an age of increasingly instantaneous mass communication, "democracy," as we have understood the term in the past, is even possible—or desirable.

Edward Bernays

During the Great War, George Creel's Committee on Public Information hired a young former journalist and theatrical press agent. Edward Bernays (1891–1995) was assigned to the CPI's New York office to concentrate on gaining Latin American business support for the US war effort, an activity he described as "psychological warfare."[51] At the war's end, he was part of a team of sixteen public relations agents working for the CPI at the peace conference at Versailles, kept, however, from playing a leading role.

A double-nephew of Sigmund Freud (his mother, Anna Freud Bernays, was Sigmund Freud's sister; and his father, Ely Bernays, was brother of Freud's wife, Martha Bernays), Bernays was a pioneer in the use of many of his uncle's psychological principles in propaganda. Bernays believed that human beings were possessed of powerful—and dangerous—unconscious urges welling up from the libido; these unfulfilled animal urges were the source of all human conflict and violence. Without the leadership of an educated and enlightened elite, society would eventually collapse, as historically it has always seemed to do, into chaos. But he also claimed to believe that it was possible to build a utopian society where these urges could be controlled and sublimated, through the agency of an educated elite redirecting and channeling those inherently irrational desires into the mass consumption of manufactured goods. We desire a certain material

50. Lippmann, *Public Opinion*, 138.

51. Ewen, *PR!*, 162.

commodity not for itself, but because we have "unconsciously come to see in it a symbol of something else, the desire for which" we are ashamed to admit.[52] Business, therefore, could both satisfy the unconscious cravings of what Bernays considered to be the inherently irrational masses, and at the same time provide a powerful stimulus for consumption and economic growth. "Intelligent men," he wrote in 1928, "must realize that propaganda is the modern instrument by which they can fight for productive ends and help to bring order out of chaos."[53]

In his unapologetic manifesto *Propaganda*, Bernays makes the case for the same sort of elitist, antidemocratic leadership of society suggested by Le Bon, Tarde, and Lippmann, from whose ideas he borrows heavily.

> The conscious and intelligent manipulation of the organized habits and opinions of the masses is an important element in democratic society. Those who manipulate this unseen mechanism of society constitute an invisible government which is the true ruling power of our country . . . We are governed, our minds molded, our tastes formed, our ideas suggested, largely by men we have never heard of.[54]

The role of the propagandist—or in Bernays's words, "counsel on public relations"—is to take a malleable and volatile public opinion and to "crystallize" it; to create "a compact, vivid simplification of complicated issues."[55] Starting from the assumption that an elite group of intelligent and educated individuals are more capable of leadership and decision-making than the masses, Bernays laid the foundation for propaganda 2.0. "Abstract discussions and heavy fact," he wrote, "are the groundwork for [the public relations counsel's] involved theory, or analysis, but they cannot be given to the public until they are simplified and dramatized. The refinements of reason and the shadings of emotion cannot reach a considerable public."[56] This, of course, has profound and dire implications for both objective journalism and democracy. Insisting that it is the counsel on public relations, and not the masses, who knows "what news really is,"[57] Bernays wrote in very clear terms that the propagandist "must not only

52. Bernays, *Propaganda*, 75.
53. Bernays, *Propaganda*, 168.
54. Bernays, *Propaganda*, 37.
55. Bernays, *Crystallizing Public Opinion*, 170.
56. Bernays, *Crystallizing Public Opinion*, 169.
57. Bernays, *Crystallizing Public Opinion*, 179.

supply news—he must create news. This function as the creator of news is even more important than his others."[58]

Bernays's definition and description of propaganda displays an uncanny recognition of the principles of propaganda 2.0, and anticipates Jacques Ellul's own model of "total propaganda."

> Modern propaganda is a consistent, enduring effort to create or shape events to influence the relations of the public to an enterprise, idea or group . . . The important thing is that it is universal and continuous; and in its sum total it is regimenting the public mind every bit as much as an army regiments the bodies of its soldiers.[59]

Unwilling to condemn propaganda like much of the postwar world, Bernays constructs elaborate arguments about its moral neutrality—"I am aware that the word 'propaganda' carries to many minds an unpleasant connotation. Yet whether, in any instance, propaganda is good or bad depends upon the merit of the cause urged, and the correctness of the information published"[60]—as well as its ultimate inevitability:

> Formerly the rulers were the leaders. They laid out the course of history, by the simple process of doing what they wanted. And if nowadays the successors of the rulers, those whose position or ability gives them power, can no longer do what they want without the approval of the masses, they find in propaganda a tool which is increasingly powerful in gaining that approval. Therefore, propaganda is here to stay.[61]

In all his writings Bernays stressed the necessity for propaganda and the benefits it provides for democratic society. He argued that propaganda, for the sake of society, must be executed only by persons of integrity and high ethical ideals. Yet none of his books or articles describe exactly what those ethical ideals might be, or what social groups might benefit more from propaganda than others. And his own career provided examples of why there is cause for concern about those questions.

By exploiting the burgeoning feminism in the immediate aftermath of the passage of the Nineteenth Amendment, Bernays managed to break another old taboo, that against women smoking. Hired by the American Tobacco Company, Bernays was charged with the task of enlarging the

58. Bernays, *Crystallizing Public Opinion*, 179.
59. Bernays, *Propaganda*, 52.
60. Bernays, *Propaganda*, 48.
61. Bernays, *Propaganda*, 54.

market of smokers. The challenge was to make the image of women smoking not only acceptable, but desirable. Bernays consulted with Abraham Brill—the first psychoanalyst to practice in the United States and the translator of Bernays's uncle Sigmund Freud's work into English—who suggested that cigarettes, until that moment the sole province of men, represented "torches of freedom" for women.

At New York City's Easter Parade in 1929, Bernays had a woman friend first gather a group of female smokers who would light up at a particular moment in the parade, and then contact the press with the information that a group of women's rights marchers would light "torches of freedom" on Fifth Avenue.[62] Reporters eagerly responded to "the story." *The New York Times* April 1, 1929 edition reported, in a story about the parade with the sub-headline "Group of Girls Puff at Cigarettes as a Gesture of 'Freedom,'" "About a dozen young women strolled back and forth between St. Thomas's and St. Patrick's while the parade was at its peak, ostentatiously smoking cigarettes . . . One of the group explained the cigarettes were 'torches of freedom' lighting the way to the day when women would smoke on the street as casually as men."[63] Thanks to Bernays, the market for tobacco products doubled in size, and women were now as free as men to do irreparable damage to their health.

Edward Filene and the Economic Dimensions of Propaganda

By the late 1920s, the centrality of propaganda to American economic life was unmistakable. Recovering from the heartache and privations they suffered during the Great War, Americans were enjoying an economic boom, and both production and consumption were expanding exponentially. Herbert Hoover praised a gathering of advertising industry executives in 1929, telling them, "You have transformed people into constantly moving happiness machines that have become the key to economic progress."[64] Bernays's vision was of a populace who were not really in control of their lives, but could be made to feel as though they were. By the skilful exploitation of their unconscious desires, masses were "free" not only to consume, but to consume a diverse assortment of constantly changing products they had never before known existed, let alone desired. Capitalism provided the means to channel and control these desires to satisfy its own interests,

---

62. Museum of Public Relations, "1929: Torches of Freedom."

63. *New York Times*, "Easter Sun Finds the Past in Shadow at Modern Parade."

64. Kornberger, *Brand Society*, 8.

propaganda was capitalism's instrument, and government found that it had not only an effective means of social control, and plausible deniability of any complicity in it, but also a powerful stimulus to economic growth.

In 1931, Boston merchandising magnate Edward Filene published a manifesto for the burgeoning technoculture titled *Successful Living in This Machine Age*. Mass production, he wrote, "is production for the masses. It changes the whole social order."[65] Furthermore, he assures us (perhaps through rose-colored glasses), that "it is not standardizing human life. It is liberating the masses, rather, from the struggle for mere existence and enabling them, for the first time in history, to give their attention to more distinctly human problems."[66]

His book is a striking example of capitalist propaganda. The "machine age" offered a remedy for all the human ills that came before it—poverty, unemployment, warfare, inequality, classism, social stagnation—and Filene provided specific proposals to individuals within the mass who found themselves pressured to conform, and reassurances that they would find the quality of their lives much improved. "While there will be no leisure classes under mass production, there will be leisure—such a volume of leisure as the world has never known before. This approaching leisure is already manifesting itself in the eight-hour workday for workers and even in the five-day week,"[67] he writes, as though it had been technology and not the rising and increasingly militant voices of oppressed labor and working poor that were responsible.

Of particular interest, however, are Filene's thoughts on education in a mass society. "Mass production," he writes, "demands the education of the masses,"[68] an admirable endorsement of universal education. But what sort of education did Filene have in mind? "In the first place, the masses must learn how to behave like human beings in a mass production world . . . This civilization is founded upon production for the masses, but unless the masses play a conscious part in it, production for the masses can not [sic] go on."[69]

Explaining his vision, Filene presents a (rather utopian) scenario in which full employment is achieved through the wonders of mass production, and workers enjoy absolute economic security. Such an achievement, however, would not be without its problems:

65. Filene, *Successful Living in This Machine Age*, 1.
66. Filene, *Successful Living in This Machine Age*, 1.
67. Filene, *Successful Living in This Machine Age*, 12.
68. Filene, *Successful Living in This Machine Age*, 144.
69. Filene, *Successful Living in This Machine Age*, 144.

Would they work as faithfully if they were suddenly informed that they could not be discharged, and that the worst that could happen to them economically would be their transfer to some other job or to some other industry? Would there not be a tendency for them to lie down on the job, to take things easy, and thus to destroy the very system which makes it imperative to abolish unemployment?

Obviously, there would be such a tendency unless the masses were thoroughly educated to understand the situation. But there is little, if any, such education today. It is not being given in the home, for the average home, no matter how well equipped to teach the traditional virtues, is not equipped to interpret to its children the social relationships of the world in which those children must soon begin to do their part, and the social responsibilities which come from those relationships.[70]

"To suggest," he continues, "that the principles of mass production should be taught in the primary and elementary schools will strike most readers as fantastic."[71] But citizens in the "machine age" need to reject traditional views of schooling and embrace new ideas "if these children are to learn how to behave like human beings in this mass production world."[72]

What we have looked at in this chapter is the slow but steady evolution of thought surrounding the propaganda phenomenon, from a focus on messages and intentions to one on social interaction and information control. From Comte, Marx, and Durkheim's varying sociological views of stasis and change, through Le Bon, Tarde, Lippmann, and Bernays's concern with social control and the inherent danger of "mobs," through Creel and Lasswell's wartime theory (and practice) of propaganda, we should be able to recognize that more and more attention was paid to *the social system* and the *information structures* that support it, and less and less attention to any specific message or set of messages. We had been living in the era of propaganda 2.0 for nearly a half millennium. We were only now recognizing and acknowledging it.

---

70. Filene, *Successful Living in This Machine Age*, 145.
71. Filene, *Successful Living in This Machine Age*, 145.
72. Filene, *Successful Living in This Machine Age*, 145.

Chapter 3

Propaganda 2.0

——— Systems Theories, Cybernetics, and Information Theory

Systems Theories

S ystems theories arose in the years surrounding World War II and had their roots in the works of biologist Ludwig Von Bertalanffy, mathematician Norbert Wiener, mathematician and electrical engineer Claude Shannon, and psychiatrist William Ross Ashby, among others. Its object is to generalize and then to define certain characteristics shared by systems, with the goal of understanding their functions and purposes. Such understanding can help us to identify healthy and unhealthy systems, productive and unproductive ones, efficient and inefficient ones, etc. Over time, systems thinkers both defined what constitutes a system, and identified a number of general characteristics of systems. For my purposes, I'll define *systems* as "groups of interrelated and interdependent parts, organized in such a way that they achieve some goal." Their characteristics include:

- Systems have *a purpose.* Every system exists to perform some task (or sets of tasks) and achieve some end.

- Systems can be *natural, human-made,* or *both.* While it is easy to imagine the purposes of human-made systems, it may seem strange to ascribe a purpose to nature. Suffice it to say that nature's purpose is, at the very least, to sustain life.

- Systems have a *structure.* Their effectiveness is to a great degree dependent on their organization.

- Systems are *bounded.* Their boundaries are both spatial and temporal. There is an "inside" to a system as well as an "outside." Systems arise according to their perceived need, and they disintegrate when no longer needed or when they fail to achieve their purpose.

- Systems can be *open* or *closed*. Open systems receive and accept information from outside the system; closed systems do not. Information within a closed system tends to be conservative and static.

- Systems are *homeostatic*. They are resistant to changes that threaten their existence or proper functioning.

- Systems are *adaptable*. Despite being resistant to change, external forces often do threaten a system's existence and affect its functioning, and survival demands adaptation to environmental change.

There are numerous different types of systems, each eventually spawning its own field of study. For the purposes of this investigation, I wish to focus on two: *cybernetics* and *information theory*.

Cybernetics

The cybernetic view of human society is that of a system; a bounded, self-regulating organization of human beings, their ideas, and their techniques, that seek stability and homeostasis but at the same time need to be adaptable to change (whether planned or unplanned) for the purpose of performing some function or attaining some goal. Cybernetics, in Ross Ashby's terms, is "a 'theory of machines', but it treats, not things but ways of behaving. It does not ask 'what is this thing?' but 'what does it do?'"[1] Cybernetics is concerned with the *telos* or purpose of systems; is a given system, for example, functioning as it ought to, and if not, is the system prepared to remedy a failure? "Cybernetics deals with all forms of behaviour in so far as they are regular, or determinate, or reproducible."[2]

Information (emphasized here because its meaning, as we shall see, is more than its popular definition suggests) is central to all systems and critical to their survival, smooth operation, and hopes for success. For the most part, systems are predictable; each constituent part of a system, having been conditioned to function in the way that he, she, or it was trained, taught, or programmed, plays its part as expected. The interdependence among the system's various constituencies makes it necessary to do so. When one element in a system is not functioning optimally, it affects the other elements, who will then very likely report on that failure.

1. Ashby, *Introduction to Cybernetics*, 1.
2. Ashby, *Introduction to Cybernetics*, 1.

There is an inevitable variance in every system, in its individual constituents as well as among its various constituent groups. There is occasional divergence from the norm, deviation from expectations. Sometimes these deviations are normal and can be anticipated (illness, incapacitation, or death of a constituent) and therefore can easily be remedied, but sometimes they are unanticipated (malicious intent on the part of a constituent or constituent group, for example, to disrupt or even destroy the system) and threaten the system's stability—if not its very existence. When this occurs, the system must be able to respond to this deviation and correct it.

Cybernetic Learning

It is critical to the stable functioning of any system that there be a mechanism (a "feedback loop") to monitor, instantly and continuously, its proper functioning and constituent parts, thereby allowing for adjustment and therapeutic remediation of deviations from the norm. Here we see the system's techniques of self-regulation in the service of both stability and homeostasis, as well as adaptation. Feedback is the key; remediation is the goal. "Learning" is a mere by-product. Feedback, Wiener tells us,

> is a method of controlling a system by reinserting into it the results of its past performance. If these results are merely used as numerical data for the criticism of the system and its regulation, we have the simple feedback of the control engineers. If, however, the information which proceeds backward from the performance is able to change the general method and pattern of performance, we have a process which may well be called learning.[3]

This cybernetic view of learning is not restricted to, but is certainly predominated by, a conditioned reflex approach and is directed toward the maintaining or improving the performance of the system.[4]

Notwithstanding the essential uniform characteristics of systems, there is, however, no necessary uniformity to systems. Each system is founded and therefore dependent upon some piece or pieces of information—its purpose, its goal, its ethos. A system (society) founded on the idea of communalism and guaranteeing human equality, for instance, will function very differently from one dedicated to the idea of private property and maximization of profit. An organic, oral culture will be predicated on the idea of stability and tradition, while the technologically developed culture will find its "stability"

3. Wiener, *Human Use of Human Beings*, 61.
4. Wiener, *Cybernetics*, 129.

in constant change and expansion or where, as the saying goes, "the only constant is change." In the organic culture, stability is ensured by tradition, by the passing down of sacred stories and myths; in the technological society, stability is ensured by the propagation of an ethos of openness to change and a fetishization of "newness." In the organic culture, feedback identifies heretics and apostates; in the technological society, it identifies "Luddites." In either culture, the remedies can be severe.

Ultimately, every system (society) operates on the basis of the information upon which it was founded, which rationalizes its goal, and which justifies its existence (its ethos). The ability of its constituents and constituent groups to learn, their ability to recognize, consider, and assimilate new information and viewpoints, is in a very real way constrained and regulated by that ethos and its congruence with the system's structure. The system itself is predisposed to remain stable and to self-perpetuation or survival, and will filter or "self-censor" messages that threaten its stability. As Weiner stated,

> we are now no longer concerned with the study of all possible outgoing and incoming messages which we may send and receive, but with the theory of much more specific outgoing and incoming messages; and it involves a measurement of the no-longer infinite amount of information that they yield us.[5]

Information Theory

Claude Shannon's and Warren Weaver's information theory concerns itself not with content per sé, but with the efficient transmission of information. Claude Shannon's contribution to information theory (and admittedly his contribution constitutes the essential majority of *The Mathematical Theory of Communication*) limits itself to questions of efficiency in the transmission and reception of information. However, Warren Weaver's often overlooked contribution interprets and contextualizes Shannon's in very important ways. Referring to Shannon's contribution as a solution to the Level A "technical problem" ("How accurately can the symbol of communication be transmitted?"),[6] Weaver suggests that there are not one, but three levels of communication problems, including a Level B "semantic problem" ("How precisely do the transmitted symbols convey the desired meaning?"), and a Level C "effectiveness problem" ("How effectively does

---

5. Wiener, *Human Use of Human Beings*, 21.

6. Shannon and Weaver, *Mathematical Theory of Communication*, 4.

the received meaning affect conduct in the desired way?").[7] In this interpretation of the relationship between engineering and pragmatics of communication, Weaver provides a model for analysis and understanding of propaganda, and extends Shannon's pragmatic theory beyond the mere technical to the ethical and aesthetic realms, allowing us to make value judgments about the quality of information.

The Meaning of Information in Information Theory

The word *information*, in the context of information theory, does not necessarily mean what we might usually think. Weaver tells us, "The word information, in this theory, is used in a special sense that must not be confused with its ordinary usage. In particular, information must not be confused with meaning."[8] In information theory, he continues, the word information "relates not so much to what you do say, as to what you *could* say. That is, *information is a measure of one's freedom of choice when one selects a message*."[9] (My emphasis.) The less information one has, the less freedom exists to choose among messages, and the higher the probability that any given message might be chosen. The more information one has, the more freedom exists to choose among messages, and it becomes very difficult to predict what that person will say next. I think it is significant that Weaver not only points out, but emphasizes this particular point in Claude Shannon's work. It indicates Weaver's qualitative judgment of support for more rather than less information, and an equally supportive attitude toward openness and learning.

Information in information theory, then, does not refer to what you know; information is *what you don't know*. If you already know something (i.e., have information about it), then someone telling you about that something is not information. It is redundancy (which we shall examine shortly). For the purposes of information theory, sameness is not information. Difference is. As Gregory Bateson put it, "A difference which makes a difference is an idea. It is a bit, a unit of information."[10] By this he meant that even in what appears to be a disordered system, a system that appears to be chaotic and nonsensical, a system that we will soon identify as *entropic*, if we are able to actually discern a pattern amid the chaos, we are presented with the possibility of finding meaning where none is readily apparent.

7. Shannon and Weaver, *Mathematical Theory of Communication*, 4.

8. Shannon and Weaver, *Mathematical Theory of Communication*, 8.

9. Shannon and Weaver, *Mathematical Theory of Communication*, 8–9.

10. Bateson, *Steps to an Ecology of Mind*, 271–72.

Even though we are more accustomed to the textbook and dictionary definitions of the word *information*, we seem idiomatically aware of Shannon and Weaver's stance. A sarcastic response of "Tell me something I don't know" to a juicy bit of gossip is an acknowledgement of Shannon and Weaver's use of the term *information*. What we already know is *not* information. It's "old news." What is predictable is *not* information. What we are comfortably accustomed to is *not* information. What everybody accepts to be true is *not* information. On the contrary, when we confront what is alien, uncomfortable, confusing, and perhaps even frightening, we can be pretty certain that we are encountering information. And if we're smart and take the time to examine, question, and consider that piece of information, we just might learn something that we don't already know. Curiosity may have killed the cat, but for his first eight lives we can be certain he learned a lot.

The Shannon-Weaver Information Theory Model

Shannon and Weaver's model consists of six constituent parts: an information source, a transmitter, a medium (which is subject to the influence of some noise source), a receiver, and a destination. Let's look closely at each of these parts:

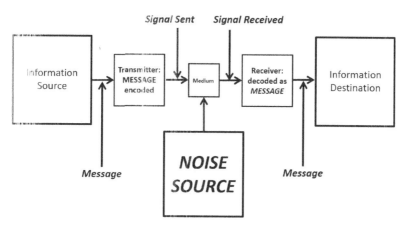

1. *The information source* selects a desired message out of all the possible messages it contains.[11] Messages are "constructed" from discrete bits of information. This implies a significant responsibility on the part of the information source for choosing bits of information (and not choosing others) and organizing them in such a way that they not only have meaning, but the particular meaning that the information source wants to convey. It also implies a considerable level of intelligence necessary in both the choice and construction of messages. Furthermore, we can recognize that the information source is constrained in the construction of messages by the amount of information that he, she, or it has learned. The information source cannot construct comprehensible messages from information it does not have. This is not to say that an information source cannot lie or "make things up." But every lie and every fantasy must come from some sort of internalized experience and conveyed in such a way as to make it comprehensible at its destination.

2. *The transmitter* encodes the message into a symbolic form (or "code") that allows it to be conveyed through some medium to a receiver. In the case of writing, the information source is our brain, the transmitter is our hand and a pen or pencil, and the code is the written form of the spoken language. In the case of speech, the information source is our brain, the transmitter is our vocal mechanisms, and the code is some spoken language.[12] However, in the case of (interpersonal) speech, we are also encoding information nonverbally, in paralinguistic codes (tone of voice, articulation, speed at which we speak, loudness or softness of our voice, etc.), in kinesthetic codes (our posture, hand gestures, facial expressions, dynamic movement or rigid non-movement, etc.), and proxemic codes (how the information source uses space to orient itself to the receiver). Unlike writing, which lacks these other channels of encoding, speech demands not only that the information source choose the correct words to make the message meaningful, but that the presentation of the information is consistent with and supports the desired meaning.

On the other hand, one of the reasons why effective writing (in either the pragmatic or aesthetic sense) is so difficult is that it lacks the emotional presence and layers of meaning typical of interpersonal conversation.

3. *A medium* is the technology or conduit through which a message passes from transmitter to receiver. In the case of oral speech, the air itself,

11. Shannon and Weaver, *Mathematical Theory of Communication*, 7.
12. Shannon and Weaver, *Mathematical Theory of Communication*, 7.

modulated by the vibrations caused by our vocal mechanism, is the medium. In the case of writing, the medium consists of two pieces of technology: something to write with, and something to write on. In the case of a broadcast medium like radio or television, the transmitter and receiver are parts of the medium, but the electromagnetic spectrum, upon which electronic signals are modulated, is part of the medium as well.

4. The receiver, Weaver tells us, "is a sort of inverse transmitter, changing the transmitted signal back into a message, and handing this message on to the destination."[13]

5. The idea of **the destination** should be self-explanatory, but still calls for deeper investigation. In the case of interpersonal speech (conversation), the information source conveys a message to the destination. But it is expected that the destination will then respond, becoming in turn the information source and conveying his, her, or its own message to the destination (who only seconds earlier was the information source). Also in the case of interpersonal speech, there is an intended destination, but there may also be one or more unintended destinations (for example, a conversation in a crowded room or on a train).

However, in the case of mass-mediated communication, the intended destination is always a large group of people—for the purposes of technologically complex mass communication, the largest group possible. In such situations, the mass of people who constitute the intended destination remain the destination at all times. There is never any opportunity for them to "change hats" and become the information source.

6. The communication event is always subject to the influences of a **noise source**. Anything that disrupts the efficient flow of messages in a communication event is a form of noise. In Level A technical problems, the noise source is related to the medium used. However, we can easily apply the idea of noise to Level B semantic problems. If you are not a native speaker of a given language, but have been trained to perform at a rudimentary conversational level, you will likely get the meaning of messages spoken to you, but not feel a great deal of confidence in your comprehension because there were some words that you just didn't understand. Those words are a form of semantic noise. Similarly, having a conversation in a crowded room, perhaps with police sirens screaming out the window, you may misunderstand—or

---

13. Shannon and Weaver, *Mathematical Theory of Communication*, 7.

miss entirely—some of the words spoken to you. In this case, we can use the word *noise* in a very literal sense.

Noise is one manifestation of a powerful physical force that is present in all systems, whether biological, geological, chemical, or mechanical—entropy. But "noise" is not a mere synonym for entropy. Entropy takes many forms in every communication system.

Entropy

The first law of thermodynamics (also known as the law of conservation) states that the energy of the universe is finite. Energy cannot be destroyed, and new energy cannot be created. Energy is, instead, transformed from one physical state into another (e.g., from light into heat, from work into organization, etc.). With every transformation from one physical state to another in an isolated organized system, however, the energy of that system decreases, being transferred to another system. To keep a system infinitely organized demands an infinite expenditure of energy. This is impossible as energy is finite, and its finitude underlies the second law of thermodynamics.

What the second law states, essentially, is that all ordered systems tend toward disorder. The energy in any given ordered system is insufficient to keep that system ordered. A constant expenditure of energy must come from beyond an ordered system to maintain that system's order. This, of course, would mean utilizing energy that might otherwise be used, for example, for work, heat, light, or ordering *some other system*.

Entropy, then, can be seen as the measure of the degree of randomness or disorder in a system. Entropy is the natural tendency of all ordered systems to move toward disorder and chaos as the energy in the system dissipates. In terms of communication systems, entropy is the introduction of randomness into the communication process (or, again, the removal of organizing energy). In most—if not all—cases, the influence of entropy is subjectively experienced as noise. Entropy is at work when we say one thing, but our communication partner hears or perceives something else. Entropy is at work when we sit in a classroom and nineteen students hear the professor say X but one is absolutely certain that the professor actually said Y. It takes an enormous expenditure of energy to keep our communication systems focused and working efficiently. To let down on the energy, even a little bit, is to invite entropy to do its mischief.

Entropy, being a measure of randomness in a communication system, has a strong, positive correlation with ambiguity and uncertainty. How do we fight entropy? With redundancy.

Redundancy

Redundancy is the rule-based part of any system that allows it to be ordered and predictable; redundancy can be thought of as negative entropy. It is that part of the message which is not determined by the free choice of the sender. Redundancy has several forms: repetition, amplification, parallel-channel reinforcement, structural redundancy, and others.

- Repetition is often necessary just to get a piece of unfamiliar information to "stick" in one's mind. "Rote learning" is an example of repetition, and we see it used frequently in early childhood education.

- Amplification has both Level A and Level B implications; we amplify a signal being transmitted across a lengthy span of cable to fight against the inevitable signal loss that occurs due to the natural resistance of the cable. But we also "amplify" ideas by definition, exemplification, and application.

- Parallel-channel reinforcement (or channel redundancy) also has Level A and Level B dimensions; on the technical level, "old technology" linear, nondistributed (centralized) networks suffered from the weakness of single-channel routing. Any break in the network left all points beyond the break in the dark. The signal could not travel beyond the break. That's one of the reasons why a consortium of universities, businesses, and government agencies in the middle of the last century started developing distributed (decentralized) networks—networks of networks—that would not be broken if one point in the network failed. (I refer here, of course, to the internet.) On the semantic level, parallel-channel reinforcement is evident in many situations; in the use of nonverbal cues (gestures, vocal intonation, facial expressions, etc.) to reinforce spoken words, in the use of pictures to illustrate complex (or even simple) concepts, etc.

- Structural redundancy is the redundancy that is "planned into" the system (whether that planning was conscious and deliberate or unconscious and accidental). The fact that spoken languages have grammars, syntaxes, parts of speech, etc., and that written languages share those traits but add things like spaces between words, punctuation, capitalization, etc., are all examples of structural redundancy.

Each of these techniques of redundancy has a few things in common: for one thing, they are all, unlike entropy, inventions—human techniques developed over the ages to bring greater clarity and certainty to human communication. Entropy is a force of nature and therefore inevitable;

redundancy is a set of techniques invented by human beings to fight the forces of entropy. But another thing these techniques have in common is that they all demand an expenditure of energy, dedicated to limiting the effects of entropy and assuring a workable level of certainty in communication, *which cannot then be devoted to the transmission of additional information*. The more energy one expends making sure that a message will be received and comprehended as intended, the less energy remains available for the transmission of new messages.

Redundancy, then, has a strong positive correlation with certainty. The more redundant we are in the communication process, the more certain we may be that the process will be successful; that is, that the message received will be identical—or, at least, very, very close—to the message sent. Redundancy is the reason why teachers don't only assign textbooks for our classes, or why we don't only ask students to attend lectures, or why we don't only provide PowerPoint presentations, or why we don't only expect students to take lecture notes. The more channels through which we receive information, and the more time we spend studying it, the more likely we are to understand it, internalize it, and assimilate it.

Here we must remind ourselves of Shannon and Weaver's definition of information—"a measure of one's freedom of choice when one selects a message"—and (what may seem to many to be) the curious relationship pointed out by Warren Weaver of entropy to information, for we are very likely to find ourselves rooting right now for the great guarantor of certainty, redundancy, against the "dark forces" of entropy. But perhaps we should think again. "[W]hen one meets the concept of entropy in communication theory," Weaver says,

> he has a right to be rather excited—a right to suspect that one has hold of something that may turn out to be basic and important. That information be measured by entropy is, after all, natural when we remember that information, in communication theory, is associated with the amount of freedom of choice we have in constructing messages. Thus for a communication source one can say, just as he would also say it of a thermodynamic ensemble, "This situation is highly organized, it is not characterized by a large degree of randomness or of choice— that is to say, the information (or entropy) is low."[14]

Entropy and redundancy might be thought of as the yin and yang of human communication, appearing, as do night and day, to be working at cross purposes; but actually complementary and interdependent parts of the

14. Shannon and Weaver, *Mathematical Theory of Communication*, 13.

system, each necessary, on its own merits, in any healthy system of human communication. For without redundancy, it is very difficult for human beings to speak to one another; without entropy, we have very little to say.

Learning in the Context of Information Theory

We can now contrast the idea of "learning" in information theory with that of cybernetics and present a sort of elaborate syllogism, a set of six axioms or propositions which derive logically from Shannon and Weaver's work, and a seventh that derives logically from the previous six. The first six, as I said, are axiomatic—they are not only self-evident but empirically verifiable. The seventh, however, while equally axiomatic, is not at all self-evident, but in fact extremely counterintuitive—which is to say it goes against the generally accepted assumptions of the mass:

- Entropy correlates positively with ambiguity
- Entropy correlates positively with uncertainty
- Entropy correlates positively with information
- Redundancy correlates positively with clarity
- Redundancy correlates positively with certainty
- Redundancy correlates negatively with information

Therefore:

- Entropy must correlate positively with *the learning of new information*.

Entropy, in other words, is inherent in propaganda 2.1, and the opposite of propaganda 2.0. And redundancy is propaganda 2.0's best friend.

Propaganda 2.0

—————— Ellul's Technological Society and Total Propaganda

J acques Ellul was one of the most important thinkers of the twentieth century. The author of fifty books (not all yet translated into English) and literally hundreds of articles, his areas of expertise spanned the fields of philosophy, sociology, mass communication, and theology. The bulk of his writing is theological in nature, but his sociological works set the standard for scholarship in technology and communication. It is not my goal to attempt an in-depth exegesis of Ellul's work. But understanding his thinking in *Propaganda* (and a few other sociological works) is critical to any genuine understanding of the phenomenon, and in this chapter I'd like to provide a (relatively) brief overview of his thoughts.

Ellul argues that human civilization has reached a point where *technique* suffuses every facet of society at every moment. Whereas earlier civilizations' realities were negotiated through a dialectic process among a number of competing social forces—capital, division of labor, ownership of property, etc.—today all social forces are subsumed into the dominant and dominating force: *technique*. Everything we do, every step we take, every thought we have, everything we know—all are unconsciously influenced by and dependent on technique.

Ellul defines technique as "*the totality of methods rationally arrived at and having absolute efficiency* (for a given stage of development) in *every* field of human activity."[1] (Ellul's emphases.) However, Ellul is not limiting our attention to what we commonly refer to as "technology," although machinery and mechanization, like all other social forces, are certainly subsumed into the technological phenomenon as well. Accompanying every

—————————————
1. Ellul, *Technological Society*, xxv.

technology is a method, and a method implies a particular behavior or set of behaviors. With every behavior comes a set of assumptions about right or wrong, appropriate or inappropriate, effective or ineffective, efficient or inefficient. At the same time, we must recognize the hidden but corollary proposition that every method also *excludes* particular behaviors or sets of behaviors; and so *questioning* right or wrong, appropriate or inappropriate, efficient or inefficient becomes moot. Technique not only defines the parameters of our cognitive reality, it defines what must thereafter be deemed unthinkable. What we're describing here is a mindset, a worldview: *technique is a value system based on rationality and efficiency.*

Reflex vs. Reflection

Ellul warns us that the technical worldview, so attuned to the algorithmic methods we have adapted, is a reflexive one rather than the reflective mindset of the person living more in tune with the natural rhythms of life.

> Reflection means that, after I have undergone an experience, I think about that experience. In the case of a reflex you know immediately what you must do in a certain situation. Without thinking. Technology requires us no longer to think about the things. If you are driving a car at 150 kilometers an hour and you think you'll have an accident. Everything depends on reflexes. The only thing technology requires us is: Don't think about it. Use your reflexes.[2]

A reflex demands no conscious thought, no decision-making process; the reflexive process takes place entirely on the level of the unconscious. To be conscious of your actions, to make value judgments about them, moral or ethical, to make decisions about whether to do something or not—these are the antitheses of reflex, and undermine the technical worldview.

The Values of the Technological Society

Over many years of reading Ellul I have seen his emphasis on the rationality and efficiency of technique (predominantly efficiency, I must say) repeatedly hammered home. I understand his point. But if efficiency and rationality are the primary values of the technological society, I'd like to suggest a list of secondary or complementary values based on my own observations of the technological society: productivity, profit, progress,

2. Ellul, "Betrayal by Technology."

ease (of use), convenience, maximization, utility, pragmatism, and consumption. These, along with rationality and efficiency, make up the value system of the technological society.

Technique is as old as our species; the technological society is very new. Technique precedes science; indeed, science would never have developed as a social institution in the absence of technique.[3] Older technologies, however, were developed only when they were needed and were generally subordinated to the demands of religion and tradition; they were, like their societies, relatively stable and unchanging, passed down from generation to generation with very little modification. They were more geared toward survival and sustainability than toward profit and innovation, and the "morality" of early technique did not extend beyond judgment about whether or not you had used it for the correct task, the one for which it was created. Social values, mores, and taboos rationalized the uses of technology, not the other way around.

However, after science is firmly established in the West following the development of the technique (and machinery) of moveable-type printing, techniques proliferated at a constantly accelerating rate, and the demand for their use became motivated by profit. Handicrafts began to disappear, manufacturing, in time, became a mass technique, and manufactured goods became exact copies of one another. The loss of the uniqueness and sense of "authenticity" of handmade goods was offset by the novelty of new ones or the innovation and improvement of old ones.

Standardization, based on the technologically imposed methods of manufacture, followed naturally; standardization of products, standardization of production procedures, standardization of appearance (first of the products and then of the people making, buying, using, and wearing them), standardization of speech and spelling, standardization of thought, but most importantly standardization of behavior.

The Inevitability of Technique

Here is an axiom concerning our technological society: *what technique makes possible, it also makes inevitable.* Techniques "are always put to immediate use."[4] While the possibility of random or accidental invention exists, one should be able to assume that a technique is never formulated for no reason; every technique is an attempt to solve a specific problem or answer

3. Ellul, *Technological Society*, 7.
4. Ellul, *Technological Society*, 10

a question. Therefore it is natural also to assume that once a new technique or technology is created, it will be used.

But in the technological society, the stakes are raised to mass proportions. Primitive techniques were created as a means directed at some end; in the full flowering of the technological society, techniques are developed before any particular end has been identified. They are created as commodities and become both means and ends in themselves. They are used because we have them and they do *something*; whatever it is they do is something that we were unable to do without them (and never realized there was a need for doing). So the fact that technical potentiality quickly becomes technical inevitability is not an insignificant one.

Ellul presents to us what he calls a *characterology* of technique, outlining several characteristics of modern technique, a few of which I will discuss: *automatism, self-augmentation, monism, technical universalism,* and *autonomy*.

Automatism As we noted earlier, when a society formulates a specific technique to address some issue or solve a problem, if it is efficient it will be adopted. It is "the one best way."[5] Here we see the rationality of technique. To consciously avoid adopting the technique would make no sense. To opt for a less efficient solution would be equally irrational. The rationality and efficiency of the technique *alone* determines its adoption (underlining again the inevitability of technical adoption). This phenomenon is what Ellul refers to in his idea of the *automatism* of technique.

Self-augmentation A successful technique formulated to serve one dimension of human civil, social, political, or social life will eventually find its way into another, and eventually *all the other dimensions* whether that is desirable or not. Technique seeps from one element in the technoculture to another by virtue of its rationality and efficiency, even when its effects on the new element will almost certainly not be the same as the first.

Ellul furnishes us with two laws of self-augmentation: 1) in a given civilization, technical progress is irreversible; and 2) technical progress tends to act, not according to an arithmetic, but according to a geometric progression.[6] Technique moves from level to level, from discipline to discipline, from social institution to social institution until we find it suffuses our entire culture.

---

5. Ellul, *Technological Society*, 79.
6. Ellul, *Technological Society*, 89.

Another aspect of self-augmentation that Ellul presents to us concerns the fact that technique tends to be self-perpetuating. Technical systems being *systems*, every technique will eventually reveal its flaw, and those flaws threaten the stability of the system. When feedback reveals a technical problem, it is necessarily addressed by a new technical solution—a "patch," perhaps on the present technique, the addition of a supporting technique, or the formulation of an entirely new technique taking into account the failings of the older one. The solution to a technical problem is *never* the removal of technique.

Technical Universalism

Ellul tells us that universalism manifests itself in two dimensions: a geographic and a qualitative one.[7] He describes a process in which technique unifies all who live under its sway, so that not only is it an inevitability that the so-called developing nations of the world will eventually reach the same level of development as the rest of the technoculture, as did the now-independent postcolonial world, but will be using the same techniques, in the same ways, for the same purposes as the developed nations of Ellul's technological society. At the same time, the peoples of the not-yet-developed world will be forced to abandon anything that stands as an impediment to the spread of technique—traditional customs, behaviors, and cultural mores, traditional handicrafts and means of agriculture, cultural identity—in order to enjoy the benefits of technical development.

We can see this happening today in the phenomenon of globalization, both economic and cultural. Developing nations, seeking foreign direct investment, agree to regulations set down in 1948 in the General Agreement on Tariffs and Trade (GATT) and monitored since 1994 by the World Trade Organization (WTO). Foreign direct investment helps the poor not by alleviating any immediate crisis (e.g., buying and delivering food to relieve starvation, supplying medicine to alleviate disease, etc.) but by bringing investment, technology, jobs, manufacturing, and construction. These nations must prepare themselves to trade on a global market and put no artificial restrictions on imported goods. They must prepare their governmental bureaucracies to focus on the types of administrative tasks necessary to moderate international trade, and they must rethink the role of their legislatures in facilitating it. They must restructure their educational institutions to prepare citizens to meet the demands of a technological society. The changes the developing nations have been experiencing over the

7. Ellul, *Technological Society*, 116.

last three decades are enormous, and only the poorest and least developed retain the traditional behavioral patterns of their past, and await their own turn to throw off the shackles of traditional culture.

We see how technique expands geographically, in the past by invasion and colonialism, in the present by economic and cultural development. Qualitatively, technical universalism expresses itself in the commonality of thought and behavior shared by all involved in the same technique.

Looking at it from the point of view of specific "micro-techniques," a heart surgeon in Bavaria has the same knowledge and learns the same skills as the heart surgeon in Boston. People who write code for computer software have the same concerns whether they work in Palo Alto, Paris, or Peoria. Long-haul or interstate truckers have the same skills and stresses (and, very likely, drugs to help them stay awake) whether they're driving between London and Edinburgh, Moscow and Helsinki, or Chicago and San Francisco.

From a more "macro-technical" point of view, no matter where we look, and no matter what micro-technique one is engaged in, every day across the technological society—in the United States, the European Union, Russia, China, Japan, Australia, Indonesia, and Malaysia, Caracas, Bogota, Buenos Aires, and other places—we will witness masses of people being awakened by a technical device (once the alarm clock, then the clock radio, and increasingly frequently now, the smartphone), eating a mass-produced packaged breakfast heated in a microwave, driving, biking, cab-bing, or Ubering to work (or to mass transit), checking their messages or social media posts during the commute on some device (through which they're probably also listening to music), doing their highly specialized task in a much larger and complex work environment, at some point eat-ing a meal (at a restaurant or, again increasingly likely, a fast food joint like McDonald's), going back to work, commuting home, eating more packaged food, and watching television. The deep-structural patterning of behavior is the message of the technological society.

Ellul's model of the technological society dovetails neatly into his work on *Propaganda*. Ellul defined propaganda as "an instrument of ma-nipulation to obtain an objectively conforming behavior (orthopraxy). That is to say, that it obeys, exclusively, principles of efficacy, technical rules of a psychological or sociological nature, the usage of instruments which are themselves techniques."[8] Propaganda, as described by Ellul, does not simply consist of lies, manipulations, or falsehoods, and it is not "brainwashing." It is, however, a systematic creation and explanation of a

8. Ellul, "Ethics of Propaganda."

shared social "reality" within which individuals are led to believe that they enjoy freedom of thought, of choice, and of behavior, while at the same time they are adapting and conforming to the values of the technological society. Propaganda is *mass-manufactured reality*.

Propaganda Is Systematic

The technological system—like all systems—strives to maintain its balance, momentum, and structural integrity. Propaganda is the integral part of the technological system whose purpose is to make consistent and predictable (i.e., redundant) in its behavior that part of the system which is, by its very nature, the most inconsistent and unpredictable (i.e., entropic)—*human behavior*. As a technique, propaganda is made up of a number of other human techniques including techniques of communication, psychological techniques, commercial techniques, and techniques of authoritarian government.[9]

Systematic Propaganda Is Total Propaganda

The mass society must use *all* technological means at its disposal at *all* times. Each individual technology can address a specific dimension of the propaganda message in its own way, thereby giving the illusion of diversity of messages. Movies can entertain us and appeal to our emotions by the symbolic evocation of mythic themes (e.g., bravery, patriotism, undying love, transformation through hardship, etc.), while televised sports provides credible support for the value of competition—a central, fundamental value of the technological society. News programming allows us to feel involved in the public life of society, to form opinions about those issues of which everyone is speaking. Entertainments divert our attention from the harsher realities of life in the technological society.

Different technologies are particularly suited to a certain type of propaganda—for instance, newspapers are better at presenting rational discourse than television news programs, and television and other visual media are better at presenting an artificial image of reality and evoking the emotional responses of personal experience—but all must be used in concert for effective propaganda to take place.

---

9. Ellul, *Technological Society*, 91.

The Continuity and Duration of Propaganda

Propaganda must be continuous (no gaps) and continual (never ending). The citizen must live in a seamless sphere of information, stepping into one technological environment as he steps out of the previous. Wake to an alarm clock or a smartphone, read a newspaper or news aggregator with breakfast, listen to music while showering, check Facebook or Instagram posts on the train, text your friend while walking to the office, spend several hours in a cubicle, very likely at a computer and working either online or offline, take calls from clients and friends throughout the day, listen to iMusic (or Pandora or Spotify) on the train ride home, text more friends, check more posts, settle in for dinner, then Netflix. After that, into bed, check messages, texts, and posts one more time, check the alarm, sleep, and repeat.

This continuous propaganda creates an excess of redundant information which impedes—by overwhelming—the individual's capacities for attention or adaptation to constantly changing information and thus his abilities to critically analyze or resist propaganda. This creates what Neil Postman calls "information glut, information as garbage, information divorced from purpose and even meaning."[10]

Orthopraxy, Not Orthodoxy

In the popular mind, propaganda is often viewed as a form of "mind control" or "brainwashing." Most people believe its aim is to change our ideas, to somehow remove unwanted thoughts from our heads and replace them with "acceptable" thoughts. Nothing could be further from the truth. As Joseph Goebbels said (echoing Harold Lasswell),

> There is really little point to discussing propaganda. It is a matter of practice, not of theory. One cannot determine theoretically whether one propaganda is better than another. Rather, that propaganda is good that has the desired results, and that propaganda is bad that does not lead to the desired results. It does not matter how clever it is, for the task of propaganda is not to be clever, its task is to lead to success.[11]

Effective propaganda aims at *participation*, at *action* (of some sort). The individual interior response to propaganda should not be expected to be reasoned or logical, but to exist on the level of emotion and instinct—the

---

10. Postman, *Building a Bridge to the 18th Century*, 89.
11. Goebbels, "Knowledge and Propaganda."

knee-jerk reaction. The behavioral response to propaganda *may* make sense; it simply doesn't have to. Propaganda far prefers doing without thinking to thinking before doing, prefers walking the walk to talking the talk. Talk is cheap, after all, and actions speak louder than words. The participation which propaganda seeks, however, may be *active* or *passive*. At first glance "passive participation" seems an oxymoron. The active participant will be one who, for instance, donates money to a cause, or campaigns for a candidate, or starts a petition drive, or votes regularly (probably on a strict party line), or sleeps in a tent in front of the Apple Store to be the first to buy the new iPhone, or telephones ICE (Immigration and Customs Enforcement) to report those he suspects to be undocumented aliens living in his neighborhood. The passive participant will be the one who either a) takes no action but psychologically supports a cause or a candidate, or b) opposes any or all of those things but neither speaks out against them nor takes action to oppose them. Eldridge Cleaver once said that if you're not part of the solution, you're part of the problem. And if you're not actively opposing the object of propaganda, you're passively participating with it.

Knowledge of the Psychological Terrain

Propaganda is not magic. It is not mind control and it is not brainwashing. It is a human technique based on social sciences like mass communication studies and social psychology (as Edward Bernays correctly noted). A certain knowledge of what Ellul calls *the psychological terrain* is therefore necessary. When we think about psychological manipulation we're usually imagining the manipulation of an individual. This is an error in thinking; effective propaganda works on the individual *only* through the mass. Propaganda that seeks to provoke an individual to abandon his or her most strongly held and firmly established beliefs will fail. Propaganda cannot contradict what an individual believes to be true but instead must aim to excite and then exploit the shared cultural symbols, stereotypes, fears, aspirations, etc., of the mass in order to move the mass to action (of some sort). The best and most effective propaganda seeks to obtain participation without demanding intellectual consistency.

Knowledge of the Fundamental Currents in Society

The propagandist must be knowledgeable of the fundamental currents in society—its social attitudes, values, ideologies, myths, etc., because these are the foundation upon which effective propaganda is built. To evoke a response rooted in deeply internalized myth rather than expressing a demand for a particular action provides the individual with a sense of personal ownership of whatever action he eventually takes. When jobs are lost to automation, for example, one could simply tell workers that it is necessary to decrease labor costs, increase productivity, and bolster the overall profit margin of a company; it is helpful, though, to have a workforce that believes deeply in the speed and efficiency of technology, and the righteous inevitability of "progress." Such workers will leave quietly and without much of a fight. When a political party that once stood firmly on the principles of workplace democracy, collective bargaining, and a fair wage begins talking about legislative support for "right to work" laws, they can simply tell their constituents that with the influx of corporate money into the political system, refusal to accept campaign donations from corporations is political suicide and it therefore becomes necessary to do at least a portion of corporate America's bidding; but it might be better to have a constituency that believes deeply in pragmatism and the need for compromise. Such voters who put pragmatism over principle will get not what in principle is right, but instead only that which those in power will give them.

Timeliness of Propaganda

Propaganda must also be *timely*. When Ellul wrote of timeliness he was still writing in an era when information moved (relatively) slowly. Newspapers dominated the information environment; radio was focused more on music than on news, and television was just ascending to a position of power. He did not anticipate cable television stations dedicated to nothing but news, the rise and spread of the internet, the twenty-four-hour news cycle, and the explosion of information that we have witnessed over the last twenty-five years. Timeliness, therefore, is an even more critical factor in propaganda today than it was when Ellul was writing.

When Andy Warhol famously said that in the future everyone will enjoy fifteen minutes of fame, he was, no doubt, referring to the effects of the newly dominant medium of television on cultural attention spans. The faster information moves, the more information we get, and processing enormous quantities of information becomes very difficult. This phenomenon is the previously mentioned information glut—the situation we face when there is too much information (frequently decontextualized, disjointed, and, on the face of it, meaningless) coming at us, far too quickly, through too many conduits, and from too many directions for us to make any sense of it at all. As a consequence, we tend to construct cognitive filters, and focus only on two types of information: 1) what we find relevant to our lives (this in itself is problematic, for without sufficient exposure to diverse experiences and bits of information it is impossible to have a genuine sense of what is relevant), and 2) that information which is most *timely*; entertaining or diverting, sensational, controversial, or popular for the next few weeks (or days, or minutes), during which time it will be the topic of conversation for the majority of the nation.

This, of course, partially explains the shift in news reporting from issues to personalities of the moment, as well as the growth over the last three decades of such new genres of journalism as entertainment news, lifestyle news, sports news, ambush journalism, investigative journalism (that doesn't really investigate much of anything), technology journalism, and others. These new genres of journalism have acted to focus our attention not on the news itself, but on the people (and personalities) currently in the public arena who make the news. Rather than explaining, for instance, the geopolitical circumstances that have catalyzed terrorism in the last generation (postcolonialism in Africa and the Arab world, poverty, sweatshop exploitation in a global "free-market" capitalist system, etc.), our journalism tends to focus on the terrorists themselves; to this end, the image of an Osama bin Laden flashed onto our screens every few weeks acts as a vividly frightening icon of the death and destruction wrought by violent fanatics, and keeps us in anxious expectation of the next attack. We don't concern ourselves with the root causes of terrorism, we simply obsess anxiously over its existence.

Newsworthy circumstances can languish for long periods of time before they become timely enough to be reported as news. It is widely known, for instance, that Russia has been engaged in a long-term campaign of cyber warfare with the United States (as has China, Israel, and the United Kingdom, and in fairness to the subject I must include the US, engaged in cyber warfare with all of them as well—along with ISIS, the international group of hackers known as Anonymous, and individual hackers around the globe), but it was not until the presidential campaign of 2016 that Russian hacking became a powerful propaganda meme.

There's a very curious sidebar to the story: the US establishment media have ignored several key elements that might make the story more understandable, but would certainly change its overall meaning and weaken its propaganda power: 1) Key former US intelligence operatives have said that any Russian hacking of the Democratic National Committee's server was unlikely;[12] 2) WikiLeaks founder Julian Assange has publicly claimed on sev-

---

12. McGovern and Binney, "Emails Were Leaked, Not Hacked."

eral occasions that the leaked DNC/John Podesta emails did not come from a hacker, but were leaked from an internal source;[13] 3) Former UK Ambassador to Uzbekistan Craig Murray told the *Daily Mail* that he received the leaked email directly from a disgruntled member of the Democratic National Committee and hand-delivered them to WikiLeaks,[14] calling the US establishment narrative of Russian hacking "bullshit";[15] and 4) In March of 2016 WikiLeaks published a cache of files and documents leaked from a high-security network inside the CIA's Center for Cyber Intelligence (CCI) in Langley, Virginia, revealing a top secret program called "UMBRAGE" which, among other things, "collects and maintains a substantial library of attack techniques 'stolen' from malware produced in other states including the Russian Federation" and allows hackers working (on contract) for the CIA to hack into a private network and "misdirect attribution by leaving behind the 'fingerprints' of the groups that the attack techniques were stolen from."[16]

Let me say at this point that I am in no way explicitly contradicting the January 6, 2017 declassified Director of National Intelligence assessment of Russian interference in the 2016 US presidential election. I have no solid evidence to do so. But that is also my point: no one has enough evidence to either support or refute it, yet our news media have reported it as though it were a fact.[17] The Office of the DNI, in its assessment, provided no evidence to support its conclusions, stating that "the release of such information would reveal sensitive sources or methods and imperil the ability to collect critical foreign intelligence in the future," and therefore "while the conclusions in the report are all reflected in the classified assessment, the declassified report does not and cannot include the full supporting information, including specific intelligence and sources and methods."[18] In other words, we must accept the conclusions of the assessment on faith, despite the fact that the same US intelligence community was complicit in a year-long campaign of disinformation culminating in the illegal 2003

13. Bowerman, "Russian government not the source."

14. Goodman, "WikiLeaks operative claims Russia did NOT provide emails."

15. Gayle, "CIA concludes Russia interfered."

16. "Vault7—Home."

17. One of the problems here may be that it *is* a fact that the CIA published this assessment. The various media reported *this* fact. So far there is no problem. But in the ensuing months since the publication, the media narrative has shifted from the fact of the CIA's assessment and the *factuality of* the assessment, and this has not (in fact) been established. I don't believe this would be a problem if every time someone in our media mentioned "the Russian hacking" they would say "the Russian hacking that allegedly occurred according to a CIA assessment for which no supporting evidence has been presented . . ."

18. Office of the Director of National Intelligence, "Assessing Russian Activities."

invasion of Iraq (more on that invasion later), and despite the fact that there was not only ample motive but also the opportunity and technical capability of the CIA to make it appear that Russia hacked the 2016 US presidential election. Our news media have reported the official story with Homeric diligence; the part of the story actually supported by first-person eyewitness and documentary evidence has been either entirely ignored or dismissed, with Orwellian contempt, as "conspiracy theory."

Still, the official US government Russian hacking story (without regard to either its truthfulness or its accuracy) was an extremely timely one, and dovetails neatly with another of Ellul's points: what makes news *news* is how it is interpreted, *not* its objective reality.

"Expert" Analysis

Things happen (an "event") and we can witness them, either directly through our senses, or through the mediation of some technology of communication. But the meaning of the event is not necessarily clear—especially in light of the glut of information provided by the technological society—and certainly ought to be considered part of its inherent reality. As a consequence, news media in the United States have, over the last several decades, taken on the role of providing viewers, listeners, and readers with a proposed meaning behind events. This is called news analysis, and while potentially a helpful thing, the objectivity of the analyst (also frequently known as a "pundit") ought to be a matter of our interest. As Ellul points out, "[Edgar] Morin shows that the powers that are threatened by the power of information have no recourse but to change it into an instrument of obfuscation . . . 'The Powers systematically practice pseudo-information. The spread of lying in this field is the answer to the potential spread of truth through the rise of the media.'"[19]

Many of the so-called analysts who provide us with the meanings of events have ties to the corporate world or to the defense establishment—or both.[20] Others are partisan political operatives whose opinions reflect only the views and policies of their parties, potentially tainting the political process.[21]

Analysts not directly connected to the government, defense industries, or political parties are often unworthy of our unquestioning trust as well. When otherwise widely loathed US president Donald Trump

19. Ellul, *Technological Bluff*, 88.
20. Barstow, "Behind TV Analysts, Pentagon's Hidden Hand."
21. Editorial Board, "Using Political Flacks as News Analysts."

launched a missile strike on a Syrian military airbase in April of 2016 in response to a disputed Syrian chemical attack that had occurred earlier in the week, CNN's Fareed Zakaria gushed, "I think Donald Trump became president of the United States last night . . . I think this was actually a big moment."[22] *The Washington Post's* David Ignatius, speaking as a news analyst on MSNBC's *Morning Joe* program told host Joe Scarborough, "In terms of the credibility of American power, I think most traditional Washington commentators would say he's put more oomph, more credibility back into it."[23] And a very emotional Brian Williams, on his MSNBC show *The 11th Hour* soliloquized while watching Defense Department footage of the missile launches, "We see these beautiful pictures at night from the decks of these two U.S. Navy vessels in the eastern Mediterranean . . . I am tempted to quote the great Leonard Cohen: 'I am guided by the beauty of our weapons.' They are beautiful pictures of fearsome armaments making what is for them a brief flight over to this airfield." It was only afterward that he asked his guest, "What did they hit?"[24]

This is, perhaps, a troubling enough phenomenon. Pundits cannot be expected to present the objective truth to an audience. But while so-called news analysts might suggest a particular meaning to a news event, they can't get away with lying. Which brings us to Ellul's next point: propaganda must be *factual.*

Factuality

"The idea that propaganda consists of lies (which makes it harmless and even a little ridiculous in the eyes of the public) is still maintained by some specialists," writes Ellul. "But it is certainly not so. For a long time propagandists have recognized that lying must be avoided."[25]

If propaganda is to be effective it must make use of accurate facts; any falsehood lies only in the intentions and interpretation of facts by the propagandist, in order to evoke a similar interpretation from the audience. "If one falsifies a fact, one may be confronted with unquestionable proof to the contrary . . . But no proof can be furnished where motivations or intentions are concerned or interpretation of a fact is involved."[26] In the case of Donald Trump's Syrian missile attack, there was no lie in stating the fact

22. Hensch, "Donald Trump Became President."
23. Cawthorne, "David Ignatius: Trump Has Restored."
24. Hawkins, "Brian Williams Is 'Guided by the Beauty of Our Weapons.'"
25. Ellul, *Propaganda*, 53.
26. Ellul, *Propaganda*, 57.

that he did, in fact, hit the airbase in question—with fifty-nine Tomahawk cruise missiles. The falsehood exists in the media commentators' tendency to portray this as a great success and not as the (possibly deliberate) exercise in futility it might, in fact, have been. To have claimed a missile strike where none existed would have been a lie easily exposed. But to overstate its effectiveness is little more than opinion—an opinion, however, distributed to millions of Americans through numerous media outlets.

Categories of Propaganda

Total propaganda must utilize different forms, the more efficiently to monopolize our attentions. Ellul provides us with a list of eight categories of propaganda: political and sociological propaganda, agitation and integration propaganda, vertical and horizontal propaganda, and rational and irrational propaganda. We'll look at just a few of those categories here.

Political Propaganda

Political propaganda is archetypal; it is the image of propaganda that we carry around with us in our heads. When we protest that we can "recognize propaganda when we see it," we're usually, whether we're aware of it or not, referring to political propaganda. Political propaganda is that which is used by a government, a party, a pressure group, or a political action committee in order to influence public attitudes or behaviors.[27] Political propaganda has both strategic and tactical dimensions; the strategic dimensions, for instance, would be outlined in the various positions and proposals of a party platform or shared with the nation in a president's State of the Union address, while the tactical dimension would be the formulation of the specific propaganda campaigns necessary to accomplish each of the various proposals. Tactical political propaganda may be directed at building (or diminishing) support for a specific piece of legislation, or policy, or military action, or a candidacy, etc.

Because the work of government is constant, new laws are continually being passed, old policies overturned and new ones instituted, and internal and external threats identified, political propaganda must consist of ongoing campaigns, both simultaneously and serially, and its methods must be deliberate and calculated.[28] Its goals will be precise but limited:

27. Ellul, *Propaganda*, 62.
28. Ellul, *Propaganda*, 62.

to build support for (or opposition to) a piece of legislation, persuade the people that a particular nation is a threat (or an ally), reassure them about the health of the economy (or, for an insurgent candidate, its weakness), warn them of the consequences of inaction on the climate (or that climate change is a hoax), etc.

The political propaganda of democracies provides the same illusion of a diversity of content that we find in most other forms of propaganda. In the United States, the political propaganda of the two major parties suggests very strongly that there are major ideological differences between the two. As we shall see later in this chapter, however, this appearance of ideological diversity, like all appearances of diversity in a total propaganda system, is a "necessary illusion."[29]

Sociological Propaganda

Unlike political propaganda, sociological propaganda is invisible to most of us. We are unaware of its existence as propaganda, even as we engage with it on a daily basis. It is not an obvious form of propaganda made up solely of discrete campaigns, but rather is multifaceted and complex, flowing constantly through our collective lives like a deep river whose water runs swiftly at the surface and slowly at the riverbed. It doesn't turn off at the end of the day, and you're rarely out of its presence. Sociological propaganda is "the group of manifestations by which any society seeks to integrate the maximum number of individuals into itself, to unify its members' behavior according to a pattern, to spread its style of life abroad, and thus to impose itself on other groups."[30] Its purpose is to integrate us into the technological society, to help us conform to its values—productivity, profit, progress, ease (of use), convenience, maximization, utility, pragmatism, consumption, and above all, efficiency—and to spread those values in our dealings with an increasingly global culture.

Sociological propaganda expresses itself through a diversity of media—movies, TV, radio, computers, the internet, technology in general, education, advertising, etc. What is being expressed in sociological propaganda is the uber-ideology of the technological society: a way of life, a value system, right and wrong ways to live. This ideology penetrates the individual by means of its sociological context—the shared experience of the "reality" of life in the technoculture.

29. Chomsky, "Necessary Illusions."
30. Ellul, *Propaganda*, 62.

Sociological propaganda is not necessarily overtly planned in the sense that a political, advertising, or public relations campaign is planned. It is implicit in the life of the technological society. It springs up spontaneously; it does *not* need to be a deliberate, willful act.

In the technological society, technoculture itself becomes an export. In the 1980s, years before the fall of Soviet Communism, young Muscovites paid as much as (US) $140 for a pair of American Levi's jeans. Blue jeans, said Yale law professor Charles Reich at the time, "express freedom and wholeness of self."[31] Levi Strauss and Company believe that the very American symbol of the blue jeans resonated deeply with a population living under Soviet Communism; the image of the gold miner and the cowboy on his horse, riding the open plain, the postwar motorcycle rebel, the "wild one," Marlon Brando, the 1960s counterculture, the anti-war protester, the hippie.

> When the Berlin Wall finally came down, television viewers around the world saw young people jumping, climbing, pulling down, and sitting on the wall as nearly twenty years of imprisonment came to an end. They also saw a blending of two important symbols: the destruction of what kept people apart, by men and women wearing what brought them together: jeans.[32]

Black market VCRs and bootlegged American films flooded the Soviet Union in the 1980s, subverting a state monopoly on information that would shape public opinion.[33] And at least one Romanian filmmaker believes that the presence of those illegal movies helped to bring down Communism.[34] "It was amazing to do something illegal during Communism, something not Communist," said one young Romanian. "Watching imperialist movies."[35]

Aside from Levis and movies, the list of only the American portion of the technological society's cultural exports to the world is staggering and impossible to present in its entirety, but includes: Coca-Cola, McDonald's, Kentucky Fried Chicken, Marlboro cigarettes, baseball, (American) football, basketball, Elvis impersonators, Pabst Blue Ribbon beer, the personal computer, the smartphone, and Facebook.

We can recognize, then, that even though it is spontaneous, sociological propaganda is *not* undirected or random. It is directed by the same

31. Coakley, "Blue Jeans."
32. Staff, Uzipped, "Jeans as a Symbol of Freedom."
33. Shanker, "Soviets' VCRs Often Wrapped In Yards Of Red Tape."
34. Calugareanu, "VHS Vs. Communism."
35. Calugareanu, "VHS Vs. Communism."

agencies that, by and large, are responsible for political propaganda—the US government, American corporations, American media, etc.

Propaganda of Agitation

Propaganda of agitation (or agitprop) is another example of "obvious" propaganda. We know it when we encounter it.

Agitprop is the propaganda of the oppressed, of the desperate, and of the hopeless. It is the propaganda of those to whom the dominant propaganda of the technological society sounds hollow. It is the propaganda of the people who benefit least, when they benefit at all, from the promises of technique.

Agitprop "attracts attention because of its explosive and revolutionary character."[36] It is frequently—if not always—subversive, undertaken by a party or parties seeking to destroy an established order,[37] and seeks to induce individuals to push their energies to the limit. Consequently, agitprop cannot be long-term propaganda. Crises pass, energies and resources drain, moments of opportunity are lost, and the agitation propagandist must await the *kairos*, the next opportune moment to move people toward radical change.

Agitprop generally provokes a crisis or attempts to take advantage of an existing crisis, always operating on a level of fundamental human needs—nourishment, housing, freedom, survival, etc. It is, of course, most effectively directed toward society's weakest, poorest, least educated—those left disenfranchised by technique, living on the fringes of the technoculture.[38] And so it uses correspondingly simple media—poster, pamphlet, speech, rumor.[39]

One of the interesting things about agitprop in the United States is that, until very recently at least, there's been so little of it. Injustice (systematic racism) has been a constant in our country since its founding, poverty has historically plagued our African American population far more so than the white, and inequality between the wealthiest and the poorest has been growing drastically for three decades, increasing the financial burden of the middle class. Yet, nearly the only time we witness anything remotely resembling agitation propaganda is when an innocent Black person is shot by a police officer, or a police officer is acquitted of criminal homicide in the

36. Ellul, *Propaganda*, 73.

37. Ellul, *Propaganda*, 71.

38. Ellul, *Propaganda*, 74.

39. Ellul, *Propaganda*, 73.

death of a Black person, and loud (and sometimes violent) protests break out. It is a testament to the power of our propaganda system that there have not been more examples of agitprop to point out before today.

Propaganda of Integration

Propaganda of integration is the propaganda of the technologically developed nations, largely unknown before the twentieth century.[40] It is a propaganda of conformity—the technological society demands total adherence to its attitudes, values, and behaviors. Predicated on the concept of society as a collective organism, propaganda of integration seeks to maximize the efficiency of collective institutions and their processes. Its aim is to stabilize society, unify it, and reinforce it. For this reason integration propaganda is the preferred instrument of government, even though propaganda of integration *does not* have to be political propaganda, and is more likely to be an example of sociological propaganda.[41]

Ellul provides one final, but extremely important, note about integration propaganda: "the more comfortable, cultivated, and informed the milieu to which it is addressed, the better it works."[42] In the same way that agitprop is the propaganda of the oppressed, propaganda of integration is the propaganda of the privileged, and is most effectively directed toward society's most comfortable, affluent, and educated members. These people call it "reality"; the poor and disenfranchised call it "bullshit."

Conditions for the Existence of Propaganda

In order for propaganda to exist in any society (let alone to work), certain political, social, and cultural conditions must be present. Ellul describes several conditions necessary for the systematic, total propaganda of the technological society. We'll look at a few of them.

The Individual and the Mass

Society must embody two paradoxical qualities: a strong ethos of individualism contained within a uniform mass structure.[43] This seems impossible.

40. Ellul, *Propaganda*, 74.
41. Ellul, *Propaganda*, 75.
42. Ellul, *Propaganda*, 75.
43. Ellul, *Propaganda*, 90.

In my readings of Ellul over the years, I have discerned a way out of this paradox of which, I'd like to believe, he would approve.

Elsewhere (in his 1948 book *The Presence of the Kingdom*), Ellul provides us with an intriguing description of what he considers genuine individuality to be. The genuine individual is first of all *aware*; aware of both his strengths and his failings, and the fact that he shares the same strengths and failings with everyone else, with whom he is linked inseparably in reality. Awareness

> means the refusal to accept appearances at their face value, and of information for information's sake, the refusal of the abstract phenomenon, the refusal of the illusion given by the present means, the consoling illusion of "progress," and of the improvement of situations and of men, by a sort of benevolent fatalism of history.[44]

The genuine individual is also committed to finding objective reality, "to discover the facts of life led by the people who surround me."[45] Ignorance of the world, whether willful or involuntary, is the unfortunate and paradoxical condition of the information society.

Thirdly, the genuine human being will be empathetic, grasping reality on a human level.

> We must refuse energetically to be detached from this sphere, a level which is not very high, but is the only significant one. This means that first of all we must get rid of evasion, in all its forms—in the ideal, in the future, in abstraction. We must no longer think of "men" in the abstract, but of my neighbor Mario. It is in the concrete life of this man, which I can easily know, that I see the real repercussions of the machine, of the press, of political discourses and of the administration.[46]

"All other knowledge of the world," he cautioned, "through statistics or news, is illusory, and keeps us tied to the outlook we have been discussing,"[47] an outlook which was, incidentally, an early and partial description of the technological society.

My way of working around the paradox of the need for a powerful ethos of individualism contained within the structure of a mass society is this: we're really talking about two related, but entirely different,

44. Ellul, *Presence of the Kingdom*, 98.
45. Ellul, *Presence of the Kingdom*, 98.
46. Ellul, *Presence of the Kingdom*, 98.
47. Ellul, *Presence of the Kingdom*, 100.

phenomena. Individuality is a human phenomenon characterized by an individual's distinctiveness from the mass; individualism is an ideology that elevates individual needs and opinions over the common good. It is therefore possible to have a strong ethos of individualism in a mass utterly devoid of genuine individuals. Indeed, as Ellul tells us, individualism actually spurs the growth of mass culture by weakening the traditional regional, tribal, and communal bonds characteristic of life in a more "organic," less technologically developed culture.[48]

One of the effects of this ethos of individualism is to subject the individual to pressures and influences not encountered in those more organic, communal societies. Furthermore, while the breakdown of local, regional, and traditional loyalties, values, relationships, etc., frees the individual from the homogeneity of thought typical of a more rural organic culture, the loss of those influences in a mass society promotes its own homogeneity of thought and behavior. This is because in order to have a mass culture in the first place, techniques of public opinion, mass communication, and propaganda must be in place.

Mass Media of Communication

An opinion cannot form itself in an entire society without the active presence of mass medium of communication.[49] Therefore, propaganda as such is impossible without some mass medium or media. As a corollary to that idea, we should note that once mass media made their appearance in Western culture, the development of a mass culture was inevitable, and equally inevitable was propaganda.

For systematic, total propaganda to be successful the mass media must be subject to centralized control but diversified with regard to content.[50] And as Ellul tells us, whether that centralized control is at the hands of the state or of private ownership is irrelevant.[51]

The chauvinism of technological attitudes causes us, perhaps, to recoil from these statements; or at the very least to doubt them. Certainly, we reason, a state system is more controlled than a commercial system; there is but one state owner and there are many owners in a commercial system. And just as surely content in a commercial system must be far more diverse, with far less censorship and other forms of intrusion, than in a state system.

48. Ellul, *Propaganda*, 90.
49. Ellul, *Propaganda*, 102.
50. Ellul, *Propaganda*, 102.
51. Ellul, *Propaganda*, 103.

Without, once again, trying to make a case for one structure being superior to the other, I respond by simply restating what Ellul has told us: if centralized control exists, it doesn't matter whether that control is in the hands of some government office or distributed within a collective "free market."

For example, television in the former Soviet Union was remarkably similar to Western television. The Soviet government had five television stations; in addition, each of the Soviet Republics and Autonomous Republics had stations. In the 1980s, the *Gorizont* satellite network consolidated regional broadcasting, making all programming—regional and national—available to the entire geographical Soviet Union.

Contrary to popular (and stereotyped) belief, Soviet programming had about the same diversity as US programming. There were movies, children's programs, cartoons, sports events, news programs and news interview programs, and by the 1980s, talk shows and game shows. None of them would have seemed terribly out of place if you were to find them on an American television network, local station, or public broadcasting station. One could, of course, make the case that all of these programs were going to be pushing the party line, that is to say promoting the Soviet way of life, encouraging participation in (sham) political processes, putting a uniquely Soviet spin on the national and world news of the day, and making sure that nothing that called Communism into question or suggested the superiority of capitalist consumerism would ever appear. And anyone making this case would be absolutely correct.

Of course, then, in order for that point to have any significance it would be necessary to demonstrate that American television networks and stations were not promoting the American way of life (through the consumption of material commodities and the expansion of "free trade"), encouraging participation in (sham) political processes, putting a uniquely American spin on the national and world news of the day, and that there was a diversity of views broad enough to call capitalism into question, or suggest the superiority of any sort of regulated economy. And this is demonstrably untrue.

Anticipating the deregulatory policies of Ronald Reagan's FCC, Ellul also made the following prophetic statement:

> To make the organization of propaganda possible, the media must be concentrated, the number of news agencies reduced, the press brought under single control, and radio and film monopolies established. The effect will be still greater if the various media are concentrated in the same hands.[52]

52. Ellul, *Propaganda*, 102.

Since the passage of the Communication Act in 1986 under Reagan, and the Telecommunication Act of 1996 under Clinton, control of broadcasting in the United States has tightened in the hands of a constantly dwindling number of corporations who are enjoying hundreds of billions of dollars in profits through the use of public airwaves. Whereas there were roughly fifty corporations who controlled the US mass media in 1980, today the five largest media corporations in America[53]—Comcast, Disney, News Corporation, National Amusements (Viacom/CBS), and Time Warner—control over 90 percent of everything we see, hear, and read.[54]

Ellul explained the dangers of this type of media conglomeration to us in 1965. "Only through concentration in a few hands of a large number of media can one attain a true orchestration, a continuity, and an application of scientific methods of influencing individuals," he wrote, adding presciently, "A state monopoly, or a private monopoly, is equally effective. Such a situation is in the making in the United States, France, and Germany—the fact is well known."[55] He wrote that prophetic passage, I must repeat, more than a half century ago.

The Complicity of the Propagandee

When I ask my students to describe the medium of television, they always describe the box (or more likely today the screen) that sits in their living room, their family room, their bedroom, even their kitchen. Rarely, if ever, does the thought come to their minds that somewhere far from their homes there is a place with cameras, microphones, lights, miles of cables, signal processing devices, recording devices, amplification and modulation systems, and transmitters. These are all part of the television medium, and they are extremely expensive to own as well as to operate.

So what we see—at least during the time of Ellul's work, the era of mass media and broadcasting—are highly technologically complex media that, by their nature, cannot be owned by everyone, but by an elite few: wealthy families, investors, and corporations. But, as in the case of the printing press and books, there's one piece of the medium that's always designed to be inexpensive so that it is, in fact, accessible to the mass. In the case of television, this is the receiver. The businesspeople and entrepreneurs who

---

53. Media reports on this issue vary between five and six. It is five. Many reports ignore the fact that a seventh company, National Amusements, recently swooped in and purchased both Viacom and CBS.

54. Lutz, "These 6 Corporations Control 90% of the Media in America."

55. Ellul, *Propaganda*, 103.

built our mass media systems knew that in order to have any effect at all (in other words, in order to make money) you had to design as great a degree of accessibility into your product as possible.

It is precisely here, according to Ellul, that we locate the complicity of the propagandee in the process of systematic, total propaganda. "If he is a propagandee," he says, "it is because he wants to be, for he is ready to buy a paper, go to the movies, pay for a radio or TV set."[56]

Propaganda without mass media means propaganda without an audience, and what this actually means is that you've got no propaganda at all. But looking at the statistics, we appear to be more than happy to buy into the system.

Even though the number of American households with television has been declining (slightly) over the past decade, more than 97 percent of households still have at least one set, and 39 percent have three or more.[57] As of January 2017, 95 percent of Americans own a cellphone of some kind and 77 percent of Americans own smartphones.[58] Nearly nine out of every ten Americans now use the internet; 73 percent use high-speed internet via broadband connection, and 69 percent use social media of some kind.[59] Six in ten US households have at least one person who plays video games regularly (three or more hours per week).[60] Furthermore, US adults now spend more than twelve hours each day engaged in some sort of media use,[61] five of those twelve hours on a mobile device,[62] more than two hours a day using social media.[63]

Most Americans don't find any of these statistics troubling. But then again, most Americans don't believe that the virtually infinite amount of content—music, status updates, photos, advertisements, videos, television shows, video games—to which they expose themselves all day long, day after day after day, is propaganda.

56. Ellul, *Propaganda*, 103.
57. Berry and Woodward, "Average Number Of Televisions."
58. "Mobile Fact Sheet," 2017.
59. Smith, "Record Shares of Americans Now Own Smartphones."
60. Entertainment Software Association, "2017 Essential Facts."
61. "US Adults Now Spend 12 Hours 7 Minutes a Day Consuming Media."
62. Perez, "U.S. Consumers Now Spend 5 Hours Per Day on Mobile Devices."
63. Mander, "Daily Time Spent of Social Networks Rises to Over 2 Hours."

Objective Conditions of Total Propaganda

The need for an average standard of living

At the risk of lapsing into tautology, one of the reasons that systematic, total propaganda has worked as well as it has is that the complex system of which it is a central part—*the technological society*—itself has worked so well. Technique has made it possible to have mass societies of millions and even hundreds of millions of people and administer law, provide essential goods like food, clothing, shelter, and even provide opportunities for higher-order needs like relaxation, entertainment, and arts. These are all important to both the proper functioning of the technological society and the effectiveness of propaganda. In order for total propaganda to be effective, an average standard of living is necessary.[64]

However, the technological society has never been able to deliver all the needs to all its subjects at the same level or in the same quantities. We've always had some level of unemployment and, consequently, a similar level of poverty. Social, political, and economic inequality make some types of propaganda powerless. Modern integration propaganda, for example, cannot affect people living in poverty or near poverty and on the fringes of society.[65] From a Maslovian perspective, we might say that it is impossible to satisfy the higher-order needs offered by integration propaganda when the lower-order needs of survival remain unmet. From a more streetwise point of view, however, it is possible that when you feel abandoned by your society, its propaganda of integration simply sounds like bullshit. It is amazing to consider then, as I mentioned earlier, how placid the American sector of the technological society actually remains, how few people are engaging in agitprop, how very few are calling for even radical change let alone revolution (and even then they are largely ignored in the mass media).

But even as systemic racism survives in the United States, the majority of our 45 million poor people remain Black and Latino, Black Americans (a minority of 13 percent of the population) make up a plurality (40 percent) of the two and a half million people in our prisons, and a frightening number of Black Americans are killed by police officers, our streets, until recently, are quiet. It's an example of what Noam Chomsky calls "the spectacular achievements of propaganda."[66]

64. Ellul, *Propaganda*, 103.

65. Ellul, *Propaganda*, 103.

66. Chomsky, *Media Control*.

The Need for an Average Culture

Most people believe that propaganda works, it just doesn't work on them. It works on everyone else. The (until recently) increasingly educated middle class tells themselves "I read the news. I study history. I know what's going on. I'm too intelligent to be manipulated by propaganda." This is true, by the way, on both the political left as well as the right. People tend to believe that education inoculates them from the effects of propaganda. The reverse, in fact, is true. Modern integration propaganda cannot affect people living in ignorance; a common education is a prerequisite.

It is in the institutions of elementary and secondary education—along with family and place of worship—where much of the integration propaganda is introduced into young people's lives. Integration propaganda is the propaganda of conformity,[67] and where do we first teach our children how to learn by rote repetition, recite by memory, and color within the lines? It is in elementary and secondary schools that children learn the fundamentals of the technological culture: Western history and values, Western arts and literature, Western techniques and science, etc. Children learn to read in school, they learn to write, they learn to memorize and "spit back" what they hear. What they do not learn is how to think. The important thing, Ellul tells us,

> is not to be able to read, but to understand what one reads, to reflect on and judge what one reads. Outside of that, reading has no meaning (and even destroys certain automatic qualities of memory and observation). But to talk about critical faculties and discernment is to talk about something far above primary education and to consider a very small minority.[68]

Especially since the advent of No Child Left Behind and its Obama-promoted sequel Race to the Top, the resulting implementation of Common Core State Standards, and the phenomenon of teaching to the test, the pressure to conform has only risen. While there is no US national curriculum, there are the national Common Core standards for the development of curricula. These standards are pragmatic and useful—if we ignore the explicit statement of their ultimate purpose, to prepare students for "success in college, career, and life in today's global economy," that is to say to meet the demands of the technological society. However, the implementation of these standards by each state, and the mandate for yearly testing, has brought with it some additional problems, such as over-testing, de-emphasizing

67. Ellul, *Propaganda*, 74.
68. Ellul, *Propaganda*, 108.

the arts, history, and social sciences, the constant threat of teacher firings and school closings, and the introduction of corporate influence into state and local curriculum development. The Bill and Melinda Gates Foundation funded—and promoted—the Common Core initiative to the tune of $200 million by 2014 alone.[69] States began awarding hundreds of millions of dollars of Gates's and Department of Education funds in contracts to businesses including Pearson, McGraw-Hill Education CTB, Houghton Mifflin Harcourt, the Educational Testing Service, and Apple.[70]

New York University research professor of education and privatization critic Diane Ravitch believes that Common Core "has nothing to do with improving education or creating equality of opportunity but everything to do with cutting costs, standardizing education, shifting the delivery of education from high-cost teachers to low-cost technology, reducing the number of teachers, and eliminating unions and pensions."[71]

The Need for Information

Opinions, it has been said, are like a particularly fragrant part of the human anatomy: everybody has one. To be uninformed does not in and of itself necessitate indifference; ignorant people have opinions too. However, since the *informed opinion* is indispensable to propaganda, information in a mass society is necessary in the process of opinion formation.[72]

Mass information, however, is a very different phenomenon than information gathered through individual experience. Effective propaganda is not founded on errors or lies, but on "facts." In the more organic, low-tech past, most of the facts learned by individuals came either through direct experience, or through interpersonal interactions with trusted members of their communities or authority figures. In the technologically developed world, however, we now get the vast majority of our facts from our mass media. When all individuals in a society have been informed of the same facts, unified action becomes more likely. And the more information a mass of people receive, the stronger the impetus to respond *en masse*.

In an image-based visual culture, such as the one the technological society has developed in the last century, information will most likely come to us as images rather than words, or images with a few carefully selected words explaining or interpreting them. Images affect a viewer in a

69. Layton, "How Bill Gates pulled off the swift Common Core revolution."

70. Cavanagh, "Common-Core Testing Contracts Favor Big Vendors."

71. Strauss, "Everything you need to know."

72. Ellul, *Propaganda*, 113.

very different way than words affect a reader. Images are *nonpropositional, nondiscursive codes* that, rather than making any sort of a statement, present an *analog of reality*—they look like the things, events, and phenomena they represent. This is even more true of moving images. Unlike words, moving images defy critical thought. They can't be parsed, criticized grammatically, or put to a test of linear logic. They simply are what they appear to be, and nothing else.[73]

The growing role of the pundit or "expert commentator" in television news is directly attributable to the dominance of visual images. A picture, they say, speaks a thousand words, and we hear that phrase as a testament to the value of images rather than a warning of their danger. Every image, however, can be interpreted in a number of ways; a thousand people will have a thousand different impressions of an image. And this is precisely what makes the political pundit a mainstay of television news. Pundits explicitly tell us how they see the image, implicitly telling us how *we ought to see it.*

Ideology and Myth

In consequence of the fact that Ellul never really defines what he means by *ideology*, I've found it necessary to come up with my own definition, one which I've found useful and productive: *The body of ideas reflecting the social needs and aspirations of a group, class, or culture; a set of doctrines or beliefs that form the basis of a political, economic, religious, or other system; the objectification of a subjective set of beliefs, values, or attitudes; the universalization of personal philosophy.*

An ideology—if it is truly an ideology—will always have these characteristics:

1. It is not necessarily true, but is seen as true by those who believe and profess it; evidence of an ideology's weaknesses or faults will be ignored or denied systematically by its adherents.

2. It is absolute and inflexible; ideology resists compromise or dilution.

3. It is seen, by those who profess it, as universal; it must be true not only for those who believe it, but for everyone.

4. Consequently, an ideology provides its own rationale for expansion, conversion, and hegemony.

5. There is an almost sacred quality to an ideology; it must be accepted as *the one true way.*

73. Fallon, *Metaphysics of Media,* 211.

Most ideologies find their origin in a personal epiphany: Adam Smith's ideas about a marketplace rationally regulated by self-interest, Marx's idea of the arc of history bending toward the worker's ownership of the technologies of his labor as well as his labor itself, Mao's idea that the peasant farmer was superior to the industrial worker because it is within the peasantry you will find the motivation for a permanent revolution, etc. These personal epiphanies appeal to groups of people who share the same worldview as the persons who created them and become institutionalized in some social or religious movement, or political party. These movements or parties, then, implement techniques of propaganda to spread the ideology, often with an almost religious zeal.

What is paradoxical about all this is that ideologies, while appearing to their adherents as something very like sacred doctrines to be propagated among the unconverted, tend to desacralize (if not secularize) human thought. They emphasize the pragmatic and technical over the transcendent and mystical. They force a backing away from the contemplative and empathic potentials of human nature (reflection) and encourage purposeful, goal-oriented action (reflex). They are detours around the hazardous byways of critical thinking, and shortcuts to positive action. They are, essentially, another type of technique, and this has been, until recently, what has made ideology as valuable as it has been to propaganda.

Myth, on the other hand, is a universal human phenomenon. Every culture on Earth has its myths; the technological society is no exception. While the traditional myths of the ancient world may have lost their hold on us, and the grand narrative of the Enlightenment recedes into darkness, we technologically developed humans have been developing newer and more meaningful (for us) myths to explain reality, the world, and life.

Myths are, essentially, explanatory stories. They are stories we create to explain to ourselves the meaning of some great mystery. Early human myths often dwelt on the mystery of *being*; they answered, among others, the questions "Where did we come from? Who are we (as a people)? Why are we here (is there a purpose to our existence)? What is the good life and how do we live it? What is the nature of good and evil and how do we determine them?" These myths formed the bases of many of our religious traditions.

Myths are neither true nor false, in anything like an objective, empirical sense. Myths do not have to be—and in truth rarely are—statements of fact. But they present stories that reflect the dominant ethos and moral code of the people who create, preserve, and relate them to the next generation. Rather than being "true," myths have "the ring of truth" to them. Eric Havelock, in *Preface to Plato*, has described how the Homeric tradition, with its mythic tales of gods and heroes interacting, usually at some distance, with mere mortals, encapsulated the structure of Athenian society, exemplifying its mores, formulas, prayers, protocols, and relationships—both hierarchical and horizontal.[74]

These mythic tales were meant less to function as a unified, formal legal or moral code than as overall descriptive—and prescriptive—formulas.

> This is the way in which the society does normally behave (or does not) and at the same time the way in which we, its members, who form the poet's audience, are encouraged to behave. There is no admonition: the tale remains dispassionate. But the paradigm of what is accepted practice or proper feeling is continually offered in contrast to what may be unusual or improper and excessive or rash.[75]

The Enlightenment narrative gave us a number of myths, many of which survive in a somewhat changed and, perhaps, diminished form. These, too, were created to explain to us certain mysteries that wracked human minds at the time. The myth of progress is still a powerful one, although, as we saw earlier, its contemporary power lies purely in the symbol of the tool created and used through the agency of reason, and bears no necessary connection to the ends to which the tool is directed. The myth of human freedom remains strong as well; but the concept of freedom has changed radically in the last three centuries, having more to do with consumption of material goods than with personal sovereignty, autonomy, and selfhood. The myth of democracy in recent decades, however, has taken something of a beating.

The technological era has its own myths which, like the myths of every other era, explain the mysteries of our lives to us in ways that are both understandable and appealing to our technology-drenched sensibilities. For the sake of brevity I wish to consider only two: the myths of technology and of matter.

Technology itself has taken on mythic attributes: we tend to *believe in* technology unquestioningly; technologies provide solutions to the problems (mystery being reduced to the mere material and pragmatic dimension) of life; they give us enhanced human powers and allow us to do things we would otherwise be unable to do; they provide us with an unerring guide to living and finding meaning in life, etc. So we can confidently point to a *myth of technology*, or, to use Lewis Mumford's phrase, "the myth of the machine." We can also speak, at the same time, of a *myth of matter*. Technology has had a profound effect on the metaphysics of the present-day world in that it has concentrated our attention on the material and sensory dimensions of

74. Havelock, *Preface to Plato*, 71–73.

75. Havelock, *Preface to Plato*, 87.

reality at the expense of the immaterial, intuitive, imaginative, and empathic dimensions. We create technologies to do *things*, to take actions, to shape and move and build and destroy; then we *use the technologies* to do *things*, to take actions, to shape and move and build and destroy. More specifically, we create communication technologies to do things as well: to move information, to store information, to sort and manipulate and edit information. One facet of the myth of matter that has changed our very conception of humanness can be observed in the drive to develop what is being called machine intelligence or artificial intelligence. Artificial intelligence, or AI, is more faith than science and dovetails very neatly with the myth of matter, exalting the material dimension of human biology over the imaginative, contemplative, or spiritual dimensions of human life.

The Traditional Relationship Between Propaganda and Ideology

Ideologies can expand and propagate themselves without physical, military, or political force only through the use of propaganda. Such propaganda can appear in either a spontaneous or organized manner, as circumstances demand; it is organized when planned by a party or institution, spontaneous when driven by the zeal of the ideology's adherents.[76]

The traditional relationship suggests that propaganda organizes itself in conformity with the prevailing ideology of a society, and Ellul emphasizes that in such a case the propaganda message, rather than being interchangeable with other messages, is of critical importance: "what counts here is to spread the content of that ideology."[77] In other words, the propaganda does not try to take possession of, or dominate, or manipulate the individual, but merely to transmit certain beliefs and ideas, the content of the ideology.

This, Ellul tells us, is the traditional relationship of propaganda to ideology. In an ideology-driven world, this is the form you would expect the process to take. However, this description no longer bears much resemblance to the actual relationship that arose in the latter half of the twentieth century.

The propaganda of the early twentieth century—based on the propaganda techniques recognized no more or less by Leninist Communists and by the Nazi propagandists of the Third Reich than they were by George Creel, Edward Bernays, and the propagandists of American capitalism—reshaped the necessary ethical relationship between *means* and *ends*. The

76. Ellul, *Propaganda,* 193–96.
77. Ellul, *Propaganda,* 194.

world of the twentieth century—as it is today—was a world of rapidly proliferating means; there were more means to any end at our disposal than any time in human history, and we should—and did, and continue to—make use of as many of them as possible.

The widespread availability of means encouraging—and facilitating—the irresponsible exercise of power, in all cases, trumped the defense of ideological purity and weakened the future structural integrity of the various ideologies, whether capitalist, Communist, or National Socialist. In the twentieth century, human ends became of secondary importance to means "or, in many cases, of no importance at all."[78]

Thus the ends or goals of our behaviors have been completely transformed by the profusion and proliferation of means. And while the various ideologies continue to exist, spread, and attract adherents, they can no longer possess the motive force over our behavior that they lost in the twentieth century.

The New Relationship

Propaganda's task is less and less to propagate ideology; neither does propaganda need to obey or follow an ideology. Being both a technique and a central component of the technological society, propaganda becomes autonomous and drives rather than follows ideology. In a sense, propaganda—as the public manifestation of technique, as the representation of the technological society in which we all live—becomes, more and more, ideology itself.

Ideology becomes integral to propaganda and dependent upon it. No ideology beyond technique itself can any longer have a real hold on the propagandist's convictions. There is no need for the propagandist to believe the ideology on whose behalf he does his work.[79] "More and more," Ellul writes, "the propagandist is a technician using a keyboard of material media and psychological techniques; and in the midst of all that, ideology is only one of the incidental and interchangeable cogs."[80]

Ideology, then, becomes mythologized, reduced to the status of the *brand* in marketing: an open, ambiguous symbol representing a vaguely appealing idea that may open one up, at some point, to learning more about the person, organization, or party with which it is associated. But beyond the brand there is no longer any meaningful ideology.

78. Ellul, *Propaganda*, 195.

79. Ellul, *Propaganda*, 196.

80. Ellul, *Propaganda*, 197.

Whether one refers to "the deep state," the "permanent government," or the military-industrial-information complex, it is hard to deny that, regardless of which political party holds power over what branch of government, US policy—foreign, economic, military, fiscal—remains fairly constant and overwhelmingly favorable to those corporations, executives, and managers that constitute the technological society. No ideology, of either left or right, seems capable of weakening its hegemony. Few, in fact, seem to be trying.

The Need for Propaganda

The traditional view of propaganda casts the propagandist as a villain, propaganda as a weapon, and the propagandee as a victim. By this view, the propagandee appears not to be responsible for a social phenomenon seen as originating entirely outside of himself rather than as an active participant in a process,[81] which is in fact the case.

It also loses sight of the fact that propaganda is only one of a number of human techniques meant to help adapt the individual to life in the technological society. Ellul seeks to establish and explain two points here: 1) that there is an obvious and objective need for the state to establish a system of total propaganda; 2) that there is a less obvious but equally compelling need on the part of the individual, not only to accept subjection to propaganda, but to actively seek it out.

The State's Necessity

Propaganda is needed in a mass society for a number of reasons, but foremost is the simple fact that the masses have come to participate in political affairs.[82] While it is true that democracy as an ideology is dead (government by hundreds of millions is impossible), the myth of democracy (ideology reduced to a *brand*) is strong enough to make people want to *feel* as though they are in control of their own destinies. In a mass culture, however, democracy cannot be seen in the same way we thought about democracy in the past. Individual opinion is no longer relevant. Only public opinion.

In a democracy, the citizens must believe they have a stake in the decisions of the government—"to have wanted what the government is doing, to be responsible for its actions, to be involved in defending them and making

---

81. Ellul, *Propaganda*, 118–19.

82. Ellul, *Propaganda*, 122.

them succeed, to be 'with it.'"[83] But it is in the nature of public opinion to be fundamentally irrational, unstable, unsettled, and unpredictable.[84]

Take for example the shift in public opinion on climate change that occurred in 2009. This was the year of the so-called Climategate scandal, when a server at the Climate Research Unit at the University of East Anglia in the UK was hacked and thousands of emails posted on climate change-denying websites.[85] The scandal was reported widely in the American mainstream media. Climate skeptics claimed the emails proved that anthropogenic climate change was a hoax, a "deliberate fraud" and "the greatest deception in history,"[86] but there was no real information contained in the emails that legitimately called into question the findings of the Intergovernmental Panel on Climate Change, and really only showed a handful of scientists being dismissive of climate skeptics, being rude, and being "jerks."[87]

Still, the affair had a serious effect on public opinion (helped along by record cold weather in the eastern US and record snowfalls in the southern and mid-Atlantic states). The Brookings Institution found a significant decrease between 2008 and 2009 (from 72 percent to 66 percent) in public confidence that there was "solid evidence" of rising temperatures[88] and an even greater drop in personal confidence (from 58 percent to 40 percent) "that the average temperature on earth is increasing."[89] A Yale University study showed a similar serious shift between 2008 and 2010. More than 3,000 respondents were asked, "Do you think that global warming is happening?"

> In 2008, 71 percent of Americans said "yes," global warming is happening. By 2010, however, this number had dropped significantly to 57 percent. Meanwhile the proportion that said "no," global warming is not happening doubled from 10 to 20 percent, while those who said "don't know" increased to 23 percent of the public . . . Those respondents who said "yes" were then asked how sure they were that global warming is happening. By 2010, only 59 percent said they were "very" or "extremely sure" global warming is happening—a 13 point drop from 2008 . . .

---

83. Ellul, *Propaganda*, 127.

84. Ellul, *Propaganda*, 124–25.

85. Leiserowitz et al., "Climategate, Public Opinion, and the Loss of Trust."

86. Henig, "'Climategate.'"

87. Henig, "'Climategate.'"

88. Rabe and Borick, "Climate of Belief."

89. Rabe and Borick, "Climate of Belief."

Respondents who said "no" global warming is not happening
did not become significantly more certain of their views . . . [90]

Here we see evidence of Ellul's claim that if a "democracy" is to be
stable, if it is to administer policy consistently and deliberately, it cannot
follow public opinion.[91] But neither can government ignore public opinion and continue to support a claim to being democratic. Ellul presents the
proposition, then, that if government cannot follow public opinion, public
opinion must be made to follow the government.[92]

> One must convince this present, ponderous, impassioned mass
> that the government's decisions are legitimate and good and
> that its foreign policy is correct. The democratic State, precisely
> because it believes in the expression of public opinion and does
> not gag it, must channel and shape that opinion if it wants to be
> realistic and not follow an ideological dream.[93]

In an age of mass communication, Ellul is saying, dictatorship is only
possible with the "manufactured consent" of the masses. The mechanisms
of propaganda—news, public relations, public opinion polling, as well as
entertainments and diversions—transform democracy into a peaceful
totalitarian dictatorship because we refuse, or are unable, to see that the
democratic ideology has been reduced to myth.

If power is legitimate when it derives from the sovereignty of the
people, and expresses and follows the will of the people, can any political power be legitimate that does not follow public opinion but seeks to
have public opinion follow its actions? Yes, if that is the social contract we
define and agree to.

The Individual's Necessity

Perhaps the most compelling part of Ellul's model of systematic, total propaganda rests on a few provocative questions:

- Does propaganda in any way help the individual in the technological
  society?

- Does the individual benefit at all from being the subject of a systematic
  and total propaganda mechanism?

90. Leiserowitz et al., "Climategate, Public Opinion, and the Loss of Trust," 3.
91. Ellul, *Propaganda,* 126.
92. Ellul, *Propaganda,* 126.
93. Ellul, *Propaganda,* 126.

- Or is the individual really no more than a stooge, willingly victimized in exchange for comfort and stability?

These are difficult questions to answer as technique in general, and propaganda specifically, present themselves to us as *faits accomplis*. We are without options, it seems, powerless but to accept our fate. The individual, deeply rooted in the technological society, has no real choice but compliance with the values and goals of technique; which, after all, offer certain material and economic benefits, if no particular spiritual ones. What are those benefits?

One benefit is participation in the life of society. Most people desire to participate rather than not participate in the public life of their society, even when that means expressing opinions on issues—political, economic, foreign policy—about which they know nothing.[94] All people believe in the validity—and the importance—of their own opinions, and feel obliged to share them publicly. But without assistance, they can't possibly form opinions on things they've never experienced or don't understand.

There is, in fact, too much information in the world for the average human being to be conversant in, let alone to understand. On any given day, an average of thirty-four wars are going on somewhere on Earth.[95] On any given day, 794 million of the world's people are starving or malnourished.[96] On any given day, 168 million children ages five to fourteen are employed in factories in the developing world, many of them sweatshops.[97] On any given day, the United States is spending $2,005,478,452.05 on its military.[98] And yet on any given day we tend not to hear or read about these things.

It has long been noted that our mass media have an agenda-setting function, that is to say that they filter through the myriad possible bits of information that happen on *any given day* and decide which ones are going to be news stories and which ones are not. As one scholar put it, in words that reflect the true nature of propaganda, our mass information system "may not be successful much of the time in telling people what to think, but it is stunningly successful in telling its readers what to think *about*."[99]

Propaganda supplies not only the opportunities for "participation" (the individual perceives public opinion as driving the actions of government),

---

94. Ellul, *Propaganda*, 139.

95. "SIPRI Yearbook 2020: Armaments, Disarmament And International Security," 2.

96. "World Hunger, Poverty Facts, Statistics 2016."

97. "11 Facts about Sweatshops."

98. "Ranking: Military Spending By Country 2015."

99. Cohen, *Press and Foreign Policy*, 120.

and the means of becoming and remaining "informed" (for neither propaganda nor dictatorship is possible without an informed populace) but also the very framework of myths, values, and ideologies within which the aforementioned sacrifices are rationalized. Noam Chomsky writes bluntly about "empty concepts like Americanism."

> Who can be against that? Or harmony. Who can be against that? Or, as in the Persian Gulf War, "Support our troops." Who can be against that? Or yellow ribbons. Who can be against that? Anything that's totally vacuous.
>
> In fact, what does it mean if somebody asks you, Do you support the people in Iowa? Can you say, Yes, I support them, or No, I don't support them? It's not even a question. It doesn't mean anything. That's the point. The point of public relations slogans like "Support our troops" is that they don't mean anything . . . Of course, there was an issue. The issue was, Do you support our policy? But you don't want people to think about that issue. That's the whole point of good propaganda. You want to create a slogan that nobody's going to be against, and everybody's going to be for.[100]

Psychological Effects of Propaganda

Ellul sets the stakes high in beginning his discussion of the psychological effects of propaganda. Ellul makes it clear that there is a serious price paid by the propagandee for active, willful participation in the process of propaganda:

> A person subjected to propaganda does not remain intact or undamaged: not only will his opinions and attitudes be modified, but also his impulses and his mental and emotional structures. Propaganda's effect is more than external; it produces profound changes.[101]

We are rarely shocked out of our propaganda-mediated dream, but when we are—soldiers in the midst of combat, victims of violent crime, witnesses to disasters or terrorism (as we all were on September 11, 2001)—the experience is frightening and traumatic. When you find yourself face-to-face with such a stark, inescapable reality and your response is

---

100. Chomsky, *Media Control*, 24–25.

101. Ellul, *Propaganda*, 161.

"it was just like a movie,"[102] this is a sure sign that the reality you believe you live in is false.

Anxiety

What, exactly, are the "profound changes" we undergo as a result of our constant exposure to propaganda? There are several that Ellul mentions in *Propaganda* (and some of his other works). I'll look at two. The first Ellul speaks of is anxiety.

> Anxiety is perhaps the most widespread psychological trait in our society. Many studies indicate that fear is one of the strongest and most prevalent feelings in our society. Of course, man has good reasons to be afraid—of Communist subversion, revolution, Fascism, H-bombs, conflict between East and West, unemployment, sickness. On the one hand, the number of dangers is increasing and, because of the news media, man is more aware of them; on the other, religious beliefs, which allowed man to face fear, have disappeared almost entirely. Man is disarmed in the face of the perils threatening him, and is increasingly alarmed by these perils because he keeps reading about them.[103]

Much more so than in more organic, traditional societies, life in the tightly structured, highly connected, time- and space-compressed technological society imposes a sort of *psychic trauma* on those who have no choice but to live within the boundaries of its "reality." There is so much to fear, and we see it, hear it, and read about it constantly.

We fear, first of all, the brutal randomness of nature—the floods, droughts, fires, lightning strikes, heart attacks, aging, sickness, and death. These are existential fears, natural to our species, and we place a great deal of trust in technology to protect us from them. But along with these natural fears are others that we bear specifically as a result of living in an environment of systematic, total propaganda. A perceived threat of violence (real or not) pervades our lives and we live with a constant dread that the peace we have managed to achieve and maintain in our homes, our communities, and our minds will be unexpectedly shattered. We fear the intentions of others to harm us—other nations, other ideologies, other races, other people.

We also, however, fear losing the promised benefits of technology that are part and parcel of the technological society and its propaganda

---

102. Greydanus, "September 11 and Hollywood."

103. Ellul, *Propaganda*, 153.

message. We fear poverty, for instance (a condition that arises only in an environment of mass prosperity). We fear being "left behind" or looked down on by others (a condition heightened by our competitive, consumerist, image-based culture). We fear being "out of the loop" ("information poverty"—a condition created by the transformation of information into a commodity). We fear living "meaningless" lives, even as the only meaning our lives might have is provided by propaganda.

Then, beyond the existential and social fears, there is the anxiety of everyday life in the technological society.

> Psychologists and sociologists are aware of the great problem of adjusting the normal man to a technological environment—to the increasing pace, the working hours, the noise, the crowded cities, the tempo of work, the housing shortage, and so on. Then there is the difficulty of accepting the never-changing daily routine, the lack of personal accomplishment, the absence of an apparent meaning in life, the family insecurity provoked by these living conditions, the anonymity of the individual in the big cities and at work. The individual is not equipped to face these disturbing, paralyzing, traumatic influences.[104]

In making necessary our adaptation to an unnatural environment (that all agree is "natural"), propaganda imposes a sort of *societal neurosis* that we perceive to be perfectly normal.[105] Propaganda in the technological society strips the individual of his own individuality by making him a part of an indissoluble mass, even as he continues to cherish his individualism. It despoils his individuality by inhibiting his critical thought and personal judgment, even as he congratulates himself on his intelligence and advanced education. It wrenches his individuality from him by making him responsible for a public opinion that has no power to drive or direct government, even though he is convinced that he has spoken his political will. We can no longer be whole, organic individuals; we become creatures violently shaped in the soulless crucible of the technological society, human manifestations of technique, and our natural cognitive and affective processes—even our autonomic functions—are conditioned to respond to the sensory data that come to us, not directly through our senses, but through the mediation of technology in our mass-manufactured "reality."

Technological man's interactions with his economic world cannot remain untouched by technique. The values of the technological society— productivity, profit, speed, consumption, convenience, maximization,

104. Ellul, *Propaganda*, 143.
105. Ellul, *Propaganda*, 154.

etc., but above all efficiency—suffuse technical man and his entire culture and provide a context for his own values, attitudes, beliefs, and behaviors. And those values, attitudes, beliefs, and behaviors reflect the underlying fundamental *violence* of technique and of the systematic propaganda that supports it.

> The competition that goes with the much-touted system of free enterprise is, in a word, an economic "war to the knife," an exercise of sheer violence that, so far, the law has not been able to regulate. In this competition "the best man wins"—and the weaker, more moral, more sensitive men necessarily lose.[106]

Alienation through Propaganda

As a consequence, the propagandee finds himself in a most uncomfortable position: alienated not only from himself, his conscience, his true individuality, his free will; but also from his actual (as opposed to virtual) community—his neighbors (to whom he says hello each day but with whom he has never actually had a conversation), his friends (with whom he shares the same mass-mediated information that they discuss, argue over, and laugh about without ever touching on the reality of their lives), his workmates (whom he sees more as competitors than as people), his peers (about whom he knows very little), and the strangers he passes on the street (whom he barely notices). He is most intimate with, and clings most desperately to, not the human members of his actual community, but to the technologically mediated members of his mass-manufactured virtual "reality": the characters he "knows" from television, the celebrities whose escapades he follows on the internet, the athlete who dominates his favorite sport, the "friends" he's never met on Facebook, the popular yenta he "dishes dirt" with via text messages. These are the predictable and dependable daily constituents of his life: images, avatars, icons, profile pictures, and disembodied data. These are his constant companions. The propagandee thus finds his every waking moment mediated by some technology—or in the case of the much-vaunted multitasker, by a variety of different technologies. To the propagandee this is all entirely normal. But somewhere deep inside does the propagandee—the *mass individual*—actually recognize the paradox of his situation and question the normalcy of it all?

---

106. Ellul, *Violence*, 86.

This scenario represents the "new nature,"[107] the "new normal." The technological milieu is the "natural" habitat of technological man; to propose a world with limited technologies seems patently unnatural, even deviant. There is no questioning technology's legitimacy or its reality to the denizen of the technological society; to do so poses an existential threat to both the technical system and to all those who live within it. Even worse, it is impractical and inefficient. This is just the way it is. This is the way it is meant to be. This is what is right. This is life. This is "natural."

Effects on Political Parties

Propaganda 2.0 makes inevitable the linking of partisan politics to money. Political propaganda is becoming more and more expensive, because of the volume of information needed to flow through the system and the rising costs of the instruments of delivery. A party that wishes to make propaganda must have the means to express its messages strongly,[108] and that means that marketing research consultants, public relations advisors, audience research specialists, and all available media, but particularly the mass media, must be employed to support a particular policy, platform, or candidate, necessitating a constant search for big-money donors to underwrite those media campaigns. Paradoxically, however, the stronger the link between the political system and sources of money, the less meaningfully distinct the partisan differences will be, since the parties' sources of funding are, by and large, identical. The funding of propaganda 2.0 will always be from core constituents of the technological society (corporations, wealthy individuals, foundations, etc.) and the overall message system of the technological society will inevitably support, rather than subvert, its values.

The turn of the new millennium, however, and the rise of digital technology and social media have revealed the power of propaganda 2.1 to transform this stagnating political dynamic. We will investigate in greater detail the characteristics of the propaganda 2.1 information environment in the following chapter. But for now it may instructive to observe, in retrospect, this political transformation from a system of total information control to one of uncontrolled and—so far—uncontrollable information.

Since the Reagan era, we've seen Democrats—and their party leadership—increasingly supporting policies and legislation that mirror those of the Republican Party, favoring capital and its accumulation, and abandoning the last vestiges of their populist, New Deal roots. This has earned them

107. Ellul, *Technological Bluff*, 15.

108. Ellul, *Propaganda*, 216.

the sobriquet Republican Lite.[109] Embracing smaller government with lower taxes (usually for the wealthy "job creators"), the privatization of the public commons, the rollback of regulations in order to "liberate business," the expansive use of American military force to "spread democracy" (or, far more probably, capitalism) and to support and defend the growing global free market, and the continued dependence on fossil fuels, the Democratic Party is barely distinguishable from the Republican Party, except in so far as they exploit the competing themes of identity politics vs. culture wars.

The "controversies" that exist between the two parties are well known; indeed, most people have at least a vague idea where each party stands on abortion, the status of gays and lesbians in society, and the need for a social safety net to protect the poorest among us, because our news media focus on these hot-button issues at the expense of other, perhaps more important stories that affect *all* of us; for example, precisely what restrictions on freedom any given piece of legislation represents, or the fact that the US is the world's largest manufacturer and exporter of weapons of mass destruction, or that the economic technique we call capitalism, as the game is currently being played, is economically and ecologically unsustainable and destructive of both democratic ideals and the very fabric of civilized society. Both parties have supported and passed legislation that serve the interests of the technological society and have harmed not only the rights of women, but of the LGBTQ community, of African Americans and Latinos, of the poor, and of the working class. But by focusing on the (admittedly significant) surface differences between the two parties while ignoring the deep-structural similarities, propaganda 2.0 protects the interests of the technological society and its elites.

This is a result of the fact that political propaganda demands vertical (top-down) liaison among party organizations; it will fail with any attempt at horizontal liaison.[110] Centralization, "message control" (a euphemism, directly from the realms of marketing and public relations, for various forms of censorship), and the exercise of other techniques of public relations are at the heart of politics in the technological society; party leaders rather than rank-and-file members must have complete control over policy decisions, reflecting the "dictatorship by consent" relationship of government and propaganda as a whole. Rights get a lot of lip service, but are not as advantageous to the imperatives of technique as a mass of underpaid and overstressed workers, broad underemployment and/or unemployment, and forty-five million people living in poverty. At the

109. "Republican Lite."

110. Ellul, *Propaganda*, 216.

end of the day, the differences between the two parties are based more in the surface of the technological society than in its deep structure. It is not unreasonable, I think, to claim that we are talking about a one-party political system in the United States today (the Technics Party? The Capitalist Party?) constituted of two wings: a socially moderate wing, and an extremely conservative, even reactionary wing.

In order to maintain this corrosive status quo, political propaganda, like politics generally, focuses on social control by projecting *power*. Political leadership implies the possession and wielding of power. As a consequence propaganda demands a schism between a political party's leadership and its voters,[111] separating them into subject and objects. Masses admire power, Ellul notes,[112] and therefore "leadership," "strength," "wisdom," etc., especially as it is embodied in some prominent and recognizable individual. In the four decades since the "Reagan revolution," political leadership has been based more and more on the subjectively perceived *personality* of a potential leader rather than on vague and ill-defined notions of ability. As Fred Greenstein notes, "Political institutions and processes operate through human agency. It would be remarkable if they were not influenced by the properties that distinguish one individual from another."[113] The political leader, then, is a celebrity—in Daniel Boorstin's admirable phrase, a "human pseudo-event"[114]—and his or her *personality* is not in fact a personality at all, but *an image*, carefully constructed and maintained by highly paid consultants and coaches who craft speeches, give public speaking tips, encourage expressive body language, and even help choose a candidate's wardrobe.[115]

When propaganda *does* occasionally focus on the actual experiences and abilities of potential leaders, it is always from the point of view of technique. Candidates for high office in the US, and particularly for president, come overwhelmingly from four areas central to the technological society: the legal profession, government, business, and the military. The founders and early presidents of the United States included farmers, surveyors, printers, and inventors, so we can be fairly certain that they did not see experience in law, politics, commerce, or war to be prerequisites to leadership. However, of the ten presidents in the last half century, four have been governors, three have been vice presidents, four have been senators, three have been businessmen, three have been lawyers, and five have served in the military. In the

111. Ellul, *Propaganda*, 216–17.

112. Ellul, *Propaganda*, 217.

113. Greenstein, "Can Personality and Politics Be Studied Systematically?"

114. Boorstin, *Image*, 57.

115. Abnett, "Styling Politicians in the Age of Image Wars."

116th US Congress (January 3, 2019 through January 3, 2021), there were 145 House members and forty-seven senators from the legal professions, 183 representatives and twenty-nine senators from business, 184 representatives and forty-seven senators with prior political experience, ninety-six veterans or active military in the House and twenty in the Senate, seven members of the military reserves in the House and one in the Senate, and seven members of the National Guard, all in the House.[116] In no circumstances should we assume that all or any of this aggregated "experience" worked to the detriment of technique; the only moral judgments technique tolerates, after all, concern resistance to their implementation and use.

Watching the 2016 US presidential campaign, we saw both the ideas of personality and ability being exploited by the mass media. Many people believe that Donald Trump was and is uniquely unqualified to be president of the United States, on both the bases of personality (or character) and ability. Specifically, he was called "temperamentally unfit to be commander-in-chief" by then-president Barack Obama before the election.[117] The view was echoed over and over in the mainstream, establishment media.[118] Yet that message didn't seem to register with a sufficient number of Americans to deny him the presidency. At the same time, many Americans appear to have responded favorably to Trump's abrasive, abusive, and wildly undisciplined personality, which evoked masculine values that apparently appealed to his base, but which have prompted pundits to refer repeatedly to his election as "a victory for toxic masculinity and patriarchy."[119]

By contrast, Hillary Clinton was touted early on as "the most qualified candidate for president in our lifetime."[120] Later in the campaign, then-president Barack Obama upped the historical ante on this particular meme, hyperbolizing that "there has never been a man or a woman—not me, not Bill, nobody—more qualified than Hillary Clinton to serve as president of the United States of America."[121] Hillary supporters in both the mainstream and social media made sure that this meme was constantly repeated and reinforced in the minds of American voters.

However, the "qualifications" they chose to emphasize were not necessarily going to be ones that registered positively with Americans in general and Democratic voters in particular. They typically noted her time as First

116. Manning, "Membership of the 116th Congress."
117. "Obama: Trump 'Uniquely Unqualified' to Be President."
118. "Trump Unqualified to Be President."
119. Hazen and Holloway, "Patriarchy and Toxic Masculinity."
120. Payne, "Commentary: The Most Qualified Candidate."
121. "Obama: Hillary Clinton Most Qualified Presidential Candidate Ever."

Lady, US senator from New York, and secretary of state, missing or ignoring the fact that as First Lady she supported the North American Free Trade Agreement that many Americans blame for the loss of skilled manufacturing jobs over the previous two decades, as well as the 1994 Crime Bill which expanded the death penalty and accelerated mass incarceration, putting millions of Black Americans behind bars. They tended to miss or ignore the fact that as US senator, Hillary Clinton voted for the disastrous and illegal invasion of Iraq. They tended to miss or ignore the fact that as secretary of state, Hillary Clinton supported Arab Spring uprisings that destabilized the region and strengthened ISIS, helped arm Sunni rebels in their fight against Assad, which ended up in the hands of terrorists, abetted a coup in Honduras against a democratically elected president resulting in the persecution and murder of labor, human rights, and LGBTQ activists, and promoted the expansion of fracking around the world.

Nor did the former First Lady fare well in terms of personality. A Washington Post-ABC News poll in August of 2016—just weeks after her success in winning the Democratic nomination—showed that only 41 percent of Americans had a favorable impression of Hillary Clinton, while 56 percent viewed her unfavorably.[122]

As all this was going on, another candidate was rising to unexpected prominence, a candidate whose very career stood in stark contrast to the values of the technological society. On April 30, 2015, Bernie Sanders, the independent senator from the state of Vermont, declared his candidacy for president of the Unites States—a candidacy that would have been virtually impossible before the rise of digital technologies, social media, and propaganda 2.0. Sanders was, in many ways, the least likely presidential candidate to have emerged as a legitimate threat to the status quo in decades. His major policy proposals were radical—by establishment standards—and populist, and proved to be very popular among not only left-wing Democrats, but a sizeable portion of the Republican base: anti-establishment conservatives.[123] Rectifying income inequality, reforming the tax code, breaking up banks that are "too big to fail," instituting universal healthcare through a single-payer system, a massive infrastructure program that would create millions of jobs (paid for by the closing of business tax loopholes), reforming campaign finance and corporate lobbying, forcing businesses to increase vacation time and provide paid family and medical leave for their workers, curtailing the ability of the US government to spy on its citizens, tuition-free higher education, raising wages and working conditions (and *not* "spreading democracy")

122. Blake, "Record Number of Americans Now Dislike Hillary Clinton."
123. Foran, "Meet the Lifelong Republicans Who Love Bernie Sanders."

in the developing world[124]—this was a list of proposals designed to roll back some of the biggest gains the technological society had achieved in the last half century. He was destined to lose.

Despite attracting the largest crowds for any candidate of either party in the primary season; despite a virtual tie in the Iowa caucuses (.25 percent difference); despite winning twenty-three primaries and garnering more than thirteen million popular votes; despite having the highest favorability rating of any candidate at the moment Hillary Clinton accepted the Democratic nomination (54 percent)—Bernie Sanders's candidacy was finished before it began. The Democratic wing of the Capitalist Party could not allow any candidate to win who might threaten the continued global dominance of technique, nor could their allies in the mass media. So together they fought a counterinsurgent war[125] against the former Democratic Socialist mayor of Burlington, Vermont, and what appears to be a highly effective propaganda war against the single candidate that had acted as a consistent irritant to the technological society's global aspirations.

During a long primary season with an ascendant left-wing candidate, the cameras and microphones of the nation's mass media were focused, essentially, on two people: Donald Trump and Hillary Clinton. There was very little of Bernie Sanders to be seen in the mainstream media. A searchable database, powered by Google's GDELT project, on the Internet Archive's Television News Archive website, provides a picture of unequal coverage. The database measures GDELT's monitoring of the number of times each candidate is mentioned in a number of national media outlets. Between 2015 and August 3, 2017, Donald Trump had been mentioned 1,893,804 (that number is skewed, of course, because he had, at that moment, been president for six months), Hillary Clinton had been mentioned 684,808 times, and Bernie Sanders 202,102 times (this, despite the fact that Sanders was the most popular candidate during the campaign and remained "the most popular active politician" throughout the period covered).[126] Reacting

124. "Bernie Sanders on the issues."

125. Ironically, at the very same time the mass media appeared to have empowered Donald Trump's candidacy by giving him an unusually disproportionate amount of attention, even though a few of his policy positions—opposition to TPP and free-trade agreements, an end to military interventionism, enforced accountability of the intelligence community—were equally inimical to the goals of the technological society. It seems likely that this was less a concerted effort by the mass media to till the primary election in Trump's favor than it was a case of collective journalistic *cognitive dissonance* and no one actually believed he could win. Or it could have been profit-driven shortsightedness. As CBS chairman Les Moonves said at the time, Trump's candidacy "may not be good for America, but it's damn good for CBS."

126. Easley, "Poll: Bernie Sanders Country's Most Popular Active Politician."

to readers' complaints about the unequal coverage, *The New York Times*' public editor Margaret Sullivan defended her paper—but admitted the criticism was not without merit. "The *Times* has not ignored Mr. Sanders's campaign," she wrote on September 9, 2015, "but it hasn't always taken it very seriously. The tone of some stories is regrettably dismissive, even mocking at times. Some of that is focused on the candidate's age, appearance and style, rather than what he has to say."[127]

The Shorenstein Center for Media, Politics, and Public Policy at Harvard described Sanders's situation:

> By summer, Sanders had emerged as Clinton's leading competitor but, even then, his coverage lagged. Not until the pre-primary debates did his coverage begin to pick up, though not at a rate close to what he needed to compensate for the early part of the year. Five Republican contenders—Trump, Bush, Cruz, Rubio, and Carson—each had more news coverage than Sanders during the invisible primary. Clinton got three times more coverage than he did . . . Name recognition is a key asset in the early going. Unless poll respondents know of a candidate, they're not going to choose that candidate . . . But even as late as August of 2015, two in five registered Democrats nationally said they'd never heard of Sanders or had heard so little they didn't have an opinion.[128]

Despite the early (and continuing) snub from the mainstream mass media, Bernie Sanders went on to achieve a virtual tie in the Iowa caucuses (breaking 50.75 percent to 49.25 percent for Hillary Clinton), a commanding 60 percent–32 percent win in New Hampshire, and a loss by only six percentage points in the controversial Nevada Democratic caucus. Some portions of the media were now beginning to take his candidacy a bit more seriously than they previously had.

However, whatever advantage Sanders might have gained was dampened by the fact that during these early primary contests the bulk of the media coverage was focused not on the Democrats, but on the Republican candidates (primarily Donald Trump). The early Republican primaries received 58 percent of media attention compared to 42 percent for the Democratic contests.[129]

Meanwhile, angry allegations of Democratic Party attempts to "rig this primary for Hillary Clinton, by minimizing and delaying the debates, by

127. Sullivan, "Has the *Times* Dismissed Bernie Sanders?"

128. Patterson, "Pre-Primary News Coverage of the 2016 Presidential Race."

129. Patterson, "News Coverage of the 2016 Presidential Primaries."

counting superdelegates as if they vote before July's convention, and by surreptitiously funneling money to her campaign that was solicited for down-ticket candidates"[130] were only exacerbated on October 7, 2016 when WikiLeaks released 19,252 DNC emails and an additional 8,034 attachments showing a very clear pattern of preferential behavior on the part of the DNC toward the Clinton campaign. The Clinton campaign and the DNC immediately accused Russia of being responsible for the hacking of their email system.

WikiLeaks founder Julian Assange, however, quickly denied the claim. "The Clinton camp has been able to project a neo-McCarthyist hysteria that Russia is responsible for everything," he said during an interview on Russian cable station RT in November of 2016. "Hillary Clinton has stated multiple times, falsely, that seventeen U.S. intelligence agencies had assessed that Russia was the source of our publications," which, if true, was an interesting claim for Clinton to make as the Directorate of National Intelligence did not publish their assessment until January 6, 2017. "That's false—we can say that the Russian government is not the source."[131]

Muddying the waters further, former UK ambassador to Uzbekistan Craig Murray, a friend and associate of Assange, called the Russian hacking claims "bullshit," adding: "They are absolutely making it up . . . I know who leaked them. I've met the person who leaked them, and they are certainly not Russian and it's an insider. It's a leak, not a hack; the two are different things."[132] In another interview Murray claimed he received the email files from insiders and passed them on to WikiLeaks. "Neither of (the leaks) came from the Russians," Murray insisted. "The source had legal access to the information. The documents came from inside leaks, not hacks," he said, emphasizing his belief that the leaker was motivated by "disgust at the corruption of the Clinton Foundation and the tilting of the primary election playing field against Bernie Sanders."[133]

What the emails disclosed was a series of fairly banal and clichéd exchanges among DNC leaders which, although filled with disdain for Sanders and the progressive "revolution" he was leading, were probably criminal only for their disgraceful disdain for the common good. When Bernie Sanders criticized the Paris climate accords for not going far enough, Clinton campaign manager John Podesta emailed his associates, saying, "Can you believe that doofus Bernie attacked it?"[134]

---

130. Brasunas, "Only Voter Suppression Can Stop Bernie Sanders."

131. Sharkov, "Julian Assange Denies Russia Fed Clinton Emails to WikiLeaks."

132. Gayle, "CIA concludes Russia interfered to help Trump win election."

133. Goodman, "WikiLeaks operative claims Russia did NOT provide emails."

134. Podesta, "Fwd: Fwd: Congratulations On Paris."

Discussing ways to throw cold water on a campaign many were now calling "the Bern," DNC chief financial officer Brad Marshall suggested questioning Sanders's religion.[135]

> It might may (sic) no difference, but for KY and WVA can we get someone to ask his belief. Does he believe in a God. He had skated on saying he has a Jewish heritage. I think I read he is an atheist. This could make several points difference with my peeps. My Southern Baptist peeps would draw a big difference between a Jew and an atheist . . .[136]

The leaked emails also revealed that interim chair of the Democratic National Committee Donna Brazile had tipped the scales in favor of Hillary Clinton in one of the primary season's town hall debates, providing the Clinton campaign with specific questions the candidates would be asked. Hours after the email was posted on WikiLeaks, Brazile released a statement denying it, saying flatly "I never had access to questions and would never have shared them with the candidates if I did."[137] But in a subsequent essay in *Time* magazine she admitted that "among the many things I did in my role as a Democratic operative and D.N.C. Vice Chair prior to assuming the interim D.N.C. Chair position was to share potential town hall topics with the Clinton campaign . . . sending those emails was a mistake I will forever regret."[138] In the same essay, however, Brazile remained consistent with the DNC's "Russian hacking" narrative. "By stealing all the DNC's emails and then selectively releasing those few," she insisted, "the Russians made it look like I was in the tank for Secretary Clinton."[139]

On January 6, 2017, the Office of the Director of National Intelligence, James Clapper, released the assessment claiming that Russia had hacked the DNC/Podesta emails as part of a campaign to influence the 2016 presidential election. They made this assessment on the basis of what they implied was concrete evidence—*evidence that they couldn't identify and wouldn't publicly release*. "The Intelligence Community rarely can publicly reveal the full extent of its knowledge or the precise bases for its assessments, as the release of such information would reveal sensitive sources or methods and imperil the ability to collect critical foreign intelligence in the future . . . Thus, while the conclusions in the report are all reflected in the classified assessment, the declassified report does not and cannot include the

135. East, "Top DNC staffer apologizes for email on Sanders' religion."
136. Marshall, "No Shit."
137. "18 revelations from Wikileaks' hacked Clinton emails."
138. Brazile, "Russia DNC Hack Played Out Exactly as Hoped."
139. Brazile, "Russia DNC Hack Played Out Exactly as Hoped."

full supporting information, including specific intelligence and sources and methods."[140] Instead of evidence, the assessment offered numerous facts about its method, the skill and experience of its analysts, their intelligence, objectivity and clear judgment, and the diligence with which they did their jobs. Then they presented their key findings:

> We assess Russian President Vladimir Putin ordered an influence campaign in 2016 aimed at the US presidential election. Russia's goals were to undermine public faith in the US democratic process, denigrate Secretary Clinton, and harm her electability and potential presidency. We further assess Putin and the Russian Government developed a clear preference for President-elect Trump.

> We also assess Putin and the Russian Government aspired to help President-elect Trump's election chances when possible by discrediting Secretary Clinton and publicly contrasting her unfavorably to him.[141]

Interestingly enough, they also provided the following disclaimer:

> We did not make an assessment of the *impact that Russian activities had on the outcome of the 2016 election.* [My emphasis.] The US Intelligence Community is charged with monitoring and assessing the intentions, capabilities, and actions of foreign actors; it does not analyze US political processes or US public opinion.[142]

The remainder of the assessment is essentially a banal and pointless critique of the Russian cable television station RT. Ellul would classify all of this as an example of propaganda through the use of *innuendo*:

> Facts are treated in such a fashion that they draw their listener into an irresistible sociological current. The public is left to draw obvious conclusions from a cleverly presented truth, and the great majority comes to the same conclusions. To obtain this result, propaganda must be based on some truth that can be said in few words and is able to linger in the collective consciousness.[143]

140. Office of the Director of National Intelligence, "Assessing Russian Activities and Intentions in Recent US Elections," 1.

141. Office of the Director of National Intelligence, "Assessing Russian Activities and Intentions in Recent US Elections," ii.

142. Office of the Director of National Intelligence, "Assessing Russian Activities and Intentions in Recent US Elections," i.

143. Ellul, *Propaganda*, 56–57.

Say what you will about the strength of the intelligence community's case for Russian tampering of the 2016 US presidential election, its strength is based on an *appeal to authority*, not on evidence. It is based on *trust*; it is we who must trust the collective word of those "seventeen intelligence agencies" and trust the intentions of not only the agency directors, but of the Obama administration. In the face of this tacit demand for trust, we should remember what has happened to that loose cluster of separate and competing institutions we euphemistically call the "intelligence community" over the last few decades. The shake-up that occurred in 2004 arising from the George W. Bush administration's frustration with "liberals" in the CIA who were "disloyal" to that administration and its agenda gave us the Director of National Intelligence (DNI) in the first place. Until 2005 the nominal head of the intelligence community was the Director of Central Intelligence (DCI—who also served as the director of the Central Intelligence Agency). The *Intelligence Reform and Terrorism Prevention Act of 2004* was passed—ostensibly—to remedy some of the "intelligence failures" that led to the attacks on US citizens and property on September 11, 2001. However, agency insiders claim that the CIA resisted Bush administration efforts to cherry-pick only the data that supported the invasion and ignore all the rest. The "reforms" were made when intelligence professionals balked at this *dictat*. Paul Pillar, a veteran CIA officer who did intelligence assessments about the Middle East at the time, wrote in the March-April 2006 issue of *Foreign Affairs*, "What is most remarkable about prewar U.S. intelligence on Iraq is not that it got things wrong and thereby misled policymakers; it is that it played so small a role in one of the most important U.S. policy decisions in decades."[144]

One of the provisions of the act was the establishment of the DNI, thereby displacing, demoting, and emasculating the DCI. This demotion was not incidental or *pro forma*; it was a calculated and emphatic act meant to give the Bush administration—and all subsequent administrations—greater control over how information was gathered, what sorts of information would be gathered, and how it would be used. It accompanied a purge at the CIA under its new director Porter Goss. As a former high-ranking official of the CIA told *Newsday* in 2004, "Goss was given instructions . . . to get rid of those soft leakers and liberal Democrats. The CIA is looked on by the [Bush] White House as a hotbed of liberals and people who have been obstructing the president's agenda."[145]

---

144. Shane, "Ex-C.I.A. Official Says Iraq Data Was Distorted."
145. Sealy, "Purging the Disloyal at the CIA."

Since that time, the CIA has lost a lot of responsibility, a lot of its power, and a lot of its independence. Other, more clandestine agencies are doing the intelligence gathering, and the CIA has become little more than a public relations spokesman for the foreign policy agenda of whatever administration happens to be in power. As Pulitzer Prize-winning investigative reporter Seymour Hersh wrote in 2005, "The C.I.A. will continue to be downgraded, and the agency will increasingly serve, as one government consultant with close ties to the Pentagon put it, as 'facilitators' of policy emanating from President Bush and Vice-President Dick Cheney. This process is well under way."[146] It would be smart to remember these facts when thinking about the "threat to democratic institutions" that Russia currently poses.

On July 13, 2016, a class-action lawsuit was filed in the United States District Court in the Southern District of Florida against the Democratic National Committee and its chair, Debbie Wasserman Schultz, on behalf of the millions of Americans who donated to the doomed campaign of Bernie Sanders. (Very few people—aside from Bernie Sanders's supporters—are even aware of this fact, due to a nearly complete blackout on the part of the mainstream mass media.[147] A Google search of the term *DNC lawsuit* will yield more than 9 million results; the vast majority of them coming from either left-wing websites or, interestingly enough, right-wing sites; but very few mainstream sources.)[148] The lawsuit argued that

> the DNC was biased in favor of one candidate—Hillary Clinton—from the beginning and throughout the process. The DNC devoted its considerable resources to supporting Clinton above any of the other Democratic candidates. Through its public claims to being neutral and impartial, the DNC actively concealed its bias from its own donors as well as donors to the campaigns of Clinton's rivals, including Bernie Sanders.[149]

The Democratic Party showed no signs of settling the case and, in fact, considered its actions to be consistent with the normal workings of the American political system:

> The most recent court hearing on the case was held on April 25, during which the DNC reportedly argued that the organization's neutrality among Democratic campaigns during the primaries

146. Hersh, "Coming Wars."

147. Riotta,"Was the Election Rigged Against Bernie Sanders?"

148. "DNC Lawsuit—Google Search."

149. Wilding, et al. v. DNC Services Corporation.

was merely a "political promise," and therefore it had no legal obligations to remain impartial throughout the process.[150]

The case was dismissed on jurisdictional grounds, but not before lawyers for the DNC claimed that the party was under no obligation to adhere to any rule ensuring impartial treatment of the Sanders and Clinton campaigns, because it was "a discretionary rule that it didn't need to adopt to begin with," and was not a part of their corporate bylaws,[151] and in its final order of dismissal, the court flatly stated that "the DNC and Wasserman Schultz held a palpable bias in favor of Clinton and sought to propel her ahead of her Democratic opponents."[152] In 2019, the plaintiffs brought the case before the US Court of Appeals for the Eleventh Circuit, where the original dismissal was upheld. Meanwhile, former Democratic candidate Hillary Clinton continued to deflect blame for her failed campaign on others, and remained true to the narrative of Russian hacking. She cited Russian meddling in the election, FBI Director James Comey's involvement toward the end of the race, WikiLeaks's theft of emails from her campaign chairman, and misogyny.[153]

The total amount of money raised—most of it from pillars of technological society, corporate and/or wealthy donors, political action committees and Super PACs—is staggering. The Clinton campaign raised $1.4 billion, the Trump campaign $957.6 million.[154] The money was needed, of course, to fuel the colossal media pseudo-events we call political campaigns, with the vast majority going to the instruments of propaganda 2.0: television, radio, and print advertisements, media advisors, and logistical needs.

By contrast, Bernie Sanders refused to accept money from PACs or Super PACs, and avoided corporate donors like the plague. He still somehow managed to raise nearly $220 million, the vast majority of it from millions of individual donors, each giving an average of twenty-seven dollars, and most of it raised via the internet.[155] It is a testimony to the power of propaganda 2.1 to break the stranglehold on information exercised by propaganda 2.0 to note that, without interference from the Democratic National Committee, we might very well have been spared a Trump presidency.

150. Riotta,"Was the Election Rigged Against Bernie Sanders?"

151. Riotta,"Was The Election Rigged Against Bernie Sanders?"

152. Carol Wilding, et al., Plaintiffs, vs. DNC Services Corp.

153. Breitman, "Hillary Clinton Explains Why She Really Lost to Trump."

154. "How Much Money is Behind Each Campaign?"

155. Stein and Cherkis, "Inside Story of How Bernie Sanders Became the Greatest Online Fundraiser in Political History."

Chapter 5

Propaganda 2.1

Propaganda in the Digital Age

What is Propaganda 2.1?

Propaganda 2.0 is not the same phenomenon as propaganda 1.0. Rhetorical criticism is still useful, but it loses some of its bite when you're faced with a virtually infinite array of different media, all concentrated under the ownership of a handful of corporations, all publishing, streaming, and beaming stories to us from essentially within the same corporate narrative (support for neoliberal economic policy and neoconservative foreign policy). And we shall all be in an entirely different, and to many, frightening cognitive universe when that uniform narrative breaks down. This is the essence of propaganda 2.1.

Propaganda 2.0, the model of systematic, total propaganda described by Jacques Ellul, is a system of maximum redundancy. It is a system based on the mass manufacture and distribution of uniform bits of information, a system embodying a one-to-many flow of information. All media in the propaganda system work together, reinforcing one another. But in the digital age, the age of decentralized information, we will necessarily be exposed to diverse and often paradoxical points of view. Propaganda 2.1 is a model of competing propagandas, of uncertainty and doubt. It is a model of infinite information, and extremely high entropy. And that has turned out to be a refreshing thing for some, but an unnerving thing for many people who were raised in the environment of propaganda 2.0—and especially for those who owe their power and privilege to its existence.

Information theory tells us that, while many demands are made on our critical thinking skills, our judgment, and our sense of personal responsibility, there are opportunities for learning in such an environment, far more than the uniform narratives of propaganda 2.0 provided. Much of the new information we encounter will, of course, be questionable, much downright false. But much of it will be useful to us, and useful precisely because it is alien to our sensibilities. It becomes, then, our responsibility to sort through it, weigh it, evaluate it, and either accept it or reject it.

The Emergence of Global Society

The twentieth century quickly became the age of electronic media, and in the last half of that century the dominant medium of mass communication in the technologically developed world was television. It is here that we see Ellul's model of systematic total propaganda in its full florescence. It is here too that we recognize the formation of what Marshall McLuhan called "the global village,"[1] a place where we "share too much about each other to be strangers," where "you don't necessarily have harmony, you have extreme concern with everybody else's business and much involvement in everybody else's life." It is a place where "everybody is maliciously engaged in poking their nose into everybody else's business."[2]

McLuhan's description of life in this global village is illuminating, as it reveals the paradoxical but necessary condition of propaganda 2.0: the prerequisite strong ethos of individualism coexisting within a uniform mass.

> The electronic surround of information that has tended to make man a superman at the same time reduces him into a pitiable nobody by merging him with everybody. It has extended man in a colossal, superhuman way, but it has not made individuals feel important . . . The ordinary man can feel so pitiably weak that, like a skyjacker, he'll reach for a superhuman dimension of world coverage in a wild, desperate effort for fulfillment, or he will buy a private psychiatrist to be an audience.[3]

Along with the consequent alienation that humans experience under the influence of propaganda 2.0, we should also recognize the entropic effects of the mass media; explosions of commoditized information opening us up to new ideas, new points of view, and world events we never experienced before their existence. Think of the events that took place in the 1950s, sixties, and seventies, events that, through the new medium of television, Americans experienced as both individuals and as a mass: the civil rights movement, the

1. McLuhan, *Gutenberg Galaxy*, 31.
2. McLuhan et al., *Forward Through the Rearview Mirror*, 40.
3. McLuhan et al., *Forward Through the Rearview Mirror*, 85.

Vietnam War and subsequent anti-war movement, the massacres at Mỹ Lai and Kent State, the rise of "Black power" and radical student movements, the political assassinations, Woodstock, the awakening of a counterculture, the mind-altering drugs, the burgeoning ecology movement, the Watergate scandal and subsequent resignation of a sitting president—all of it coming into our homes on a daily basis. It was a tumultuous and, for many, frightening and disorienting time. For others, it may have seemed as though a moment of liberation was upon us.

This moment of high entropy, however, was followed, as we should have expected, by a period of increased redundancy and suppression of meaningful information—for the sake of the technocultural system's stability. Television, at the same time it was opening us up to a larger world of events, was also acting as a feedback loop, delivering all the social, cultural, and political ferment of the era to the powers that had the biggest stake in controlling the system and maintaining (and expanding) the postwar capitalist status quo. That system was, indeed, becoming increasingly unstable and in danger of collapse as a result of the growing "turn on, tune in, drop out" counterculture ethos. "From 1969 to 1972," wrote political scientist David Vogel in 1989, "virtually the entire American business community experienced a series of political setbacks without parallel in the postwar period."[4] The system's controlling powers had to do something quickly. They did. They created the myth of the "liberal media."

The Zenith of Propaganda 2.0

On August 23, 1971, Louis F. Powell (only months before becoming US president Richard M. Nixon's choice as associate justice of the Supreme Court) sent a confidential memorandum to a powerful friend in the US Chamber of Commerce, Eugene B. Sydnor Jr. At the time, Sydnor was the chair of the Chamber's Education Committee. In this memorandum, Powell described what he called an "Attack on [the] American Free Enterprise System" that had been underway, Powell claimed, for decades. The memo is notable for its Cold War rhetoric as well as for what may be some of the first glimpses of the now pervasive neoconservative ideology. In the first few pages Powell identifies the parties responsible for this assault:

> The sources are varied and diffused. They include, not unexpectedly, the Communists, New Leftists and other revolutionaries who would destroy the entire system, both political and

4. Vogel, *Fluctuating Fortunes*.

> economic. These extremists of the left are far more numerous,
> better financed, and increasingly are more welcomed and en-
> couraged by other elements of society, than ever before in our
> history. But they remain a small minority, and are not yet the
> principal cause for concern.[5]

This is almost boilerplate Cold War, paranoid anti-communist rhetoric—no real surprise, given the time at which it was written. But Powell
goes on to name other groups and social institutions which, in the coming
decades, would become familiar targets of establishment power:

> The most disquieting voices joining the chorus of criticism,
> come from perfectly respectable elements of society: from the
> college campus, the pulpit, the media, the intellectual and liter-
> ary journals, the arts and sciences, and from politicians.[6]

Powell's essential claim is that the American higher education system,
the news media, and democratic government itself were deliberately engaging in what Ellul called propaganda of agitation and·waging nothing less
than a revolutionary campaign to bring down the free market and subvert
the American way of life.

Noting that "much of the media . . . either voluntarily accords unique
publicity to these 'attackers,' or at least allows them to exploit the media
for their purposes," adding, "This is especially true of television, which
now plays such a predominant role in shaping the thinking, attitudes and
emotions of our people."[7] Powell found it ironic that "the media, including
the national TV systems, are owned and theoretically controlled by corporations which depend upon profits, and the enterprise system to survive."[8]
He then made specific suggestions about what the Chamber could do to
bring the American people back to a level of satisfaction with and support
for business. He suggested, among other things, that the television networks should be "monitored" to identify "insidious type[s] of criticism of
the enterprise system,"[9] that equal time be given to pro-corporate spokes-
persons, that "incentives" should be created "to induce more 'publishing'
by independent scholars who do believe in the system,"[10] and that corpora-

5. Powell, "Attack on American Free Enterprise System," 2.

6. Powell, "Attack on American Free Enterprise System," 2–3.

7. Powell, "Attack on American Free Enterprise System," 3.

8. Powell, "Attack on American Free Enterprise System," 3–4.

9. Powell, "Attack on American Free Enterprise System," 21.

10. Powell, "Attack on American Free Enterprise System," 22.

tions should become actively involved in US politics.[11] "As unwelcome as it may be to the Chamber, it should consider assuming a broader and more vigorous role in the political arena."[12]

The overall effect of the Powell memorandum must be seen then within the context of widespread social change. It was only a single point of inspiration—the religious right, for example, provided another—among several. But it is important to note that a number of neoconservative organizations, including Accuracy in Media and Accuracy in Academia, were created in the years immediately following Powell's missive, the corporate presence in Washington increased fivefold between 1968 and 1978, corporate lobbyists went from being insignificant to critical players in the legislative process, corporate political action committees increased from about three hundred in 1976 to more than twelve hundred by 1980,[13] and Roger Ailes[14] suggested to President Nixon that the Republican Party start their own television network.[15]

The first—and simplest—task for the US Chamber of Commerce and American business was to take control of government. In the US, the technoculture has always benefitted from maintaining a good working relationship with government (with the possible exception of the New Deal years) and with the increased presence of corporate government relations offices and lobbyists in Washington, and increased injections of money into candidates' campaigns via corporate political action committees, these relationships only improved.

The second task was to take control of the means of production and distribution of information. This was a bit more complicated because, on paper at least, the US mass media were already owned by corporations and had always operated according to the principles of the free market. Newspapers' advertising revenues far outstripped their revenues from subscription. Television advertising rates were based on the numbers of viewers each network or its shows could attract. So it was important to give the reader/viewer what he or she wanted. From the technical point of view information is, after all, information, and the job of the journalist is nothing more

11. Powell, "Attack on American Free Enterprise System," 24–26.

12. Powell, "Attack on American Free Enterprise System," 26.

13. Vogel, *Fluctuating Fortunes*, 59.

14. Ailes was a media consultant to then-candidate Richard M. Nixon in the 1968 presidential campaign. He was named the CEO of Fox News by Rupert Murdoch in October of 1996 and remained in control until July of 2016, when he was forced to resign in the face of multiple charges of workplace sexual harassment. He died on May 18, 2017.

15. Romenesko, "Memo from 1970."

than to find information and report it. But television was different from the traditional press. Because broadcasters use what was then considered to be a shared national resource—the electromagnetic spectrum—to transmit their programming, television stations were licensed by the Federal Communications Commission and in order to keep a license a broadcaster had to demonstrate that they were serving "the public interest, convenience, and necessity." As a consequence of all this, the first few decades of television journalism actually resulted in a more informed populace; more informed, at least, than they had been before the television era.

For this second task the technoculture got some assistance from Mark Fowler, the chair of the FCC under Ronald Reagan. A Friedmanian supply-sider and neoconservative who believed in market freedom, deregulation, and the responsibility of the individual consumer to choose his own products wisely, Fowler claimed that television had no greater responsibility to the public than any other home appliance, because TV was just "a toaster with pictures."[16]

In a paradigm-shifting 1982 article, Fowler redefined the idea of public service within the context of market forces, gave us a clear vision of the role of television in a competitive global society, and a preview of what a deregulated, "free market" media environment would look like:

> The perception of broadcasters as community trustees should be replaced by a view of broadcasters as marketplace participants . . . Instead of [the FCC] defining public demand . . . the commission should rely on the broadcasters' ability to determine the wants of their audience through the normal mechanisms of the marketplace. The public's interest, then, defines the public interest.[17]

Thanks to Mark Fowler and the Communications Act of 1984 (and subsequent acts) the present economic structure of television—dependent on advertising revenues for operation, owned by large and wealthy corporations (many of them multinational or even foreign-owned), competing for viewers in an ever-tightening, increasingly digital market, unburdened by the requirement to operate in the public interest—ensured and continues to ensure that we will continue to consume programming that supports, rather than challenges, the values of the technological society.[18] In other words, increase the redundancy within the system and minimize to the greatest possible extent any entropic influences.

16. Brainard, *Television*, 61.

17. Brainard, *Television*, 62.

18. Fallon, *Metaphysics of Media*, 209–10.

This was the high point of propaganda 2.0, and the general outline of the social, political, and economic context into which propaganda 2.1 is introduced at the end of the twentieth century. Propaganda 2.0—the propaganda model of Ellul's technological society—is one of virtually infinite redundancy—but redundancy that comes in a thousand different flavors and colors. The major difference (an ontological one) between propaganda 2.0 and propaganda 2.1 is the difference between the powerful conforming forces of virtually infinite redundancy on the one hand, and the often frightening and confusing feeling of liberation through virtually infinite entropy on the other. It is the difference between centralized control of information based on a one-to-many model, and a completely unregulated, multidirectional, free flow of information.

The Dilemma of Propaganda 2.1

The internet gave us that unregulated, multidirectional information flow. It was not necessarily the intentions of its creators to do so, but it was the result nonetheless. Their intention was to build a nonlinear, decentralized network of virtually infinite centers; if every point on the internet is its center, then at the same time *no single point* can be its center. To lose New York or Chicago or Washington, DC—or all of them—in a nuclear attack would not mean a loss of communication with the rest of the network; messages would simply be routed around the network's breach.

This was the revolutionary mutation in the genome of the technoculture, as it promised—for the first time in human history—individuals not only to be passive receivers of information, but active creators and distributors as well. If, as Marshall McLuhan insisted, media are the extensions of the human person, the internet represented the possibility of the global extension of *mind*: the possibility of human thought unleashed across the globe, and all that this implies. There would be, at first at least, bursts of creative and expressive energy, of intellectual ferment, of questions asked and answers proffered.

However, the rise of the internet also represented the *opposite* of all that. The internet may be the global extension of *mind*, but mind is a complex and chaotic phenomenon. Anyone who promised that the internet was going to release us from the oppressive mass manipulation of the *id* and the *superego* that we've lived under since the days of Edward Bernays and extend only the balanced *ego* was, purely and simply, lying to us. The same genomic mutation that released creative expression, intellectual ferment, and serious debate also opened the door to reactionary close-mindedness, blatant ignorance and racism, flame wars, lies, and bullying.

In a similar vein, the internet represented the opportunity to expand one's social network beyond family, close friends, acquaintances, and work colleagues, to build relationships with people from other cities and countries, other cultures, other incomes and living conditions, other educational levels, other religious, spiritual, or philosophical traditions, and, as a consequence, offered opportunities for profound personal growth. But it also allowed people to form relationships *only* with others, until only recently hidden and anonymous, who shared their views, their biases and prejudices, their hatreds, and their ignorance. The consequence of this was to remove whatever social sanctions remained against the public exhibition of behaviors that were once widely (and I believe objectively) deemed *sociopathic*—a pathological absence of empathy for others, an absence of conscience (or a malformed conscience), the need to discriminate and dominate other groups, the lack of trust in others, the need to denigrate those who are different to buttress one's own damaged self-esteem. In other words, if the internet is the extension of human mind, then it is the extension of the *fullness* of mind on a mass scale—good, bad, and ugly.

No technology, and that includes technologies of communication, is morally neutral. Each technology has its own *purpose*, a specific role it was meant to play, an end it was designed to achieve. Each medium embodies a particular set of values, a particular agenda, a particular ideology. Our problem is that, beyond the purpose and function of any new technology, we cannot always anticipate what *other* purposes a tool can be used for, what *other* unanticipated (and frequently unwanted) ends it might achieve. The internet's agenda has proven to be to remove us from the shackles of controlled information, and more specifically, increasingly corporate-controlled information. Its agenda, in other words, has been to undo all the work of propaganda 2.0. Without understanding precisely what that means (in terms of information theory), and what it will mean for the future, it is unlikely that we will be able to anticipate the internet's role as a powerful generator of entropy, and an agent in the breakdown of propaganda 2.0. To the extent that the new information we encounter contributes in a meaningful way to the lived experience of human beings, we can say that we've learned from it. In this case, we have in propaganda 2.1 what appears to be a potentially powerful antidote to the mass manufactured, homogenized pablum of propaganda 2.0. However, to the extent that new information unleashed upon us is false or manipulative, or hateful and meant to incite passions, then we flounder and are lost. The internet gives us both the opportunity to learn and the threat of being duped. But unlike the corporate-controlled mass information environment of propaganda 2.0, it is now *we* who are the agents of our own learning, and we who bear responsibility for our own stupidity. If, as John Culkin once said, "we shape our tools and thereafter our tools shape us," then it might be fair to say that at least some of the ill effects we observe or experience in our use of the internet will be of our own making.

The internet is the Frankenstein's monster of the military-industrial-academic complex; they simply could not anticipate its behavior once it escaped the laboratory. Its bias or agenda is to allow information to move freely, without restrictions, in any and every direction—from one to many, from many to many, from many to one, from one to one—without regard to content. This is a dangerous development for those with a deep stake in social control via homogenized content. The content of the internet will itself appear diverse, by virtue of the diversity of the character of each of its users, both senders and receivers of information. Naturally, then, we should have expected the internet revolution to bring with it a not insignificant amount of vulgarity and "bad behavior" along with whatever good and useful information it made available. And it is inevitable that we will encounter behaviors that will be deemed bad for no better reason than their subversion of the values of propaganda 2.0. While it is true that certain types of internet behavior are objectively bad, there is a broader range of behaviors that could be deemed bad only by more subjective judgment. Child pornography, for instance, can easily be seen as an objective evil, as can many other behaviors that are illegal in the larger world beyond the internet. Identity theft and various types of fraud, being illegal in the pre-internet world, should certainly have remained illegal in the digital world. Solicitations to murder should be banned on the internet and criminalized, just as they are in "real-world" interpersonal interactions.

However, there are other types of behavior which, while perhaps objectively "naughty," do not rise to the same level of moral imperative to prohibition as child pornography or solicitation to murder. Plagiarism, for example, is wrong—and it is something that the internet has made all too common by making it all too easy. As someone who has spent most of the last three decades teaching college-age students, I have witnessed firsthand the speedy descent of academic rigor into a cut-and-paste hell. Copyright, a child of the era of print, is endangered by the digital environment of sampling, mixing, cutting, and pasting. But who hasn't downloaded video, music, pictures, and text for their own amusement, and then shared them with friends? Gossip and rumormongering are wrong, and the internet has made them both daily global experiences. And stories masquerading as news that are sometimes grounded virtually completely in fantasy appear to many to be objectively wrong and mean-spirited—perhaps even hateful. But, to others, they are sometimes also funny and satirical, and we often enjoy them when they appear on our screens.

Ironically, there is at least one other broad category of bad behavior that very few (beyond civil libertarians) even take notice of: corporate violations of privacy, collection of data on citizens and even children, the selling of that information on the big data market, the creeping fascism of government/corporate surveillance, the bombardment of internet users' news feeds and inboxes with advertisements, and the avarice of telecommunications corporations aiming to monopolize not only the mass media ecology but its digital counterpart as well.

Despite the seriousness of this last category, governments have always been more interested in protecting the commerce function of various media than they are in the application of First Amendment protections of individual speech. So while we have watched telecom corporations devour one another, increase their power and control over the electromagnetic spectrum, and float plans to base bandwidth apportionment on audience size with virtual impunity, we have also witnessed attempts to impose both government and corporate censorship on individuals' speech on the internet.

In 1996, then-president Bill Clinton signed the Communications Decency Act into law. Its stated intent was to block the flow of pornographic material to minors (those under the age of eighteen), but also had provisions barring "indecency" and "patently offensive" content, both of which are problematically subjective judgments.

The late internet free speech activist John Perry Barlow, cofounder of the Electronic Frontier Foundation, was incensed at Clinton's signing of the CDA, and wrote a manifesto which he delivered to the 1996 World Economic Forum in Davos, Switzerland. He called it "A Declaration of the Independence of Cyberspace." In it, he summarized the dilemma facing both governments and the individual today: that dialectic tension between organized force seeking redundancy and stability, and the individual will embracing the entropy of new ideas and modes of human interaction.

"We are creating a world that all may enter without privilege or prejudice accorded by race, economic power, military force, or station of birth," he wrote. "We are creating a world where anyone, anywhere may express his or her beliefs, no matter how singular, without fear of being coerced into silence or conformity."[19]

> We have no elected government, nor are we likely to have one, so I address you with no greater authority than that with which liberty itself always speaks. I declare the global social space we

19. Barlow, "Declaration of the Independence of Cyberspace."

are building to be naturally independent of *the tyrannies you seek to impose on us.* You have no moral right to rule us nor do you possess any methods of enforcement we have true reason to fear.[20] (My emphasis.)

In the years following that Davos conference the technological society responded forcefully to Barlow's subversive manifesto on many fronts. In 2011 former French president Nicolas Sarkozy convened an "e-G8" meeting in the Tuileries Gardens in Paris, privately funded by global big tech players like Orange, Google, eBay, Microsoft, HP, and others. He challenged the internet powerhouses to behave in a "more civilized" way, and in words that seemed to respond threateningly to Barlow's manifesto, remarked, "The universe that you represent is not a parallel universe which is free of rules of law or ethics or of any of the fundamental principles that must govern and do govern the social lives of our democratic states."[21]

China had already been repressing free speech for more than a half century, and while the internet posed a challenge to Chinese censors, the country's technological infrastructure was sufficiently developed to confront and overcome that challenge. Since the introduction of the internet, the politburo has routinely blocked from the eyes and ears of 649 million Chinese internet users "subversive" content and even entire websites on the global internet that carry that content. This policy has become known as the Great Firewall of China. In recent years, the government has tried to justify its censorship by emphasizing that it is primarily seeking to ban information that is "obscene" or "pornographic," or that spreads "violence" or "terror," all reasonable concerns. But those are just a handful of examples of Chinese government-targeted content that includes "violating the basic principles [of the Chinese Constitution]," "jeopardizing the security of the nation, divulging state secrets, subverting of the national regime or jeopardizing the integrity of the nation's unity," "harming the honor or the interests of the nation," "inciting hatred against peoples, racism against peoples, or disrupting the solidarity of peoples," "disrupting national policies on religion, propagating evil cults and feudal superstitions," "spreading rumors, disturbing social order, or disrupting social stability," and "inciting illegal assemblies, associations, marches, demonstrations, or gatherings that disturb social order,"[22] most of which (with the exception of treason or publication of state secrets) would be protected speech in the United States under the First Amendment to our Constitution.

20. Barlow, "Declaration of the Independence of Cyberspace."
21. Anderson, "France Attempts to 'Civilize' the Internet."
22. Human Rights Watch, "Race to the Bottom."

Yet, neither has the government of the United States been immune to such calls for intervention and censorship, subtle or otherwise. In 1996 Democratic US senator James Exon of Nevada, appalled when he learned of the presence of pornography on the internet, told the press that "the information superhighway is a revolution that in years to come will transcend newspapers, radio, and television as an information source. Therefore, I think this is the time to put some restrictions on it."[23] In 2010 three US senators, Joe Lieberman (Independent), Susan Collins (Republican), and Tom Carper (Democrat) introduced a bill, the Protecting Cyberspace as a National Asset Act of 2010, popularly known as "the kill switch bill," that would have granted President Obama (and *all* presidents to follow) emergency power to shut down portions of the internet, or even the entire internet, if they deemed it necessary. Defending the bill on CNN, Lieberman actually cited the Chinese government's draconian system of information control as a precedent, inexplicably defending totalitarian information control. "Right now," he said, "China, the government, can disconnect parts of its internet in a case of war. We need to have that here, too."[24]

Luckily, the bill expired at the end of the 2009–2010 Congress without ever having come to a vote in either chamber. But Lieberman, Collins, and Carper's sentiments survive and, in some quarters, grow stronger as we wade more and more deeply into the entropic morass of uncontrolled information. We will likely hear future calls for a kill switch or something very much like it. And we may even feel sympathy for those calls.

The central question of this free/controlled internet dialectic is this: will the internet remain part of the global commons, a place where everyone is, for better or for worse, on equal footing with everyone else, a place where information flows freely, without external restrictions, where everyone can have their say—even when others are offended, and especially when the powerful are offended; or will it be gobbled up and monopolized, with the assistance of national governments around the world, by the commercial infrastructure of the global technological society? It's a question of critical importance, not just for the internet and its users, but for the future of democratic principles. And the truth is that, as in all things, we are the ones who will decide the future fate of the internet, and of democracy, by either the actions we take, or by the actions we fail to take.

23. Rossetto, "Cyberspace vs. the State."

24. Lieberman, "State of the Union."

Cyber Eden vs. the Wild West vs. . . . What?

To be perfectly clear about it, since the very beginning there have been at least three internets, two that existed in people's minds, and a third one more grounded in material reality. One internet people loved, one internet people feared, and the third one I will describe shortly, because we have so far been unable to come to terms with it while focusing obsessively on the other two. The first internet was going to free us, the second was going to subjugate us. One was going to join us together as a global village, one was going to separate us into tribes. One would reconsider the idea of *presence* in communication, creating a virtual *cyberspace* paradise populated by disembodied avatars of our own choosing, enjoying liberty, equality, and fraternity; the other would diminish the idea of human interaction in an actual public space, thereby diminishing both the role and the value of those forced to remain there.

While neither vision was entirely true or accurate, both visions, it turns out, were valid. The internet freed us by giving us new opportunities to interact, but also limited us by making old venues for interaction obsolete. The internet brought people together to share new and different ideas, opinions, and perspectives, facilitating learning; but it also brought people together who clung tightly to older, less enlightened, and sometimes hateful ideas. The American historian of medievalism and technology, Lynn White Jr., once wrote, "As our understanding of the history of technology increases, it becomes clear that a new device merely opens a door; it does not compel one to enter."[25] White was making reference to the fact, as Ellul did in his works, that any idea of a *technological determinism* that locks us into an inescapable future—whether good or bad—is a fallacy that must be abandoned. A new technology determines what we *may* do, not what we *must* do. We shape our tools, to be sure. But thereafter they shape us only to the extent that we allow ourselves to be shaped. It was inevitable, due to its very form, that the internet would disencumber us (at least temporarily, and only if we wanted it to) of information controlled by powerful elites. It was inevitable that it would give us new means of human association and new venues for our interactions. But the particular character of that disencumbrance, as well as of those associations and interactions, would be equally inevitably shaped by us.

25. White, *Medieval Technology and Social Change*, 28.

Cyber-Utopianism

There is a curiously spiritual, almost religious zeal apparent in most cyber-utopian literature, and that zealous sensibility is common to both the author and the reader. The cyber-utopian reader believes in *the future* in a different way than the rest of us—it is a place where people and things will not only be different, they'll be *better*. They'll be better because, unlike the older futures that we once imagined in the past, we'll design and engineer them to be better. We will *program* a future without crime, without poverty, without greed or lust for power. And our information systems will be central to all of this. We will, in fact, become one with our information systems; we will become a part of our own technological infrastructure. The "post-human future," ushered in by that moment when "machine intelligence" surpasses human intelligence—*the singularity*—will be one of cybernetic organisms (cyborgs) and disease-fighting *nanobots* facilitated and coordinated by all of the surplus intelligence of a shared cyber consciousness.

Ray Kurzweil

Perhaps no other cyber-utopian has been as influential in preaching the posthuman gospel as Ray Kurzweil. Kurzweil is the coiner of the term *singularity* to describe "a future period during which the pace of technological change will be so rapid, its impact so deep, that human life will be irreversibly transformed."[26]

> The Singularity will represent the culmination of the merger of our biological thinking and existence with our technology, resulting in a world that is still human but that transcends our biological roots. There will be no distinction, post-Singularity, between human and machine or between physical and virtual reality. If you wonder what will remain unequivocally human in such a world, it's simply this quality: ours is the species that inherently seeks to extend its physical and mental reach beyond current limitations.[27]

The internet, to Kurzweil, is a central—but not the sole or final—step in human technological evolution toward the singularity. The development of the internet, but especially its rapid growth and proliferation, is a factor in what Kurzweil claims is an exponential expansion of human knowledge we

26. Kurzweil, *Singularity Is Near*, 22.
27. Kurzweil, *Singularity Is Near*, 23.

are currently witnessing. Whereas the twentieth century saw a gradual speed-up in "the rate of progress" over the nineteenth century (about 20 percent in Kurzweil's apparently arbitrary estimation), he predicted that the twenty-first century would experience greater and faster growth, seeing

> twenty years of progress in just fourteen years (by 2014), and then . . . the same again in only seven years. To express this another way, we won't experience one hundred years of technological advance in the twenty-first century; we will witness on the order of twenty thousand years of progress (again, when measured by today's rate of progress), or about one thousand times greater than what was achieved in the twentieth century.[28]

We will use our new knowledge, Kurzweil assures us, to redefine what it means to be human—humans and machines will necessarily merge in both body and *mind*. Our media will no longer be extensions of us, they will become us, and we will wear them like we wear our own skin. We will no longer *use* the internet; we will become *part of the internet*, but of an infinitely more powerful internet, a global collective consciousness.

I'm inclined to swallow such rosy predictions only with an enormous grain of salt. Ellul tells us, of course, that technique is completely intolerant of moral or ethical judgment. So be it. Nevertheless, I believe it is more than justifiable to claim that there is a world of moral difference between some neurological surgical procedures (prosthetic hands, for instance, hardwired to nerve endings to provide the patient with motor control) and others (implanting USB ports in the brain).

But aside from the moral and ethical questions raised by the possibility of posthumanism, there is the simple question of human nature: whom do we trust to design and execute this hostile takeover of biological evolution? Will some be in positions of power—perhaps life and death power—over others? Will elites come to dominate weaker individuals and groups? Will everyone share equally in the gifts of posthumanism, or will some be left out? What will become of evil, and imperfection, and error? Will we program them out? How can we be sure? What will become of the individual who dissents from this brave new world?

And if we are upset with the internet now (while we can still, if we choose, turn it off and shut it out), how will we cope with the entropic influences of being directly connected to it, to its content, and to all of its users? Will there be filters? Whose filters? Will those filters be tunable or tweakable?

---

28. Kurzweil, *Singularity Is Near*, 25.

By whom? Will someone (or some algorithm) censor things that I write or post, or censor information that I might wish to receive?

Literary history is replete with utopian literature (most of it, admittedly, fictional), from Thomas More's *Utopia* (1516), through Francis Bacon's *New Atlantis* (1626) and Samuel Butler's *Erewhon* (1872). Like Ray Kurzweil's work (in my opinion at least), most of it can be—and has been—viewed as intentional or unintentional dystopian satire. More's perfect society is not much more exciting (or virtuous for that matter) than a cloistered monastery. Bacon's Bensalem is ruled by an elite caste of holy scientists. Butler's Erewhon has banished all machines out of fear that they might evolve the ability to self-replicate and develop something like a human consciousness.

I put Kurzweil into this category simply because he appears dismissive of the possibility that if imperfect, self-centered, and error-prone human beings are the ones to design, create, and program a new race of cybernetic human machines (and who else, besides God, will undertake such a project?), then we should not feel much confidence that this brave new world will be at all better, morally, ethically, or spiritually, than the one we're living in now. Like the rest of the technological universe, entirely engineered and constructed by human minds and hands, the approaching *singularity*—if it arrives at all—will do nothing but open a door. What happens once the door is open is completely dependent on the vagaries of human nature.

Nicholas Negroponte

I must give Nicholas Negroponte his due and admit that there's a part of me that appreciates being digital. Like everyone else, I spend an enormous amount of time on the internet and find it not only to be a great convenience, but an enormously helpful adjunct to library research. Many of the newspaper and magazine articles, reports in journals, and even a few of the texts that I used in researching this book were found on library databases, and purchased and downloaded over the internet. Almost all of the hard copy books that I used were purchased via Amazon's marketplace of used book vendors. And I have even compiled my bibliography and notes section on a website called *Cite This For Me*. I can't imagine how much longer it would have taken me to write this book (and how many sources I might have missed) if I had done all my research in the "real world."

While I consider him to be a cyber-utopian (in the sense that there is an uncritical enthusiasm in his words), Negroponte's *Being Digital* is more grounded in the reality of human relations through and with our technologies. The world it describes is not a perfect one; it is simply a "better" one and a far more efficient one. The pre-digital era was an age of atoms, a material world of scarce and expensive resources that moved no more quickly than any other material object, and of commodities that were limited by the availability of resources and the scale of manufacturing capabilities. As a consequence, markets for goods were similarly limited and commerce was hamstrung by inefficiencies. The digital world is, by contrast, a world of bits, a postindustrial world of dematerialized commodities and services of virtually infinite availability, coming to us at roughly the speed of light from their source through cable and the electromagnetic spectrum.

The digital world is also a world of choice and personalization. The world of atoms necessitated the creation of mass manufacturing and mass marketing, the production and distribution of bulk commodities. The world of bits, however, is the ultimate venue for the micro-marketing of goods and services to the world. "True personalization is now upon us," Negroponte insists.

> It's not just a matter of selecting relish over mustard once. The post-information age is about acquaintance over time: machines' understanding individuals with the same degree of subtlety (or more than) we can expect from other human beings, including idiosyncrasies (like always wearing a blue-striped shirt) and totally random events, good and bad, in the unfolding narrative of our lives.[29]

By close and constant observation of our online behavior—what we search for, what sites we frequent, what we buy, who we chat with, how much time we spend on one site as opposed to another, how much (and what) we consume, how much (and what) we create and share—internet algorithms can provide a tailor-made experience that reflects our own personalities. It must amplify, therefore, the illusion of individualism we all crave while remaining, quite firmly, part of the mass.

In consequence, *Being Digital* functions as little more than a useful handbook for life in Ellul's technological society, and an adjunct to sociological propaganda. In extolling the virtues and values of the digital revolution, Negroponte's focus is entirely fixed on economics, geared more to the consumer than to the citizen. Anticipating today's gig economy by twenty-five years, Negroponte's cavalier enthusiasm sounds cold-bloodedly unfeeling:

> As people in white-collar industries are replaced by automation, they will increasingly work for themselves. Concurrently, companies will outsource more and more and hire subcontractors.

29. Negroponte, *Being Digital*, 164–65.

Both trends are pointing in the same direction. By the year 2020, the largest employer in the developed world will be "self." Is this good? You bet.[30]

There is no pretense of genuine utopianism in *Being Digital*—unless one is awaiting creation of a shopper's or a gamer's or a cinemaphile's paradise. This is perhaps not surprising coming from a man some have called "*Wired*'s neoliberal evangelist,"[31] and others "one of the world's great salesmen."[32] "His MIT colleagues sometimes dismiss him as the P. T. Barnum of science, someone who puts on a flashy show without much substance. 'This is the red-light district of academia,' jokes a young scientist at [MIT's Media Lab]."[33]

The utopianism of Negroponte's *Being Digital* ultimately resides in its celebration of the internet as a central agent in the ongoing process of neoliberal globalization. The fact that that process is itself being governed by an unelected group of global power elites and is unresponsive to a growing chorus of democratic voices across the globe—exploited workers in developing countries, unemployed workers in developed countries whose jobs have been outsourced, human rights and eco rights activists in Africa and Latin America—gives powerful witness to the emptiness of Negroponte's utopian fantasy.

Kevin Kelly

Perhaps the most naively wild-eyed optimist of the cyber-utopians is Kevin Kelly, one of the co-founders and the founding executive editor of *Wired* magazine. In his book *What Technology Wants*, Kelly not only champions machine intelligence, but anthropomorphizes the internet, referring to it as a sentient being, an "intelligent superorganism."[34] It is the latest, but not the last, step in the ongoing evolution of what Kelly calls "the technium." The technium, he tells us, is "the greater, global, massively interconnected system of technology vibrating all around us."[35]

At the same time he likens the technium to a *system*, Kelly goes beyond mere systems theory to ascribe to the technium human, or even divine,

30. Negroponte, *Being Digital*, 240.
31. Armitage, "Resisting the Neoliberal Discourse of Technology."
32. Bass, "Being Nicholas."
33. Bass, "Being Nicholas."
34. Kelly, *What Technology Wants*, 30–32.
35. Kelly, *What Technology Wants*, 11.

characteristics. There is a mystical, almost spiritual flavor to this technium he describes. It is a force, self-directing and self-motivating, that reflects—or perhaps is even a part of—biological evolution. It not only has a purpose, it has *its own purpose*. It has *its own wants*.

> It wants to sort itself out, to self-assemble into hierarchical levels, just as most large, deeply interconnected systems do. The technium also wants what every living system wants: to perpetuate itself, to keep itself going. And as it grows, those inherent wants are gaining in complexity and force.[36]

While Kelly acknowledges—somewhat half-heartedly—that "I don't believe the technium is conscious (at this point),"[37] his words nonetheless reveal that he sees the technium as an extension of *biological life*:

> Its mechanical wants are not carefully considered delibera-tions but rather tendencies. Leanings. Urges. Trajectories. The wants of technology are closer to needs, a compulsion toward something. Just like the unconscious drift of a sea cucumber as it seeks a mate. The millions of amplifying relationships and countless circuits of influence among parts push the whole tech-nium in certain unconscious directions.[38]

In the end, Kelly assures us, the technium represents the inexorable movement toward the fullness of human life and intelligence. We should therefore, Kelly exhorts us, avoid the sins of Luddism and work in concert with the technium to achieve that fulfillment.

> The technium expands life's fundamental traits, and in so doing it expands life's fundamental goodness. Life's increasing diver-sity, its reach for sentience, its long-term move from the general to the different, its essential (and paradoxical) ability to generate new versions of itself, and its constant play in an infinite game are the very traits and "wants" of the technium . . . The technium also expands the mind's fundamental traits, and in so doing it expands the mind's fundamental goodness. Technology ampli-fies the mind's urge toward the unity of all thought, it acceler-ates the connections among all people, and it will populate the world with all conceivable ways of comprehending the infinite.[39]

36. Kelly, *What Technology Wants*, 15.
37. Kelly, *What Technology Wants*, 15–16.
38. Kelly, *What Technology Wants*, 16.
39. Kelly, *What Technology Wants*, 359.

And that, he concludes, is what technology wants.

Kelly's story echoes the ideas of the twentieth-century French Jesuit Pierre Teilhard de Chardin. Teilhard believed that evolution is a divinely directed process with a clear and unambiguous direction, that of ever-increasing organization and complexity, whose fulfillment is the fulfillment of all creation—the *Omega Point*. Biological evolution ended, Teilhard tells us, with the emergence of human beings, but the process of intellectual (and spiritual) evolution goes on, and must continue to do so in a way that reflects the principle of progress. In the presence of human intelligence, the Earth begins to don a mantle of knowledge, the *noosphere*, which spreads to all corners of the globe and deepens with each new piece of information and each new technology that disseminates it. At the Omega Point, the Earth will itself have become a sentient being, ignorance will have been eradicated, all energy will converge, and the kingdom of God will be at hand. Indeed, the fact that in 1995 Kevin Kelly's *Wired* magazine declared Teilhard "the father of the internet"[40] gives powerful evidence of Teilhard's influence on Kelly's thinking.

Kelly and Teilhard's stories are comforting and benign parables about the essential goodness of humans, human intelligence, and technology, and they are attractive to many people. But they are based on pure determinism and something very much like religious faith through and through. Even when technologies like the internet go wrong, even when they are used for ignoble ends, even when the unintended negative consequences of a technology far outweigh the intended, presumably good ends for which they were designed, it's all good, because the ultimate end of technological growth simply must be human unity and social betterment—*the rapture*.

This rosy technological outlook not only ignores the fact that every new technology, to paraphrase Neil Postman, offers us a Faustian bargain, "giving and taking away, sometimes in equal measure, sometimes more in one way than the other,"[41] but it ignores an equally important fact that *we* have a choice in the matter, *we* ultimately choose how we will use our technologies, and for what purposes. And it also ignores the fact that our choices are determined by our values, personal and social, and those values are often (if not always) strongly influenced by propaganda.

There is no reason why the internet can't bring all the people of the globe closer together, can't facilitate reasoned discourse, or can't be a powerful tool for learning. But the internet will only do those things *if that's what*

40. Chubbuck, "Wright's 'Nonzero.'"
41. Postman, *End Of Education*, 41.

we want from it. The entropic power of the internet will open the door for engagement with new ideas, but it will not compel entry.

Furthermore, the free information flow of the internet remains threatened by those who wish to maintain social control by maintaining control of information. There are powerful economic and political forces with an enormous stake in maintaining a peaceful totalitarian status quo who have no interest whatsoever in reaching the Omega Point or "expanding life's fundamental goodness." Ignoring these forces and relying on the inevitability of an ill-defined myth of progress is not only dangerous, but irresponsible.

Cyber-Dystopianism

At the other end of the spectrum, we have the cyber-dystopians, those who don't celebrate the new digital information environment, but fear it. Cyber-dystopianism is often seen as a form of *Luddism*, an irrational fear of technology. Of course, any sensible Luddite would tell you that there's nothing irrational about fearing a technology that takes away one's job, one's livelihood, one's source of income, one's traditions and habits of behavior, one's own sense of self, and leaves you with nothing more than an opportunity to use it only for the ends and purposes that the technology itself has established and propagated.

Cyber-dystopians fear imbalance; the idea that a new technology might serve to privilege one group over another. They fear not change, but specific changes, changes they don't necessarily want, and over which they exert no control. And most of all they fear precisely the kind of alienation that Ellul tells us about in *Propaganda*: alienation from the self, from the intimacy of interpersonal relationships, and from society as a whole, as we distance ourselves more and more from others through the act of self-mediation.

I have a great deal of sympathy for the cyber-dystopian objection. While I disagree with the more extreme dystopian prophecies, I have myself often been accused of having cyber-dystopian and even Luddite leanings. And even though I believe that the right technology, used responsibly toward responsible ends, can be an objective boon to humankind, I still believe that the cyber-dystopian serves a useful purpose in society as a prophet—who, after all, didn't congratulate the faithful for being as intelligent as they were, but warned them of the mortal dangers of hubris—far more than the cyber-utopian does.

Andrew Keen

Andrew Keen is one such prophet of digital doom. A Silicon Valley insider himself,[42] Keen is familiar with the road map of cyberspace and on a first-name basis with many of the netizens who inhabit it. When the dot-com bubble burst in the first few years of the new millennium, Keen rethought his early fascination with the internet. He began to write and speak publicly about its dangers rather than its opportunities, calling the internet "the greatest seduction since the dream of world communism."[43]

His 2015 book, *The Internet Is Not the Answer*, is a scathing critique of a world created by utopian speculation about the (false) promises of the internet. Keen presents an indictment of the internet on a number of serious economic and social charges—a failure to live up to its false promises—and uses the rest of the book presenting his evidence. Among the economic charges, he lists the following:

> Rather than promoting economic fairness, it is a central reason for the growing gulf between rich and poor and the hollowing out of the middle class. Rather than making us wealthier, the distributed capitalism of the new networked economy is making most of us poorer. Rather than generating more jobs, this digital disruption is a principal cause of our structural unemployment crisis. Rather than creating more competition, it has created immensely powerful new monopolists like Google and Amazon.[44]

On the docket of social crimes, Keen makes these accusations:

> Rather than creating transparency and openness, the Internet is creating a panopticon of information-gathering and surveillance services in which we, the users of big data networks like Facebook, have been packaged as their all-too-transparent product. Rather than creating more democracy, it is empowering the rule of the mob . . . Rather than fostering a renaissance, it has created a selfie-centered culture of voyeurism and narcissism.[45]

Keen is undoubtedly correct in his allegations—to a point at least. The internet has created a lot of wealth that has not seen a fair distribution. It has nurtured corporate behemoths like Amazon, Google, and Facebook. It has facilitated widespread surveillance by both corporations

---

42. Keen, "Andrew Keen on Media, Culture and Technology."
43. Keen, "Andrew Keen on Media, Culture and Technology."
44. Keen, *Internet Is Not the Answer,* 3–8.
45. Keen, *Internet Is Not the Answer,* 175.

and government. It has encouraged mob behavior. It hasn't brought out the best in us as a culture. The question is not whether, like all technologies, the internet has been at best a mixed blessing. It has. But again, at its best, has the internet done nothing of value for us beyond providing a new venue for distraction and moneymaking?

Jaron Lanier

One of the pioneers of virtual reality technology and, along with John Perry Barlow and Kevin Kelly, an early cyber-utopian, Jaron Lanier echoes some of Andrew Keen's economic concerns, but fears as well that digital technology is dehumanizing us, taking away the reflective, interior experience that makes each of us an *individual human*.

In *You Are Not a Gadget*, Lanier presents a humanist plea, not to reject all technological change or adopt Luddite attitudes, but to be careful to resist falling prey to what he calls *cybernetic totalism*. Without actually defining the term, Lanier describes it in a series of anecdotes and analogies. I'll try to give you my take on Lanier's explanation.

The core of Lanier's concern over cybernetic totalism is a phenomenon he calls *lock in*. Let's use the architecture of the internet as an example. The internet we have today is an accident of history and human choice, not an inevitability. It is not the internet we had thirty years ago when it was in its infancy, and it is not the internet that the computer geeks and technocrats who created it had in mind more than a half century ago at its birth. Everyone at the time shared the *concept* of the internet, but different people had different ideas about the programs and protocols that would make it work. Packet routing, internet protocol (IP), and transfer control protocol (TCP) make up just a part of the core structure of the internet, like a frame of steel girders and beams that are the core structure of a skyscraper, and in the early days of the internet (while it was still predominantly a tool of computer scientists at research universities and the Defense Department), the internet was not much more than this framework.

Then in 1989 a British computer scientist by the name of Tim Berners-Lee decided to put a façade on that steel framework, much like muscles, flesh, and skin cover the human skeleton. He called that façade *the World Wide Web*. The web operated according to three technologies that he designed: HTML (hypertext markup language), URL (uniform resource locator), and HTTP (hypertext transfer protocol). Berners-Lee's World Wide Web is the development that gave us *web pages* that could be opened and closed and easily switched from one to another. Before the web, a user could only access the internet through a command interface, and open or run shared programs or programs on their own computer. The introduction of the web allowed for—and necessitated—the development of graphic user interfaces (GUI) which allowed for the selection of available programs by clicking on an icon with a mouse.

At roughly the same time as the development of the web, computer geeks around the world were developing a variety of different *operating systems*, programs that manage the software, computer hardware and peripherals, and help to integrate available services. Apple's Steve Wozniak developed Mac OS, Bill Gates developed Windows for Microsoft clients (IBM was an early adopter), and a Finnish university student named Linus Torvalds wrote an operating system he called Linux. A variety of web browsers—Microsoft's Internet Explorer, Apple's Safari, Netscape's Navigator, etc.—followed close behind.

None of these later enhancements was inevitable. It was inevitable, from a pragmatic point of view, that someone would have to find an easier way to navigate through a growing number of websites if the internet were to be usable by the general public. But each particular development was more accidental than necessary. And along the way these new (and often redundant) enhancements had to compete with one another in terms of ease of use, compatibility with different computers, and expense in order to be marketable. If the changes in technologies we've witnessed over the last half century mirrored the natural processes of biological evolution, we'd have to assume that the internet we have today is the best one that could possibly exist; but they didn't, and it's not, and here's where cybernetic totalism comes into play.

Each development, once assimilated, gets locked in, threatening future enhancements. And not all of these developments have been equal. Some of them are free (of cost) and therefore facilitate the free movement of information. But some of them are proprietary, which means that the information moves freely only if you are paying for the technology that allows it to do so. Tim Berners-Lee's World Wide Web is an absolutely free and open technology, and it is so because he made a conscious decision to keep it free. Once asked if he regretted his failure to cash in on his invention, he replied, "Not really. It was simply that had the technology been proprietary, and in my total control, it would probably not have taken off. The decision to make the Web an open system was necessary for it to be universal. You can't propose that something be a universal space and at the same time keep control of it."[46]

46. Berners-Lee, "Frequently Asked Questions by the Press."

Linus Torvald's Linux operating system is also a free and open-source piece of software. Any users can download it free of charge and, once it is downloaded, alter it, rewrite it, and customize it to suit their needs. Consequently, it is a rather flexible and tolerant operating system—it supports software from numerous developers and software companies.

Windows, by contrast, is and always has been a proprietary system, and one that made Microsoft the target of a federal antitrust lawsuit in 1989. The Windows operating system was designed to make it difficult, if not impossible, to use non-Windows peripherals and programs, and their decision to include their web browser, Internet Explorer, without extra charge made it difficult for other software developers to compete. Microsoft lost the original lawsuit, but that case was overturned on appeal and they avoided the legal penalty of splitting into two companies. Still, the Microsoft lock-in may account for the ubiquity of Microsoft products and applications far better than any argument about their technical superiority. "Science," Jaron Lanier remarks, "removes [inferior] ideas from play empirically, for good reason. Lock-in, however, removes design options based on what is easiest to program, what is politically feasible, what is fashionable, or what is created by chance."[47]

Cybernetic totalism, then, is the process through which our behaviors, our language, and even our thinking get locked in to patterns that are foisted on us by new technologies and the competition between their creators. And to make matters worse, as Lanier points out, those technologies are almost always accidental and arbitrary; they were not necessary, and different technologies—or different iterations of the same technologies—could have presented us with entirely different (and perhaps healthier) patterns of thought and behavior. And in too many cases, computer designers, programmers, and technology entrepreneurs have not chosen for us those technologies which, by empirical observation and testing, will benefit us most on the basis of our humanity, but those which will return to them the greatest profit on the basis of convenience, ease of operation, trendiness, or efficiency.

Worse still, it is we who have allowed, even encouraged this to happen. We have bought into the myth of progress, and simply assume—in a knee jerk sort of way—that every new technology is a manifestation of progress rather than mere change. In doing so, we've

47. Lanier, *You Are Not a Gadget*, 9–10.

had to accept a number of anti-humanist ideas such as, for instance, the various myths surrounding the phenomenon of *artificial intelligence* (AI): machine consciousness, computers that are "smarter" than the people using them, and, of course, the *singularity*. Lanier cites the eponymous Turing test, named after the twentieth-century computer scientist Alan Turing, who emphasized the subjective nature of intelligence and suggested that if we could witness a conversation between two entities—one a human being and the other a computer—and the human being remained unaware that she was conversing with anything but another human being, that we could rightly say that the computer had achieved at least a basic level of human intelligence (and, perhaps, even consciousness). But in reality, Lanier responds, there are other possible alternatives to this conclusion that we ought, but seem unwilling, to consider. "You can't tell if a machine has gotten smarter or if you've just lowered your own standards of intelligence to such a degree that the machine seems smart."[48]

"People degrade themselves in order to make machines seem smart all the time," Lanier notes ruefully. "We have repeatedly demonstrated our species' bottomless ability to lower our standards to make information technology look good." But he cautions us to remember that "Every instance of intelligence in a machine is ambiguous."[49] He points to the triumphalism of the AI cult when IBM's Deep Blue supercomputer beat world chess champion Gary Kasparov in 1997, and the deeply ambivalent public reaction to the event. "For millennia, mastery of chess had indicated the highest, most refined intelligence—and now a computer could play better than the very best human."[50] We somehow miss or ignore the most important fact: "What happened was primarily that a team of computer scientists built a very fast machine and figured out a better way to represent the problem of how to choose the next move in a chess game. People, not machines, performed this accomplishment."[51]

"Humans are free" and not determined, Lanier reassures us, in terms reminiscent of Jacques Ellul's own views on human freedom and determinism.

> We can commit suicide for the benefit of a Singularity. We can engineer our genes to better support an imaginary hive mind. We can make culture and journalism into second-rate activities

48. Lanier, *You Are Not a Gadget*, 32.
49. Lanier, *You Are Not a Gadget*, 32.
50. Lanier, *You Are Not a Gadget*, 34.
51. Lanier, *You Are Not a Gadget*, 32.

and spend centuries remixing the detritus of the 1960s and other eras from before individual creativity went out of fashion.

Or we can believe in ourselves. By chance, it might turn out that we are real.[52]

Nicholas Carr

"The Net is, by design, an interruption system," says Nicholas Carr in *The Shallows*, "a machine geared for dividing attention."[53] Carr, referencing McLuhan's "the medium is the message," posts a warning about the dangers of attending too closely to the content of a medium at the expense of our awareness of the effects of the medium itself on our thought processes. "Media work their magic, or their mischief, on the nervous system itself."[54]

Of all the recent cyber-dystopian literature (and, in my opinion, the cyber-utopian literature as well), *The Shallows* is perhaps the most trenchant and significant, and certainly the one most grounded in empirical science rather than personal anecdote and conjecture. Carr relies on recent studies in the neurosciences to support his argument that the internet is changing the very structure of our brains—changing them in a way that literate people in a (once) literate environment could only characterize as *damaging* them. This growing body of theoretical and empirical research supports the argument that the act of reading imposes upon the developing human brain a need to reorganize its functions, remapping neural pathways and allowing new types of thought previously impossible.[55] The internet threatens to undo much or even most of that.

Carr refers frequently to *neuroplasticity* in the book; the brain's ability to "rewire" its synaptic pathways in moments of change and engagement with new experiences and ideas—a mixed blessing as it turns out. Neuroplasticity is that characteristic of the brain that allows it to retrain itself to some extent when, for instance, a portion of the brain is damaged by a stroke or other injury. The brain of a stroke victim who has lost the fine motor control of his vocal mechanisms—diaphragm, lips, teeth, tongue, etc.—and consequently cannot speak can transfer that motor control function to some other portion of the brain. Neuroplasticity also allows us to learn new skills that have not previously been a part of our repertoire of

---

52. Lanier, *You Are Not a Gadget*, 44.

53. Carr, *Shallows*, 131.

54. Carr, *Shallows*, 3.

55. Wolf, *Proust and the Squid*, 216–17.

behaviors. It allows us to learn new languages. It allows us to break bad habits and adopt new and better ones.

Neuroplasticity, however, has its limits. First of all, while neuroplasticity is a lifelong phenomenon, the level of the brain's plasticity declines over time. This is why you can learn a new language as an adult, but not as quickly and *naturally* as a young child in its developmental years. A baby born into a bilingual household will naturally learn both languages as quickly as a baby in a monolingual household learns a single language. But for many people (if not most) learning a new language as an adult can be a difficult and frustrating experience.

Second, neuroplasticity means that, in the replacement of one set of cognitive activities with another, we can actually untrain our brains from the prior cognitive activities and retrain them to perform the newer ones. This, it turns out, is the conceptual foundation of *The Shallows* in its entirety: that we have replaced the cognitive and neural functioning of the literate brain with those of the postliterate brain. Neuroplasticity, as I pointed out, allows us to break bad habits and adopt new and better ones. But it also allows us to break helpful and healthy habits and adopt newer ones that are harmful.

The crux of Carr's argument can be summed up in this passage from chapter 7 in *The Shallows*, "The Juggler's Brain."

> Dozens of studies by psychologists, neurobiologists, educators, and Web designers point to the same conclusion: when we go online, we enter an environment that promotes cursory reading, hurried and distracted thinking, and superficial learning. It's possible to think deeply while surfing the net, just as it's possible to think shallowly while reading a book, but that's not the type of thinking the technology encourages and rewards.[56]

Our reading directly influences our thinking, because the structure of print actually structures human thought patterns, changing at the same time the structure of society itself, the relationship among individuals within the society, and among individuals and social institutions. Our internet use influences our thinking as well—but in a very different way than the deep reading associated with print does. The structure of information on the internet—some text, yes, but video and images, sounds and music, and constantly changing content—is simply not conducive to sustained linear, logical thought. We ought to acknowledge the uniqueness in all of nature of the human capacity for the kind of thought nurtured and sustained by deep reading, and to recognize the precarious nature of its existence. It is a

56. Carr, *Shallows*, 115–16.

mode of thought that thrives, develops, and sharpens when it is exercised; it becomes stilted, stunted, blunted, and atrophied when not.

These, then, are the two internets that we carry around in our heads. Luckily, there is a middle ground where the cyber-utopian and cyber-dystopian narratives meet, the place where we acknowledge both the promises and the pitfalls of the digital age. It is called *reality*.

The Third Internet

If it is true, as the renowned cyber-dystopian Yogi Berra once said, that the future ain't what it used to be, it can still be better than we fear it will be, if we have the will to take control of the technologies that will ultimately help us to create it. Nor, at the same time, should we expect the internet to usher in a new Jerusalem, a final fulfillment of human progress. If the internet represents the globalization of the human mind, we should not expect it to be better, or even any different, than the mere sum of its parts.

Human beings have a long history of expecting too much of their technologies, and an equally long history of myopia in regard to their greatest strengths. Like Johannes Gutenberg, we see our new technologies through McLuhan's rearview mirror, both expecting them to be something they're unable to be, and at the same time failing to see them as they really are. Being able to recognize both what the internet does well and what it is unable to do, the opportunities it provides us and the challenges it presents, the hope for human improvement it represents and the panorama of human folly, greed, and ignorance it often comprises—these are the first steps in navigating the reality of the internet. They are also the foundation of understanding propaganda 2.1. If we can acknowledge that, to a certain extent, the internet both liberates and limits us, simultaneously facilitates both diversity and tribalism, propagates both truth and falsehood, spreads both loving concern and hateful bigotry, helps us and hinders us in our work, is at the same time both a boon to and the bane of literacy, breaks the propaganda 2.0 stranglehold on information even while it is imposing on us new demands for precisely the kind of critical thinking it seems to discourage, and emphasizes the urgent need for greater personal responsibility even as it offers opportunities for anonymity and irresponsibility—if we can, in other words, embrace the paradox of the digital information environment, we will be making great strides toward a fuller understanding of what, in the final analysis, is nothing more than a powerful extension of *ourselves*. It is, in fact, far more an extension of ourselves than the older mass technologies of television and radio could ever be, because *we make the internet happen.* It does not, if we wish, have to be something that happens to us, something that we passively watch or listen to. With mass media we have no choice. The internet offers us that choice.

Rather than consuming content mass manufactured and mass distributed by the wealthy power elite of the technological society, we now have the opportunity to become content creators and distributors ourselves—if we choose to do so. The internet opens many doors, doors to both engagement and interaction, and to passive consumption. It invites us, but does not compel us, to enter any door we please. The internet offers us the tools and the opportunity to make that choice. Mass media do not.

The internet allows—even encourages—human social interaction from a distance. We can meet, get to know, and become friendly with perfect strangers from different countries on different continents. We can exchange ideas, stories, experiences. We can share cultures. We can debate—respectfully, one would hope—issues of political and social importance. We can critique books we've read or movies we've seen or music we've heard. We can question and criticize the great unquestioned assumptions of our own, and other, societies. Or we can do none of this, and instead congregate among our own tribe mouthing the timeworn shibboleths of "our people," and continue to see the world in terms of "us and them." Either way, the internet allows us to make that choice. Mass media do not.

This third internet—the real internet, with all its warts and wonders—mirrors the human person. It embodies both peace and pandemonium, fact and fiction, hope and fear, humor and pathos. It spreads joy and it spreads hatred. It can be extremely intellectual and quite often startlingly moronic. It is, like us, a paradox.

And yet, at the same time, this real internet is more than just a mirror of the human person; it also mirrors the mass media and the corporate superstructure of the technological society that control them. Amid the chaos of uncontrolled, free-flowing information, if what you want from the internet are nothing more than the comforting and redundant narratives of capitalism, consumption, and social control, the mainstream corporate media all have a home there and are ready, willing, and eager to serve you. Again, paradoxically, propaganda 2.0 manages to live on within the very technology that has given us propaganda 2.1. That will very likely be as true in the future as it is today. If we choose not to use the internet as our own platform for free expression and decide only to use it as a receptor of other people's content, then we will have to learn to deal with the reality that propaganda 2.1 *does not* mean that we are guaranteed the truth, but only abundant information, some familiar and soothing, some alien and frightening, and that we must become more discerning not only in what sorts of information we seek, but in where and how we choose to find it.

Privacy and Social Media

By opening social media accounts we by necessity surrender a great deal of our own privacy. Whenever you post on Facebook, for instance, the terms of service agreement you accepted when you opened your account gives them an unlimited license to use your videos, images, and words, at any time, for any purpose. If you use Facebook on a mobile app, its software identifies Bluetooth signals, and records geolocation information by pinging Wi-Fi access points, beacons, and cell towers; your location is identifiable at any moment. And I'm not really certain I understand why anyone would agree to this, but if you choose to turn on Facebook's facial recognition function, Facebook can identify and auto-tag you in any photograph—even someone else's photograph taken as you were simply walking down the street while a stranger is taking a photo. Accidental photobombing can get you auto-tagged. It's a good thing not to get auto-tagged when you're walking down that street arm in arm with somebody else's significant other while you're actually supposed to be at work. You may be a scoundrel, but you still have a right to your privacy.

There is also the issue of social media companies selling users' data to so-called data brokerage firms who then sell that data—including data about your interaction with friends, your likes, what stories or ads you have read or reposted, your relationship status, as well as your age, race, sex, weight, height, education level, politics, buying habits, health concerns, vacation dreams,[57] screen names, website addresses, interests, hometown and professional history, and how many friends or followers you have, etc.[58]—to marketers for targeted advertising. Most social media sites are "free" (that is to say they don't charge you a fee in order for you to have a presence on their site), and many earn barely enough revenue on outside advertising to operate. So how do may sites survive? By harvesting, or mining, the most valuable asset they have at their disposal, then refining it, and selling it to data brokers: your personal data.

These data brokers are in the business of amassing huge files of information on internet users to sell to companies for a variety of purposes, both benign and invidious. If you've ever used one of the so-called people search sites (like Pipl, Intellius, Spokeo, or Instant Checkmate),

---

57. Singer, "Mapping, and Sharing, the Consumer Genome."
58. Beckett, "Yes, Companies Are Harvesting."

the information you've read (perhaps about yourself) has been purchased from a data broker.

Data brokers also sell information to companies that offer "risk mitigation" services that help to verify identities and detect fraud. Banks and retail outlets doing business online will frequently use these services to certify that you are the person you claim to be and not someone who has stolen the electronic identity of another person.

Then of course there is the most ubiquitous of the data brokers' clientele, the internet advertiser. Advertisers use your data to shape commercial appeals directly to you, based on your interests, age, location, likes, etc. If you've ever even looked at a product on, for instance, Amazon, and the next day you're seeing nothing but pop-up ads for that same product wherever you land on the internet, this is not a coincidence. That search you did for a kerosene lantern, or a particular brand of dog treats, or a hard-to-find European beer fed back immediately from Amazon's algorithms into a datafile of your own personal interests, available to data brokers of every stripe. And because you agreed to the terms of service, you agree to these conveniences.

As serious as these (perfectly legal) violations may be, however, they pale in comparison with the invasions of individual privacy being perpetrated on the American people—with the willing acquiescence of the social media giants—by the US government. The National Security Agency (NSA) routinely monitors the audio and video chats, photographs, emails, documents, stored data, file transfers, and connection logs of social media users, as well as their search and browser histories on search engines like Google and browsers on PCs and Apple products.

Under the code name PRISM, the NSA had secretly been tapping directly into the central servers of nine leading US internet companies, Microsoft, Yahoo, Google, Facebook, PalTalk, AOL, Skype, YouTube, and Apple, since 2007. At first, under the Protect America Act of 2007, the surveillance was limited to noncitizens or US citizens outside the United States. But with the passage of the FISA Amendments Act of 2008, which provides criminal immunity to private companies who cooperate with US government agencies in intelligence gathering, this surveillance was extended to all American citizens, both abroad and at home.

On March 12, 2013, director of National Intelligence James Clapper testified to Congress that concerns about domestic surveillance of American citizens were unfounded. He was asked directly by US senator Ron Wyden whether the NSA was spying on us. "No, sir," he responded. "Not wittingly."[59] When pressed on the issue, he added, "There are cases where

59. Contorno, "James Clapper's Testimony One Year Later."

they could inadvertently, perhaps, collect, but not wittingly."[60] All of this, of course, was a lie (Clapper later called it "the least untruthful" answer he could manage), which became evident to the entire world just a few months later when on June 5, 2013, *The Guardian* published leaked classified documents from PRISM and other examples of NSA surveillance provided to them by whistleblower Edward Snowden.

Then-president Barack Obama defended the program of systematic surveillance, downplaying its scope and potential impact. "Nobody is listening to your telephone calls," he said. "That's not what this program's about." He continued, taking considerable liberties with the truth, "I came in with a healthy skepticism about these programs. My team evaluated them. We scrubbed them thoroughly. We actually expanded some of the oversight, increased some of safeguards."[61] Unfortunately, this statement runs contrary to the fact that under Obama, domestic surveillance was broadened far beyond what began under George W. Bush.

Obama concluded with words that eerily reflect the yin and yang situation we are forced to confront in the information environment of propaganda 2.1: "You can't have 100 percent security and then also have 100 percent privacy and zero inconvenience. You know, we're going to have to make some choices as a society."[62]

Freeing Information

"Information wants to be free," Stewart Brand told the participants of the first Hackers Conference in 1984.[63] He was speaking of economics, of course, and not of any claim on a God-given right to liberty that information might possess. But he also offered a corollary to his statement—that "information wants to be expensive," an acknowledgement, for better or for worse, of information's value as a commodity. This dichotomy between the desire to know and share information freely and the desire to assume proprietary control over information is an ancient one, and one that we continue to live with in the age of propaganda 2.1.

The idea of the freedom of information is every bit as deeply ingrained in the human spirit as the belief in the ownership of private property; perhaps even more so. Neither idea exists in nature; the existence of each is dependent on the depth of societal belief in their reality. Leaving aside the

60. Ackerman, "James Clapper."
61. "Obama's Remarks On Health Care And Surveillance."
62. Acar, *Culture And Social Media*, 8.
63. Doctorow, "Saying Information Wants to Be Free Does More Harm."

nettlesome issues of copyrights, patents, and intellectual property (all of which, to paraphrase McLuhan, may have finally outlived their uselessness under propaganda 2.1), the internet has proven to be information's quint-essentially liberating medium, sometimes much to the chagrin of power-ful elites in both government and industry. The reasons for this liberating power are manifold, and include not only the software and applications the internet has provided, but also the people who have appreciated that power and have attempted to use it for our common benefit.

Web 2.0

While the structure and architecture of the internet was sufficient in its earliest days to free information from its traditional mass media restraints, genuinely free—one might even use the term *democratic*—movement of in-formation really began with the introduction of what we have come to call web 2.0, that amalgam of web-based programs and services that, along with improvements in processing speeds and capacity, encourage users to create and distribute their own content, and make websites more participatory. Web 2.0 relieved users of the need to spend money on programs and soft-ware that enabled them to create their own interactive sites. The web became a platform housing open-source software and services that users could take advantage of in order to produce applications, games, surveys, research stud-ies, and websites that would attract their own audiences. Popular websites routinely invite comments on their stories and allow commenters to debate and argue (and sometimes verbally abuse) one another. Social media sites allow us to post our own thoughts and ideas—or to steal someone else's. They allow us to share images of special moments spent with loved ones, or of our dog in a Santa suit. We can post text, images, songs, or videos we create our-selves, or the words, pictures, music, and videos of others. At every moment, the choice of exactly how we will use web 2.0 is ours to make. But the fact remains that it is in the participatory environment of web 2.0 that the truest freedom of information currently resides.

Along with social media sites, Web 2.0 also made possible the weblog or blog. While blogging may have had its heyday in the first decade of the new millennium (for a while it seemed as though *everybody* had a blog) and has since dwindled down to a few thousand (or hundred thousand) stalwarts, social media platforms have given the activity new life. Blog posts remain among the most shared content on social media. Blog hosting sites like Medium have even increased both the quantity and quality of blog con-tent. Many of the most prominent alternative news sites on the web today began as personal or group blogs: Talking Points Memo, the Daily Kos, Huffington Post, TechCrunch, Gawker, The Drudge Report, Crocks and Liars, the Daily Dish, Michelle Malkin, Breitbart, and Snopes, to name just a few. These blogs represent many segments of the political spectrum and not just the homogenized mainstream.

The open-source nature of web 2.0 has also given us the wiki—sites like Wikipedia that allow for the collaborative creation, editing, and maintenance of content by any and all who are interested. Wikis are essentially databases curated by knowledgeable users on a variety of topics. Some wikis are encyclopedic in their range (Wikipedia, for example), and some focus on more narrow topics (such as, believe it or not, Pornopedia).

There are wikis on genealogy (Familypedia), on linguistics (Glottopedia), on diplomacy (Diplopedia), on rational skepticism (RationalWiki), on quotations (WikiQuote), and on Star Wars (Wookieepedia), and cities around the world have created wikis for tourists or those interested in learning about, for instance, Davis, California (DavisWiki) or Karlsruhe, Germany (Stadtwiki Karlsruhe). Wikis, when responsibly and competently moderated, are one of the better examples of the benefits offered by the hive mind, collective knowledge of the mass being superior to the individual knowledge of any given person.

However, like the propaganda 2.1 environment generally, Wikipedia and its readers are vulnerable to pranks, hoaxes, and lies. In May of 2005, American journalist and former aide to US senator Robert F. Kennedy, John Siegenthaler, was libeled on Wikipedia by an anonymous and unregistered contributor who posted an article claiming that Siegenthaler—ironically a staunch defender of First Amendment rights—was suspected of complicity in the assassinations of both John and Robert Kennedy. The entry was eventually deleted but remained active on Wikipedia for nearly four months.

Starting in early 2006, a controversy over Wikipedia's reliability arose when staff of the US Congress began editing the entries covering the senators and congressmen for whom they worked. Investigators for Wikipedia found that edits were made in May of 2006 from an IP address assigned to the US Senate that deleted then-senator Joe Biden's history of plagiarism. In August of 2013, someone in the US Senate changed Edward Snowden's Wikipedia entry to call him a "traitor" rather than a "dissident,"[64] and a year later a House staffer edited the Wikipedia entry for United Nations High Commissioner for Human Rights, Navi Pillay, describing Edward Snowden as an "American traitor." Only a month earlier, Pillay had stated publicly that the world owed a "great deal" to Snowden and had described him as

---

64. Kloc, "Is a U. S. senator trolling Snowden's Wikipedia page?"

a "human rights defender."[65] And in December of 2014, someone using a computer with an IP address linked to the US Senate edited the Wikipedia entry for the US Senate Intelligence Committee report on the CIA's use of torture, actually removing the word *torture* and leaving the euphemistic phrase "enhanced interrogation techniques."[66]

Wikipedia—and the wiki concept generally—is propaganda 2.1 in microcosm. It provides an invaluable service to its users; but its users must be skeptical and diligent in engaging the content they find there. Lacking a broader knowledge of the historical context within which each entry is placed, one must be extremely careful; the lure of knowledge, when it is false, can be a very dangerous trap to fall into.

WikiLeaks

Despite the fact that it began its existence as a traditional wiki, WikiLeaks is now one of the most closed and tightly controlled sites on the web. While WikiLeaks invites whistleblowers from all over the world to submit leaked content anonymously, no document or entry can be posted by anyone but a WikiLeaks staffer, and none can be edited at all; only original, unedited documents appear on the site. An international, not-for-profit organization, WikiLeaks points to Article 19 of the United Nations' Universal Declaration of Human Rights as its ideological foundation: "Everyone has the right to freedom of opinion and expression; this right includes freedom to hold opinions without interference and to seek, receive and impart information and ideas through any media and regardless of frontiers."[67]

Founded by editor in chief Julian Assange and never constituting more than a dozen or so activists, WikiLeaks has made it its mission to uncover government and corporate secrecy where the release of such information is in the public interest. Historically (a brief history, to be sure) the group has been an equal-opportunity annoyance to both the political right and center-left,[68] exposing corruption in Tunisia, extrajudicial police killings in Kenya,

65. Hattem, "House Staffer Edited Wikipedia Page to Label Snowden a 'Traitor.'"

66. Bobic, "Senate Staffer Tried to Scrub 'Torture.'"

67. UN.org., "Universal Declaration of Human Rights."

68. Because of the continuing dominance of the mainstream media, we are still influenced by propaganda 2.0. Consequently, neither WikiLeaks nor Julian Assange's work gets a sympathetic hearing in the West. Assange's most consistent global support comes from the socialist left, including praise and moral support from the likes of former British Labour Party leader Jeremy Corbyn, former Brazilian president Luis Inacio Lula da Silva, British journalist John Pilger, Chinese dissident and artist Ai Weiwei, US dissident and Pentagon Papers leaker Daniel Ellsberg, internet activist John Perry

Chinese oppression in Tibet, the infiltration of the white-nationalist British National Party into the UK police, a nuclear accident at an Iranian nuclear facility, and an oil scandal in Peru. But it was in WikiLeaks' direct challenge to the American capitalist empire that the group gained its greatest notoriety and earned the enmity of the global power elite.

In February 2010, WikiLeaks released 92,000 US military documents—the so-called "Afghan War Logs"—detailing a number of civilian and friendly fire casualties previously unreported, Pakistani support for the Taliban, and the activities of an elite commando unit, Task Force 373, resulting in the deaths of 195 Afghan civilians. In April 2010, they released a gunsight video, leaked by what WikiLeaks referred to as "a number of military whistleblowers," that showed a US Apache helicopter opening fire on a group of civilians, including two Reuters journalists, killing them all. The video, now known as "Collateral Murder," also shows a van driven by family members driving up to collect the bodies being fired on as well, adding to the carnage. In October of that same year, the group published on its website a trove of 391,832 US Army field reports—the so-called "Iraq War Logs"—covering the period from 2004 to 2009. The files reveal that roughly 80 percent of Iraqi deaths in the war up to that moment had been civilians, and confirm reports that US and coalition allies had been routinely turning a blind eye to Iraqi torture of prisoners, years after the disclosure of torture and abuse in the US-run prison at Abu Ghraib.

Between 2011 and 2015, WikiLeaks continued its in-your-face challenge to US global power, releasing "the Guantanamo files," detailing the appalling conditions under which 779 mostly innocent prisoners of war were held; "the spy files," documenting the growing global mass surveillance industry; and an embarrassing set of diplomatic cables that showed that the NSA, as a matter of routine, spied on US allies, including France and Germany.

During this time, the US and other governments, unable to plug the leaks in their own bureaucracies, were trying to find a way to kill the messenger—to silence WikiLeaks by whatever means necessary. In May of 2010, WikiLeaks was temporarily brought down by a massive distributed denial of service attack (DDoS), essentially the flooding of the website's processors with more traffic, from too many different sources, than it could handle. Hacktivist supporters of WikiLeaks mirrored the site, effectively ending the attack. In November of 2010, Obama-era attorney general Eric Holder opened an investigation to determine if Julian Assange had violated the 1917 Espionage Act in publishing classified documents.

Barlow, US dissident, intellectual, and propaganda scholar Noam Chomsky, and others.

And in December of the same year Swiss bank PostFinance, along with PayPal, MasterCard, and DNS (domain name system) service EveryDNS. com blocked donations and services to the site. Hacktivist group Anonymous retaliated by inflicting their own DDoS attack on those organizations' websites and the blocks were lifted.

Perhaps the greatest finger in the eye that WikiLeaks presented to the global power elite, however, was the release of email correspondences leaked from the servers of the Democratic National Committee and Hillary Clinton's campaign manager John Podesta during the US presidential campaign of 2016. This leak, seemingly more than any other, solidified the US establishment's antipathy toward WikiLeaks and Julian Assange, culminating in the narrative that survives today, presented to the world without a single shred of evidence to support it, and delivered by a director of National Intelligence, James Clapper, who had only recently lied to the US Congress and the American people: Russia hacked the election and WikiLeaks colluded with them to do so. This narrative has done greater harm in the American mind to WikiLeaks than all the DDoS attacks in the world.

Yet at the same moment, in just a little over a decade, WikiLeaks had amassed a long and impressive list of awards for its service to free speech and to a journalism unconstrained by government or commercial pressures. They are the recipients of numerous awards, including *Time* magazine's Person of the Year (2010), The Martha Gellhorn Prize for Journalism (2011), The Global Exchange Human Rights People's Choice Award (2013), and The Yoko Ono Lennon Courage Award for the Arts (2013). And its founder, Julian Assange, was nominated for the Nobel Prize for Peace eight years in a row (2010–2018) for his work with WikiLeaks.[69]

Julian Assange

Power does not surrender power lightly. Following WikiLeaks' multiple releases of highly classified information that put the US military—and the Obama administration—under harsh global scrutiny, then-vice president Joe Biden called Julian Assange "a high-tech terrorist."[70] Then-secretary of state Hillary Clinton accused him of committing "an attack on the international community,"[71] and, according to one report[72] based on anonymous

69. International Association of Democratic Lawyers, "Written Statement."

70. MacAskill, "Julian Assange Like a Hi-Tech Terrorist, Says Joe Biden."

71. CNN.com, "Clinton Condemns Leak."

72. Cautionary note: This report was published on a conservative website, True Pundit, and should be taken with a healthy dose of skepticism. We should note,

State Department sources, asked her staff in a closed meeting, "Can't we just drone this guy?"[73] When questioned by reporters about the report, Clinton replied, "It would have been a joke, if it had been said, but I don't recall that."[74] And Democratic Party strategist Bob Beckel took to the national airwaves to call for Assange's assassination: "A dead man can't leak stuff," Beckel said. "This guy's a traitor, he's treasonous, and he has broken every law of the United States. And I'm not for the death penalty, so . . . there's only one way to do it: illegally shoot the son of a bitch."[75]

Julian Assange has been languishing in a British prison since May 1, 2019, spending twenty-three hours of each day in solitary confinement, and isolated from others during his one hour of daily exercise. The UN Special Rapporteur on Torture and other Cruel, Inhuman or Degrading Treatment or Punishment, Nils Melzer, and two medical experts visited Assange in Belmarsh prison in May of 2019 and reported that his treatment constituted psychological torture.[76]

Prior to his April 2019 arrest and subsequent imprisonment, Assange had spent seven years in the Ecuadorian Embassy in London seeking diplomatic immunity from prosecution. During his time there, his physical health began to deteriorate, and within a few years he was suffering from a number of serious ailments, including "neuropsychological impairment, weakened bones, decreased immune function, and increased risk for cardiovascular disease and cancer," according to Dr. Sondra Crosby, associate professor of medicine and public health at Boston University and an expert on the physical and psychological impact of torture, who evaluated Assange multiple times between 2017 and 2019. She added that he also displayed physical and psychological symptoms as a result of "prolonged social isolation and sensory deprivation."[77]

His legal team has stated that in the course of the hearings Assange has been handcuffed eleven times, repeatedly strip-searched, had his case files

---

however, that the website's investigative unit provided an image of an internal follow-up memo written immediately after the meeting by State Department director of policy planning Ann-Marie Slaughter and sent to Clinton, her chief of staff Cheryl Mills, and aides Huma Abedin and Jacob Sullivan titled "An SP memo on possible legal and nonlegal strategies re WikiLeaks." And the FBI report following its investigation into Clinton's use of an unprotected personal computer to do sensitive State Department work indicated that the former secretary of state was routinely involved in the process of "nominating" targets for drone strikes.

73. True Pundit, "Under Intense Pressure to Silence Wikileaks."

74. Conway, "Clinton: I don't recall joking about droning Julian Assange."

75. "Bob Beckel Calls for 'Illegally' Killing Assange."

76. Hogan et al., "Ongoing torture and medical neglect of Julian Assange."

77. Risen, "Julian Assange Suffered Severe Psychological and Physical Harm."

confiscated, and has been forced to sit in a dock encased in bulletproof glass, unable to hear the proceedings or consult with his lawyers. He missed several of his extradition hearings because of his ill health, and in September of 2020, his lawyers told presiding judge Vanessa Baraitser that Assange now suffers hallucinations and depression and is at a "high risk of suicide" if he is extradited to the United States. He has sought confession with a Catholic priest, drafted farewell letters to his family, and written his last will, they told the court.[78] The co-chair of the International Bar Association's Human rights Institute, Michael Kirby, commented: "The IBAHRI is concerned that the mistreatment of Julian Assange constitutes breaches of his right to a fair trial and protections enshrined in the United Nations Convention against Torture and Other Cruel, Inhuman or Degrading Treatment or Punishment, to which the UK is party."[79] As I write this, he remains in prison pending a US appeal of its failed extradition request.

While details of Assange's situation are easily found in the overseas press and the US alternative media, the US corporate-owned mass media have said little on his plight, and have been virtually silent on the physical and psychological toll his eight years of imprisonment have taken on him. The average American knows little about Assange, other than some vague sense of his poorly defined villainy, and even less about his current situation and condition. Even with the internet, squarely in the era of propaganda 2.1, the power of mass information control characteristic of propaganda 2.0 is still very great.

Chelsea Manning

WikiLeaks essentially acts as a feedback loop in a dysfunctional system desperately seeking to maintain its "normal" dysfunctions. As such, it is an agent of entropy. But in a closed, redundant system like the technological society, finding information to feed back to the system's constituents that would throttle them sufficiently to inspire them to take action is an enormous challenge. WikiLeaks' release and publication of the Afghan War Diaries, the Iraq War Diaries, and the Collateral Murder video, along with other as yet unreleased files, would not have been possible without the assistance of a twenty-three-year-old US Army intelligence analyst, known at the time as PFC Bradley Manning.

As Ellul pointed out, technique does not tolerate judgment. In consequence, being a whistleblower is a dangerous thing—this is why it is done

---

78. Brown, "Julian Assange a high suicide risk, extradition case told."

79. International Bar Association, "IBA–IBAHRI Condemns UK Treatment."

anonymously. Whistleblowers see something that they judge on an ethical, moral, or emotional basis to be wrong and they try to right it. Many whistleblowers at first attempt to work within the system, bringing their concerns to those higher up in their organization's chain of command, and as a last resort leak information when they are rebuffed. They know that, depending on their particular case, they might be shunned for their disloyalty, very possibly fired for their actions, or worse: they could be court-martialed, tried in a civil or criminal court, incur enormous legal debt, and possibly imprisoned. To make public ugly and inconvenient truths is to set yourself apart from your organization, your colleagues, and your bosses, and can fill you with frustration and anxiety. In a way, to tell the truth that no one else is willing to tell is to set yourself *above* all those groups, and smacks of narcissistic, moral self-righteousness. But maintaining secrets that hurt other people can simply be far too much to handle emotionally, psychologically, and even physically.

Chelsea Manning knew secrets that she was unable to live with. As an intelligence analyst, she was privy to a daily flood of strategic and tactical intelligence from the field that she would evaluate, put into context, and report to military commanders or civilian authorities in the Defense Department. She also had access to the classified files of other intel analysts and higher-ranking military intelligence officials, and she exploited them all to the fullest extent of their usefulness. But she also had her own secrets, secrets that, with equal intensity, she wished to make known to the world: she was a woman trapped at birth in a man's body. Without going into an in-depth psychological analysis of Manning's emotional state at the time she was given access to a trove of classified intelligence, it is still sufficient to say that Chelsea Manning saw great injustice in the world and wanted to do something about it.

Manning provided WikiLeaks with more than a half million classified documents detailing battles, casualties, deplorable detainee conditions, torture, and atrocities committed as part of the wars in Afghanistan and Iraq. "This is possibly one of the more significant documents of our time, removing the fog of war and revealing the true nature of 21st century asymmetric warfare,"[80] she guilelessly confided to a friend.

It was, ultimately, that lack of guile and her intense need to feel vindicated in both her personal and professional life that put her behind bars. In May of 2010, Manning began a series of online chats with a former hacker turned digital journalist by the name of Adrian Lamo. She had read about Lamo in an issue of *Wired* magazine and contacted him without warning.

---

80. Dishneau, and Jelinek, "Witness: Manning Said Leak Would Lift 'Fog Of War.'"

Over the course of these conversations, Manning not only revealed a number of leaks she had supplied to WikiLeaks, but also opened a piece of her soul to Lamo:[81]

> (May 21) **Manning:** I can't believe what I'm confessing to you. I've been so isolated so long . . . I just wanted to be nice, and live a normal life . . . but events kept forcing me to figure out ways to survive . . . smart enough to know what's going on, but helpless to do anything . . . no-one took any notice of me . . .
>
> **Lamo:** Give me some bona fides . . . yanno? Any specifics.
>
> **Manning:** This one was a test: Classified cable from US Embassy Reykjavik on Icesave dated 13 Jan 2010. The result of that one was that the Icelandic ambassador to the US was recalled, and fired. That's just one cable . . .
>
> **Lamo:** Anything unreleased?
>
> **Manning:** I'd have to ask Assange . . .
>
> **Lamo:** Why do you answer to him?
>
> **Manning:** I don't . . . I just want the material out there . . . I dont want to be a part of it . . .
>
> (May 23) **Manning:** I mean, I'm a high profile source . . . and I've developed a relationship with Assange . . . but I don't know much more than what he tells me, which is very little. It took me four months to confirm that the person I was communicating was in fact Assange.
>
> **Lamo:** How'd you do that?
>
> **Manning:** I gathered more info when I questioned him whenever he was being tailed in Sweden by State Department officials . . . I was trying to figure out who was following him . . . and why . . . and he was telling me stories of other times he's been followed . . . and they matched up with the ones he's said publicly.
>
> **Lamo:** Did that bear out? the surveillance?
>
> **Manning:** Based on the description he gave me, I assessed it was the Northern Europe Diplomatic Security Team . . . trying to figure out how he got the Reykjavik cable . . . They also caught wind that he had a video . . . of the Gharani airstrike

---

81. I've edited these excerpts minimally, changing only spelling and punctuation for the sake of readability.

in Afghanistan, which he has, but hasn't decrypted yet . . . the production team was actually working on the Baghdad strike[82] though, which was never really encrypted. He's got the whole 15-6 for that incident . . . so it won't just be video with no context. But it's not nearly as damning . . . it was an awful incident, but nothing like the Baghdad one. The investigating officers left the material unprotected, sitting in a directory on a centcom.smil. mil server. But they did zip up the files, aes-256, with an excellent password . . . so [as far as I know] it hasn't been broken yet.

Manning: I can't believe what I'm telling you . . . [83]

That same month, Adrian Lamo contacted the US Army Criminal Investigations Unit and told them he had been contacted by the person who had leaked all of that intelligence to WikiLeaks. Interviewed two years after the event, Lamo seemed to be comfortable with his decision. "I knew my actions might cost him his life," he told *The Guardian*'s Ed Pilkington. "Making the choice to interdict a man's freedom knowing it could mean his life, is something that's easy to judge but can only really be understood by living it. You either fold it into your character, come to terms and go on with your life, or you get stuck in that moment forever."[84]

Chelsea Manning was released from prison on May 17, 2017, having served seven years of a thirty-five-year prison sentence, after her sentence was commuted by outgoing president Barack Obama that January. She is appealing her military court martial, and is active on the lecture circuit. Adrian Lamo died on March 14, 2018, at the age of thirty-seven of a possible accidental drug overdose.

Edward Snowden

Perhaps the most significant example of the power of our digital information environment to free information is the case of Edward Snowden. Unlike Chelsea Manning, Snowden approached both mainstream and alternative media outlets to alert the world about secret crimes the US was committing against its own people. Since the attacks on the US on September 11, 2001, he said, the US government had been engaged in "a litany of American destruction by way of American self-destruction, with the promulgation of

---

82. This is the "collateral murder" video.

83. Zetter and Poulsen, "'I Can't Believe What I'm Confessing to You.'"

84. Pilkington, "Adrian Lamo on Bradley Manning."

secret policies, secret laws, secret courts and secret wars."[85] He believed the American people—and the world—had a right to know about them.

He had become part of a secretive network of surveillance, a "massive surveillance machine,"[86] spying not only on some "'dark conspiracy" of foreign terrorists, but on innocent US citizens making phone calls, writing emails, sending texts, posting baby pictures, flirting, having lovers' quarrels, baring their souls. And it was not only their social media interactions and email correspondences that were being intercepted and recorded, but their every movement and action as well. Every television show they viewed, every penny they spent, whether online or in stores, what they were buying, who they were with, what they were eating—all of it was making its way into NSA servers, being parsed, analyzed, and stored. The idea of due process of law, privacy, and constraints against illegal search and seizure seemed to have died in the years following 9/11.

Snowden at first tried to work within the system, bringing his concerns to supervisors, to no avail. He insists that he "made tremendous efforts to report these programs to co-workers, supervisors, and anyone with the proper clearance who would listen. The reactions of those I told about the scale of the constitutional violations ranged from deeply concerned to appalled, but no one was willing to risk their jobs, families, and possibly even freedom to go to through what [whistleblower Thomas A.] Drake did."[87]

He lived with his feelings of anxiety and guilt, frustrated that his concerns were not being taken seriously enough to provoke review of these programs, until March 12, 2013, when he decided it was time to act. "I would say . . . the breaking point was seeing the Director of National Intelligence, James Clapper, directly lie on oath to Congress. There's no saving an intelligence community that believes it can lie to the public and the legislators who need to be able to trust it and regulate its actions."[88]

Snowden, a former cybersecurity expert for the CIA, quit the CIA and began working for an NSA subcontractor, information technology consulting firm Booz Allen Hamilton, the better to collect and leak information about the US programs of domestic and global surveillance. He was stationed in Hawaii and granted administrator authority over the computer system there. He had the same or better access to classified documents as he had working for the CIA, along with a greater distance from the prying eyes of the intelligence community. It was while posted

85. MacAskill and Topham, "'They Wanted Me Gone.'"
86. Free Snowden, "Threats overview."
87. Cook, "Perils Of Whistleblowing."
88. Free Snowden, "Transcript."

in Hawaii that Snowden downloaded an estimated 1.7 million files, the largest leak of classified information in US history.

Still, he did not act immediately, for fear of reprisals against him, his job, and his life. "I understand that I will be made to suffer for my actions, and that the return of this information to the public marks my end," he wrote in May 2016 to the *Washington Post*'s Barton Gellman whom, along with Ewen MacAskill of the British newspaper *The Guardian*, independent documentary filmmaker Laura Poitras, and independent journalist Glenn Greenwald, he had approached with his story. He also warned them that until the leaks were published, their participation in the project put them in mortal danger. US intelligence services, he wrote, "will most certainly kill you if they think you are the single point of failure that could stop this disclosure and make them the sole owner of this information."[89]

Snowden took three weeks' vacation in late May of 2013 and traveled to Hong Kong to meet first with Greenwald and Poitras, and later with MacAskill. It was while in Hong Kong that he delivered the files to Greenwald and MacAskill, who would write about them for *The Guardian*. *The Guardian* won the right to publish information and stories about the documents and files first; once published in the UK, subsequent publishing in the US would be easier. On June 9, 2013, *The Guardian* ran the first of a series of front-page stories, rolling out day after day, touting headlines that said "Revealed: how US secretly collects private data from AOL, Apple, Facebook, Google, Microsoft, Paltalk, Skype, Yahoo, and YouTube," "US orders phone firm to hand over data on millions of calls," "How NSA can see 'nearly everything you do online,'" and "Europe demands answers from Obama over surveillance by US."

On June 10, with his approval, *The Guardian* and *The Washington Post* revealed Snowden as the source of the leaked documents. "My sole motive is to inform the public as to that which is done in their name and that which is done against them," he told *The Guardian*'s Ewen MacAskill.[90] He referred to the NSA *PRISM* program, and the other programs of total surveillance revealed in his leaks, as "an existential threat" to democracy.

A panicking and embarrassed US government demanded his immediate arrest and extradition. The White House warned Hong Kong officials of reprisals for failing to turn Snowden over to the US, saying, "If Hong Kong doesn't act soon, it will complicate our bilateral relations and raise questions about Hong Kong's commitment to the rule of law."[91] The Hong

89. Associated Press, "Edward Snowden's Cautious Approach."

90. Smith, "NSA Leaker Comes Forward."

91. Associated Press, "Snowden's Return to US Could Be Legal Battle."

Kong government refused the extradition order, stating simply that it "did not fully comply with the legal requirements under Hong Kong law," and Snowden remained in Hong Kong while he sought asylum in a sympathetic country. There *were* many countries sympathetic to Snowden's plight, but in order to grant asylum, they would by necessity incur the wrath of the American empire.

The US political power elite began a global campaign to discourage any country from allowing Snowden to escape American "justice." Then-vice president Joe Biden called Ecuadorian president Rafael Correa, a socialist and strong supporter of Julian Assange and WikiLeaks, urging him to refuse asylum to Snowden, who had already submitted asylum requests to Ecuador and a number of other countries.

US senator Robert Menendez, chairman of the Senate Foreign Relations Committee, warned Ecuador that giving asylum to Snowden risked a loss of US trade benefits. In a particularly assertive and snarky response, Ecuador announced that it would no longer accept trade benefits from the US, and offered to pay the US government $23 million a year to fund human rights education.[92]

The US State Department issued a statement warning countries not to allow Snowden to travel to or through their territories: "Persons wanted on felony charges, such as Mr. Snowden, should not be allowed to proceed in any further international travel, other than is necessary to return him to the United States."[93]

Venezuelan president Nicolas Maduro responded to a US demand for extradition, saying that he would reject any extradition request for Snowden and that the US government "[does] not have the moral right to request the extradition of a young man who is only warning of the illegalities committed by the Pentagon and the CIA and the United States."[94]

The US also sent extradition and arrest warrants to other countries to whom Snowden had appealed for asylum. Most of these warrants were met with barely veiled contempt. Bolivia rejected an extradition request, commenting that the request was "strange, illegal, unfounded" since Edward Snowden had not yet even entered the country. Ireland rejected US demands on a technicality, noting that the warrant presented to them failed to state where Snowden's alleged offenses took place. Iceland, too, received a demand for extradition. Pirate Party[95] member of Parliament Birgitta Jóns-

92. Free Snowden, "Political interference."
93. Free Snowden, "Political interference."
94. Free Snowden, "Political interference."
95. Iceland's Pirate Party is a left-populist party that believes in free movement of

dóttir responded, "I find it an example of U.S. authorities having lost it . . . with this letter, this request that he be arrested and extradited—before he arrives." She continued, "First of all, when we receive such a request, we're supposed to inform the public because the public should know. Then we should simply send it back because it is, for example according to Amnesty International, nothing else but a disguised threat."[96]

German vice chancellor Sigmar Gabriel told Glenn Greenwald in 2015 that the US government at the time threatened to "cut off" Germany from US intelligence if Berlin offered asylum to Snowden. "They told us they would stop notifying us of plots and other intelligence matters," Gabriel said.[97]

Snowden finally left Hong Kong on July 23, 2013, landing at Moscow's Sheremetyevo International Airport. White House press secretary Jay Carney immediately issued a statement saying that Hong Kong's refusal to arrest and hold Snowden "unquestionably has a negative impact on the US-China relationship," adding "We see this as a setback in terms of their efforts to build mutual trust and our concerns are pretty clearly stated" and said that US authorities "did not buy" Hong Kong's reasons for rejecting the extradition request.[98]

While in Sheremetyevo International Airport, Edward Snowden held a press conference where he met with representatives from multiple global human rights groups, including Amnesty International and Human Rights Watch. Jay Carney condemned the meeting, stating: "I would simply say that providing a propaganda platform for Mr. Snowden runs counter to the Russian government's previous declarations of Russia's neutrality." Alluding to the human rights organizations present, Carney was quick in attempting to reframe the narrative. "Those groups do important work. But Mr. Snowden is not a human rights activist or a dissident."[99]

The attentions of the US government and corporate media immediately shifted to Russia. President Obama canceled a meeting in Moscow with Russia's President Putin in response to Russia granting asylum to Edward Snowden. The White House issued a statement that was arguably an implied diplomatic threat: "Russia's disappointing decision to grant Edward Snowden temporary asylum was also a factor that we considered in

---

information and direct democracy.

96. Iceland Review, "U.S. Authorities Ask Iceland to Extradite Snowden.".
97. Greenwald, "US Threatened Germany Over Snowden."
98. Free Snowden, "Political interference."
99. Free Snowden, "Political interference."

assessing the current state of our bilateral relationship."[100] Later, President Obama appeared on NBC's *Tonight,* telling host Jay Leno that "There have been times where [Russia slips] back into Cold War thinking and a Cold War mentality."[101] It was eventually revealed that the US had a jet waiting in Copenhagen, Denmark, to return Edward Snowden to the US, a move they were already negotiating with Russia.

The US elite did not limit their crusade on behalf of secrecy to the whistleblower. They wanted journalists, too, to know that secrets would be revealed to the public only at great cost. On August 19, 2013, David Miranda, a Brazilian national and, since 2005, partner of the journalist Glenn Greenwald, was detained by security officials at London's Heathrow Airport under Section 7 of the (UK) Terrorism Act of 2000 while returning to his home in Rio de Janeiro, Brazil from Berlin. The security officials seized his laptop, his cellphone, video game consoles, DVDs, USB sticks, and various other materials without informing him why or whether they would be returned.

Miranda was subjected to nine hours of intense, aggressive interrogation—the maximum amount of time they could hold him under the Terrorism Act without actually charging him with some crime. "They were threatening me all the time and saying I would be put in jail if I didn't cooperate," he told *The Guardian*'s Jonathan Watts. "They treated me like I was a criminal or someone about to attack the UK . . . It was exhausting and frustrating, but I knew I wasn't doing anything wrong."[102]

Miranda believed they suspected him not of terrorism, but of involvement in the publication of Snowden's leaks. "They got me to tell them the passwords for my computer and mobile phone," he said. "They said I was obliged to answer all their questions and used the words *prison* and *station* all the time."[103]

"It is clear why they took me. It's because I'm Glenn's partner. Because I went to Berlin. Because Laura [Poitras] lives there. So they think I have a big connection," Miranda continued. "But I don't have a role. I don't look at documents. I don't even know if it was documents that I was carrying. It could have been for the movie that Laura is working on."[104]

100. White House, "Statement by the Press Secretary on the President's Travel."

101. Pace, "Obama 'Disappointed' In Russia's Snowden Decision."

102. Watts, "David Miranda."

103. Watts, "David Miranda."

104. Watts, "David Miranda."

Writing of the event in *The Guardian* that same day, Glenn Greenwald called it "a message of intimidation to those of us working journalistically on reporting on the NSA and its British counterpart, the GCHQ."[105]

> This is obviously a rather profound escalation of their attacks on the news-gathering process and journalism. It's bad enough to prosecute and imprison sources. It's worse still to imprison journalists who report the truth. But to start detaining the family members and loved ones of journalists is simply despotic. Even the Mafia had ethical rules against targeting the family members of people they felt threatened by. But the UK puppets and their owners in the US national security state obviously are unconstrained by even those minimal scruples.[106]

He concluded, defiantly, that "If the UK and US governments believe that tactics like this are going to deter or intimidate us in any way from continuing to report aggressively on what these documents reveal, they are beyond deluded."[107]

More than seven years later, in a major legal ruling handed down on September 2, 2020, Snowden, Greenwald, MacAskill, Poitras, and others who engaged with the project to publicize US illegality were vindicated. The US Court of Appeals for the Ninth Circuit said the warrantless surveillance program that secretly collected millions of Americans' digital records violated the Foreign Intelligence Surveillance Act—and may well have been unconstitutional.[108]

"I never imagined that I would live to see our courts condemn the NSA's activities as unlawful and in the same ruling credit me for exposing them," Snowden remarked in a message posted to Twitter.[109]

As a whistleblower, Edward Snowden—still under indictment in the US for espionage—knew the risks involved in upsetting a system that depended on secrecy and redundancy to maintain its power. "I was very much a person the most powerful government in the world wanted to go away," he said in 2019. "They did not care whether I went away to prison. They did not care whether I went away into the ground. They just wanted me gone," he said.[110]

105. Greenwald, "Detaining My Partner Was a Failed Attempt at Intimidation."

106. Greenwald, "Detaining My Partner Was a Failed Attempt at Intimidation.".

107. Greenwald, "Detaining My Partner Was a Failed Attempt at Intimidation."

108. Reuters, "NSA Surveillance Exposed by Snowden Was Illegal."

109. Reuters, "NSA Surveillance Exposed by Snowden Was Illegal."

110. MacAskill and Topham, "'They Wanted Me Gone.'"

But he also remained firm in his principles. "I can't in good conscience allow the US government to destroy privacy, internet freedom and basic liberties for people around the world with this massive surveillance machine they're secretly building."[111]

The High Entropy World

If propaganda 2.1 has any intrinsic value at all, then that value must be in its power to break down the comfortably redundant narratives of propaganda 2.0 and to open us up to those new—often dissenting, even troubling—points of view. Whatever value propaganda 2.1 has must come from *us*, the people who will respond to it. In the propaganda 2.0 environment, we are not in control of the information consumed by the masses. With propaganda 2.1, the responsibility to take control of our own information consumption, creation, and distribution falls on us, and we either accept that responsibility or we suffer the consequences of abrogating it. One way or the other, the meaning of propaganda 2.1 is that *we are the internet*: either it will be an agent of our will, or we will be agents of its commercial agenda. With that in mind, I want to mention several issues that we should think deeply about, because they are critically important in understanding our new situation in a responsible manner.

Fight Censorship

No one likes the word *censorship*, but many people will concede that there is often a need for it. Even though the First Amendment to the Constitution of the United States guarantees the right to speak freely, Americans have often shown themselves to be at least cautiously accepting of the need to regulate some forms of speech. Individuals, for example, are more than willing to censor themselves—to refrain from revealing their thoughts on controversial matters—if they believe that they will suffer social consequences as a result of speaking about unpopular or offensive ideas.[112] We need to be honest and acknowledge that the anonymity of the internet has changed that social dynamic. In the world of propaganda 2.0, a world of tightly controlled information and a tightly controlled social order, in order to voice unpopular or offensive ideas, you must do so in the presence of others, and take the chance that you will offend them. In the world of propaganda 2.1, the digital

111. Free Snowden, "Threats overview."
112. Hyde and Ruth, "Multicultural Content and Class Participation."

world, you can say what you want, and even surround yourself only with others who will agree with you and reinforce your beliefs.

For better or for worse, the internet today is awash in a veritable tsunami of unpopular and offensive ideas—some true, some false, some completely trivial and inconsequential. Absent the influence of censorship, by either corporations or government, this is unlikely to change. So it's a good idea to concede that some form of censorship may, from time to time, be necessary. The question is, however, what sort of censorship should we be willing to accept?

There are many legal approaches to understanding the meaning of the phrase "freedom of speech." Absolutists, for example, believe that with very few exceptions anyone has the right to say anything she wants, any time at all, and in any venue she chooses.[113] Absolutists have never been in a majority on the US Supreme Court, and I doubt the majority of average Americans are absolutists either. First Amendment absolutism appears extreme to the American mind, likely to invite speech that is irresponsible and dangerous. Other jurists and legal scholars, by contrast, believe that alleged First Amendment infringements should be looked at on an *ad hoc*, case-by-case basis, and decided on the basis of balancing the right to free speech against other constitutional freedoms. But this is a most ambiguous position for a fundamental right to occupy; by necessity it leaves the boundaries of free speech in question, and can have a chilling effect on dissent.

In the mid-twentieth century, constitutional scholar Alexander Meiklejohn wrote a series of influential papers on the boundaries of free speech. While fundamentally an absolutist in his outlook, Meiklejohn asserted that the primary purpose for the protection of free speech in a democratic society was to guarantee self-government. He unabashedly privileged political and ideological speech above all other forms of expression. The First Amendment, he said, "forbids Congress to abridge the freedom of a citizen's speech, press, peaceable assembly, or petition, when those activities are utilized for the governing of the nation."[114] While that may seem too narrow a standard for the protection of speech to civil libertarians, Meiklejohn broadened the definition of what he considered to be political speech:

1. Education, in all its phases, is the attempt to so inform and cultivate the mind and will of the citizen that he shall have the wisdom, the

---

113. Even absolutists, of course, recognized that some words might be so closely connected with producing a specific, dangerous or threatening action (such as entering into a contract with a hit man or yelling "Fire!" in a crowded theater) as to be unprotected.

114. Meiklejohn, "First Amendment Is an Absolute," 256.

independence, and, therefore, the dignity of a governing citizen, freedom of education is, thus, as we all recognize, a basic postulate in the
planning of a free society.

2. The achievements of philosophy and the sciences in creating knowledge and understanding of men and their world must be made available, without abridgment, to every citizen.

3. Literature and the arts must be protected by the First Amendment.
   They lead the way toward sensitive and informed appreciation and
   response to the values out of which the riches of the general welfare
   are created.

4. Public discussions of public issues, together with the spreading of information and opinion bearing on those issues, must have a freedom
   unabridged by our agents. Though they govern us, we, in a deeper
   sense, govern them. Over our governing, they have no power. Over
   their governing we have sovereign power.[115]

Meiklejohn's views have their critics, as do all absolutist views of the
First Amendment. But I believe that, especially when dealing with the
topic of propaganda 2.1, the Meiklejohnian approach provides a useful
and potentially effective baseline for making judgments about the need
for censorship, especially on the internet. Political speech, of whatever
persuasion, should never be censored, no matter how offensive it may
appear to us. Since the very point of political speech is to air dissenting
points of view in the hope that they might persuade undecided citizens or
even those in opposition to them, failure to protect it is an abnegation of
democratic principles and of democracy itself.

I do wish to introduce a *caveat* to what may sound like a full-throated
defense of Meiklejohnian theory. There is a part of the internet's structure
that hosts global communications most users have never seen and will very
likely never see. It is here that you will find the so-called *deep web*, and bur-
rowing down even further, the *dark web*. The deep and dark webs are not
indexed or searchable on the World Wide Web. In order to access deep or
dark websites you have two choices, either to know where you are going and
have a URL link, or to find a site more or less randomly using an unindexed
list link. Navigating the deep and dark webs demands a very specialized skill
set very few average users possess. Yet at the very same time it is estimated
that 95 percent of all internet activity takes place not on the internet that
you and I use on a daily basis, but on the deep and dark webs.[116]

115. Meiklejohn, "First Amendment Is an Absolute," 257.
116. Guccione, "What Is the Dark Web?"

Governments and businesses use the deep web for a variety of reasons: to store and access confidential information like credit card numbers, for instance, when someone purchases an item online, or your personal information—age, height, weight, driver's license number, etc.—when you register an automobile with your state's motor vehicle bureau, or your medical records on file with your doctor and whatever hospital or practice she is associated with. Information on the deep web is usually also deeply encrypted and generally well-protected from theft or illicit publication.

The dark web, however, is different. It is very much like the internet of old, populated by coders and programmers entering commands in computer languages such as Java, HTML, C++, and Python. The dark web operates beneath the layer of the internet with which we are most familiar, the World Wide Web. It is not accessible through conventional consumer browsers like Chrome, Firefox, or Edge (which replaced Internet Explorer), but only through a specific browser called Tor, a piece of free and open-source software that enables users to communicate anonymously. The dark web is part of that skeletal infrastructure that is difficult to navigate without at least some rudimentary computer science skills.

For the most part the dark web is a utility, not a venue. It is populated, as I said, by coders and programmers and geeks, many of whom are writing and testing programs that they hope to launch on the World Wide Web as websites or applications that will be salable to the general public. But it is also populated by hackers, identity thieves, drug dealers, and other bad faith actors engaged in a variety of cybercrimes, including data theft, illegal drug and weapons sales, distribution of child pornography, money laundering, digital content piracy, human trafficking, and conspiracy to commit terrorism.[117]

The dark web is also a haven for individuals and groups who wish (and need) to communicate with one another anonymously. *The New York Times*, for instance, has its own presence on the dark web which is accessible even beyond the Great Firewall of China. So, for that matter, does Facebook. Nongovernmental organizations (NGOs) like Greenpeace use the dark web to coordinate their activities. Corporate and government whistleblowers fearing the loss of their jobs, freedom, or lives can get information to trusted publishers on the dark web. Hong Kong protesters during the 2014 Umbrella Revolution used the dark web (and an app on their smartphones called FireChat) to bypass the obstructions of the Chinese government when it shut down the mobile phone networks.

---

117. McGuire, *Into the Web of Profit*.

The deep and dark webs are not the internet we know and love (or hate). They are different in a number of meaningful ways, but probably the most significant difference is the relative level of anonymity afforded the user there, and the profound limitations placed on powerful forces, whether governmental or corporate, to trace or identify users and their transactions. This makes them dangerous places, extremely difficult to regulate. Like seemingly everything else in life, this is both a good and a bad thing. Communicating with others for the purposes of stealing personal data, selling illegal drugs or weapons, distributing child pornography, laundering money, stealing intellectual property, buying and selling human beings, and planning acts of terrorism are serious issues. None of these types of communication are, or should be, protected by the Constitution, and no one should have any problem, in my opinion, in shutting them down.

But in a Meiklejohnian sense, dissent, protest, whistleblowing, the leaking of information (even classified information)—all of these are often, if not always, essential to self-government. Granted, government easily cannot shut down the deep and dark webs—they use them themselves to shield their own covert activities. But we need to become vigilant against mainstream media attacks by powerful elites on NGO websites like WikiLeaks, Amnesty International, and Greenpeace that depend on the dark web to bring us information we would otherwise be unable to receive.

There is one final point I wish to make about internet censorship. Among the traditionally protected forms of speech the courts have identified and defined is *commercial speech*. It can legitimately be argued that the average social media user encounters far more offensive messages in the form of advertisements on a daily basis than he does offensive political memes. The proprietary nature of digital giants such as Facebook, Amazon, Twitter, Instagram, and the like, and their mandated terms of service agreements in order to use their sites guarantees that the user will be subjected to nonstop intrusions in her day by algorithm-generated advertisements for all manner of products she may or may not want to know about based on her behavior.

While commercial speech nominally does not hold the same status as political speech, aggressive marketing tactics can arguably be seen as corporate violations of individuals' privacy. There is no way to effectively quantify the number of such intrusions users are subjected to on a daily basis, so I will not even attempt to do so. However, from purely personal, anecdotal experience, I would have to say I am offended far more frequently by the thousands of internet ads I'm subjected to daily than I am from the dozens or even hundreds of political or ideological posts on my Twitter or Facebook news feeds. I'd be delighted if the social media giants would subject themselves to a little self-censorship. I would be even more delighted—and, frankly, quite shocked—if governments regulated the amount and types of advertising to which we are unremittingly subjected.

Net Neutrality

Net neutrality is predicated on the principle that all information is equal, and internet service providers (ISPs) cannot arbitrarily privilege one type of information, or information coming from one internet source, over other types of information or other sources. In a truly open information environment—one with net neutrality—ISPs must provide access to all websites and content equally, without either blocking or privileging any one website or type of content. With net neutrality it shouldn't matter whether you are connecting to Facebook, MSNBC.com, FoxNews.com, Breitbart, or your neighbor's celebrity blog; your service ought to be identical in all of these cases.

We often forget that capitalism and democracy are not synonyms, and that the mythical free market is much better at providing us with useless and trivial crap that entertains us than at giving us things that we actually need, things that sustain our intellectual and physical health and our lives. To apportion bandwidth (to speak of only one aspect of the debate over net neutrality) on the basis of a website's popularity rather than on the quality of the service it provides and of the information it makes available is nothing more than Mark Fowler's redefinition of *public interest* as constituting "what the public is interested in." Some of the most important information, in terms of its utility in helping us become better citizens and more fully human beings, has for years been blocked out by the free market approach to public communication. Until the internet, political dissidence was for the most part invisible and mute in the United States. In the US, there is no need to imprison our political dissidents; we simply ignore them.

We need, all of us, to mount a robust defense of the principles of net neutrality if the promises of propaganda 2.1 are to mean anything in the future. The mass media of propaganda 2.0 have already proved themselves to be spectacularly efficient at shaping and conforming social narratives. If there is to be any dissent at all, it will only come through the digital media of propaganda 2.1.

Nationalize the Internet (and Renationalize
the Electromagnetic Spectrum)

A central principle of the twentieth century in the American territories of
the technological society was that the electromagnetic spectrum (what we
once called the airwaves) was part of the commons, owned by the people,
and administered in our name by the government. I believe it is time to
renationalize the electromagnetic spectrum (for how can the sun's energy
be privately owned?), including not just those frequencies that constitute
the airwaves, but the entire spectrum, from gamma radiation to infrared
to radio waves to microwaves to light itself. All of these energies are central
carriers of information in our communication systems, and if the concept of
free speech is to have any meaning, then the means of distribution of speech
simply can't be left in corporate hands.

The internet was built by public spending. The US Department of
Defense, working with academic computer scientists at Stanford, UCLA,
MIT, and other universities, first conceived of it in the 1960s and seventies.
By the early 1990s, following Tim Berner-Lee's development of the World
Wide Web, the private sector had both the means and the motivation to
lobby the government to cede significant control of the internet to corporations on the grounds that this new piece of electronic real estate would be
ripe for economic development. It is the private sector that is fundamentally responsible for the internet we have today, and whatever locked-in
problems we see in terms of socioeconomic stratification and information
disenfranchisement can be credited to it.

The geographic monopolization of internet service providers (ISPs)
has allowed for information inequalities among different regions and demographic groups in the country. A profit-based apportionment of technology
has negatively affected low-income and rural communities disproportion-
ately to the rest of the country. ISPs serve those geographic and demographic
groups most likely to make them a profit, ignoring those areas and groups
that promise a much lower profit margin. This, again, is the so-called digital
divide. More than one-third of Americans lack access to broadband service.
More than 50 percent of Americans with household incomes below $30,000
lack broadband; because of the systemic racism of American capitalism, this
affects Black families far more than other groups.[118] The idea of the commons has never resonated strongly in the capitalist mind. But if we want the
internet of the future to be better than it is in the present, we must resolve to
think more deeply about *the common good.*

118. Tveten, "It's Time to Nationalize the Internet."

Vermont senator Bernie Sanders is one of an unfortunately small group of public figures who have argued that high-speed internet be thought of as a basic human right, a part of *the commons*, and that as president he would propose legislation to regulate the internet as a utility, much as water and electricity are regulated. "Our tax dollars built the internet and access to it should be a public good for all, not another price gouging profit machine for Comcast, AT&T, and Verizon," Sanders wrote in 2019.[119]

There is no reason that a technology that has become so essential to the functioning of the nation's businesses and government, and so central a part of the average person's life, should be in the hands of corporations who hold profit, and not concern for the common good, as their highest priority. We should take the idea of nationalizing the internet very seriously.

Restore the FCC's Pre-1984 Definition of "Public Interest"

In order to make the internet of the future better than the internet as it exists today, we need to make our mainstream mass media of the future better as well. A more well-informed *public* will be less susceptible to gossip and innuendo than a poorly informed *market*. The proliferation of fake news in our corporate mass media following the passage of the Cable Communications Policy Act of 1984 needs to be checked. To do so we must demand that, in exchange for the free use of the public airwaves, microwaves, and other portions of the electromagnetic spectrum, corporations provide some significant number of nonprofit, commercial-free hours of public service broadcasting or cablecasting each day (for example, no less than three hours per day, at least one of which must be in the early, pre-prime time evening, one in the morning, and one in the later, post-prime time night). In addition, the US government must make a commitment to fund more fully our public broadcasting services, PBS and NPR, thereby lessening the damping effect corporate underwriting of programming has had on their content.

These changes would essentially return television and radio news outlets to a situation much like we witnessed in the 1950s, sixties, and seventies, before the Lewis Powell memo and Mark Fowler's FCC argued for the profit motive in the selection and dissemination of public information. Broadcast news directors, editors, and reporters would return to the pursuit of prestige and reputation rather than salary and celebrity status. The network news divisions of their respective corporate owners would again compete with one another for national recognition of the quality of their work in uncovering important stories of national and global significance.

119. Zakrzewski, "Bernie Sanders Just Made Internet Providers a New 2020 Target."

Use the Internet; Don't be Used by It

Of all our problems, the worst is our own rearview mirror thinking. We don't use the internet in the ways it was designed to be used. It was designed to facilitate an unrestricted multidirectional flow of information in any number of directional orientations: within groups, from individual to individual, from the mass to the individual, and from the individual to the mass. But in typical rearview mirror fashion, we treat the internet as a simple mass medium, reading a bit here and there about what's new, listening to music while doing chores, streaming shows when we sit down to relax. By failing to take advantage of the internet's opportunities for individual free speech, we become the content of the internet. The internet *uses us.*

The idea of selling audiences to advertisers is not a new one. A. C. Nielsen has been rating the content of television since 1950, and those ratings earned the company $6.6 billion in 2017 alone. Mass media in the technological society have always been dependent on profit for their operation, and that profit has either come from direct sales of content or from advertising.

But in the era of propaganda 2.1 the stakes have been raised, and the business of selling audiences has become a skin game. Tech companies compete to see who can claim the biggest portion of your daily attention. If you set up an account and agree to the terms of service on any number of social media websites—Facebook, Instagram, Twitter, TikTok, etc.—you give those sites permission to keep you under virtually perpetual surveillance. Statisticians and data analysts help programmers write algorithms—informed by the latest neuropsychological research—that provide a strong indication, based on your online behavior, of what you do or don't click on, of how long you stay on a page, of what sorts of posts or memes you like, of what topics in the news (or sports or entertainment) you're most interested in, of what products you might think about buying. They also sell your data, both public and private, which you effectively signed over to them when you accepted the TOS, to other companies interested in marketing to you. These are clear signs that the internet is using us, that corporate capitalism is its user, and that it is we who are its content.

We must prepare ourselves to use the internet more effectively than we are currently doing. We need to learn to use this powerful instrument as an agent of change, moving toward the common good, and not just as another agent of diversion and entertainment in a sea of redundant entertainments. The smartphone you carry around in your pocket or purse is not just for making phone calls to your family or sending silly texts about celebrities to your friends or emails to your boss or workmates. It is a still camera and an audio and/or and video recorder, as well as being a type-writer sufficient to sending short accounts of your world to a wider audience connected across the globe by the internet. It is a remarkable tool, perhaps even a weapon in the fight against oppression. We have the power to use this tool in real-time situations to bypass biased (or nonexistent) mainstream media coverage of important stories. The idea of citizen journalism utilizing alternative media has rankled many in the power elites over the last decade and more, but it has also forced them to cover events and stories that were previously not even on their radar.

When the Occupy movement arose in the fall of 2011, the corporate mainstream media largely ignored it, dismissing the protesters as "disorganized, violence-prone mobs"[120] teeming with "freeloaders who joined the movement for the sex, drugs and free food."[121] In May of 2012, eight months after the protests began, the extent of the corporate media's attempts to diminish them was crystal clear:

> Since September, the mainstream press in the US has systematically ignored and demonized the Occupy movement. The nakedness of the class bias in this case, however, was especially jarring: the size and significance of the protests were downplayed, reports of police brutality were largely ignored, and the movement was portrayed as violent and dangerous. Many of the most prominent US news outlets, such as *The New York Times*, practically ignored the protests altogether.[122]

It was the Occupiers themselves who reported most accurately and responsibly on their peaceful and principled protests—as well as on the many instances of unprovoked police violence that occurred during the movement's several months of activities. The use of tweets bearing the hashtags #ows and #occupywallstreet kept the world informed on a minute-by-minute basis about planned marches and general assemblies, as well as more mundane stories about feeding hundreds of protesters, providing health care, and cleaning Zuccotti Park. While Occupiers utilized social networking sites like Twitter, Meetup, and YouTube, and others to livestream and spread their story of nonviolent protests against income inequality, racism, and perpetual war, Facebook proved to be a pivotal medium. In a little over a month—from September 17 to October 22, 2011—the movement added

120. Smith, "How Elite Media Strategies Marginalize the Occupy Movement."

121. Roberts, "Park-&-wreck freeloaders."

122. Maher and Corcoran, "Corporate Media's Attempt to Kill the Occupy Movement."

more than 170,000 active Facebook users to its network, garnering 1.4 million likes for the 1,170,626 individual posts.[123]

The Occupy movement arguably set the stage for the first viable Democratic Socialist presidential candidate in almost a century, Bernie Sanders, as well as the election of a number of insurgent candidacies, such as those of Alexandria Ocasio-Cortez, Ilhan Omar, Rashida Tlaib, and others. These candidacies have differed radically from the typical establishment party's political campaigns, and have been marked by a number of common traits, all of which mirror the shift from propaganda 2.0 to propaganda 2.1: public funding by online appeals, rejection of corporate money and PACs, a calculated distancing from establishment party structures, and a powerful strain of leftist populism.

When Mohammed Bouazizi set himself on fire in 2011 in protest against Tunisian police corruption, social media sites like Facebook, Twitter, and YouTube united and activated young Tunisians who had long suffered under the strain of high unemployment, widespread and persistent poverty rates, poor education, and government corruption. The so-called Arab Spring began.

When Eric Garner, Freddie Gray, Laquan McDonald, Philando Castile, Stephon Clark, and George Floyd were killed by police in the presence of smartphone cameras, the world witnessed these killings on YouTube, Twitter, Facebook, Instagram, and other sites. While the Black Lives Matter movement was founded after the killing of Trayvon Martin by George Zimmerman in 2012, its prominence today is directly attributable to the growing number of citizens who choose to stand their ground and shoot nothing but video.

Denizens of the twenty-first century technological society no longer need corporate sponsorship or broad technical training to be functioning audio, video, or digital journalists. Propaganda 2.1 has guaranteed that we have the tools at our disposal at all times. All we need is the insight to understand that we can, at the very least, supplement the journalism that we get from the corporate mainstream—or bypass it completely when they fail to do their jobs—and the will to reject comfortable complacency and accept responsibility for finding and sharing the truth.

The Need to Read More, and More Deeply

One last fundamental point remains: if we are to be responsible citizens—and citizen journalists—in the era of propaganda 2.1, we need to *know*

123. Caren and Gaby, *Occupy Online.*

more. We need to *think more*, and think more *critically*. Returning one last time to information theory, remember that we *learn*—in the truest sense of the word—only by exposing ourselves to ideas that are not already familiar to us, and then only if we can find a pattern amid the chaos that gives that idea *meaning*. Information is not knowledge. Information is important in the construction of knowledge, but it does not in and of itself constitute knowledge. The nineteenth-century French polymath Henri Poincaré once said (I paraphrase), "Knowledge is built of information in the same way a house is built of bricks; but an accumulation of bits of information is no more knowledge than a pile of bricks is a house." There has to be a specific structure to information, there has to be organization, there has to be a context within which to fit those pieces of information before you can ever legitimately speak of having knowledge. Without these, all we really have is profoundly entropic *noise*.

Neil Postman used to talk about the "fact-information-knowledge-wisdom" hierarchy in a way that I believe is helpful. Something happens or exists: that's a *fact*, but only, practically speaking, if it is witnessed by someone. If that person reports the event to you, then you have *information* about it. If several people report it to you, then you have more information about it. But information can be wrong, and if the reports don't all agree, you have to do more work, ask some questions, use logic and your critical thinking facility, make a judgment. The more information you get, and the more you question it and filter it, the greater is the certainty of your judgment.

We can then categorize and organize information. This process yields *knowledge*: in Postman's terms, "organized information—information that is embedded in some context; information that has a purpose, that leads one to seek further information in order to understand something about the world." Those who work through this process will eventually develop *wisdom*: "the capacity to know what body of knowledge is relevant to the solution of significant problems . . . Knowledge cannot judge itself. Knowledge must be judged by other knowledge, and therein lies wisdom."[124]

The internet has proven itself to be a tremendous instrument in the pursuit of information. But we probably possess far less *knowledge* in the digital age than we did in the age of print. We have an entire universe of information at our fingertips, more than humans have had at their disposal at any time in our history. But some of that information is good and truthful and useful and intellectually nourishing, and some of it is false, trivial, and nothing more than a diversion from reality. And all of it, the good as well as the bad, lacks any discernible historical context. As

124. Postman, "Information," 495–97.

a consequence, if we're unable to differentiate between good information and bad, then the internet will likely function in our lives as an adjunct to propaganda 2.0 rather than an antidote.

As the neurosciences are learning, reading imposes upon the human brain a need to reorganize its functions, remapping neural pathways and allowing new types of thought previously impossible.[125] The power of the printed word to organize experience, to store information, to both conceptualize and to evaluate concepts, and to abstract reusable knowledge outside of day-to-day contexts, has made it the most powerful survival tool that humans have created to navigate the evolutionary processes of natural selection.[126] Sven Birkerts has written of the printed word's ability to nurture what he calls "vertical consciousness," a sense of "the deep and natural connectedness of things" that inherently encourages the development of wisdom, "the knowing not of facts but of truths about human nature and the processes of life."[127] He describes the ways in which deep and habitual reading engenders in the human psyche a belief in "the possibility of a comprehensible whole,"[128] but laments the fact that today's "explosion of data"—along with general societal secularization and the collapse of what the theorists call "the master narratives" (Judeo-Christian, Marxist, Freudian, humanist . . .)—"has all but destroyed the premise of understandability."[129] "My core fear," he concludes, anticipating Nicholas Carr's words, "is that we are, as a culture, as a species, becoming shallower; that we have turned from depth . . . and are adapting ourselves to the ersatz security of a vast lateral connectedness."[130]

"Functional illiteracy in North America," Chris Hedges notes, "is epidemic."[131] Even worse, for those who *can* read, there are too many temptations—and self-serving justifications—*not to*. "[A] culture dominated by images and slogans seduces those who are functionally literate but who make the choice not to read."[132] The majority of Americans, literate and illiterate, are born, grow, learn, and live in a mass-produced and mass-distributed *pseudo-reality*, and our mainstream news media present to us on a daily basis not news, but *pseudo-events*, information detached from

125. Wolf, *Proust and the Squid*, 216–217.
126. Fallon, *Metaphysics of Media*, 119.
127. Birkerts, *Gutenberg Elegies*, 74.
128. Birkerts, *Gutenberg Elegies*, 75.
129. Birkerts, *Gutenberg Elegies*, 75.
130. Birkerts, *Gutenberg Elegies*, 228.
131. Hedges, *Empire of Illusion*, 44.
132. Hedges, *Empire of Illusion*, 45.

material reality, presented without historical context, and therefore impossible to make judgments about. This is not information in the service of knowledge, it is information in the service of propaganda 2.0, and without the kind of wisdom necessary to construct for oneself a broad base of knowledge, bodies of knowledge based on the experience of deep and habitual reading, this will very likely only be amplified by propaganda 2.1.

This bodes ill for the survival not only of democratic principles, but of the planet. "A populace deprived of the ability to separate lies from truth, that has become hostage to the fictional semblance of reality put forth by pseudo-events, is no longer capable of sustaining a free society."[133]

> The physical degradation of the planet, the cruelty of global capitalism, the looming oil crisis, the collapse of the financial markets, and the danger of overpopulation rarely impinge to prick the illusions that warp our consciousness. The words, images, stories, and phrases used to describe the world in pseudo-events have no relation to what is happening around us. The advances of technology and science, rather than obliterating the world of myth, have enhanced its power to deceive.[134]

If we are to survive propaganda 2.1—or even better, if we can recognize in its chaos the opportunity to use it to our advantage in creating a more just world, a more equitable world; if we are to use it to express ourselves freely and openly, to build bridges between ourselves and our global community, to seek out the truth and to dispel falsehoods, to raise up the human individual and release him from the chains of intellectual servitude to powerful global corporate elites—if we are to do any of this, we must first recognize it for what it is, and stop deluding ourselves that it is what it never can be. Propaganda 2.1—and its servant, the internet—is the material manifestation of an explosion of information, nothing more, nothing less. With a broad base of knowledge, painfully wrought through years and years of depth-engagement with the ideas, principles, histories, and wisdom delivered to us through the printed book, we can be better than we are; not only better informed, but more *knowledgeable*. We can make the internet work for us instead of against us.

The choice is ours. The door is open.

133. Hedges, *Empire of Illusion*, 52.
134. Hedges, *Empire of Illusion*, 52.

Chapter 6

Propaganda 2.1

Conclusion

I n the course of writing this book, my awareness of the importance of its subject has been heightened beyond the mere clinical and academic. Several years ago I began to feel—a strong feeling, I have to say—that there was also a powerful ethical imperative for finishing it and seeing it in print. I also remembered and acknowledged my profound ambivalence about the internet and other digital technologies, an ambivalence that reflected the utopian/dystopian dichotomy described in the previous chapter.

From the beginning, I was deeply suspicious of the so-called digital revolution, so suspicious that it was a common occurrence for friends to shut down my arguments with the ever-popular charge of "Luddite!" I naturally found myself agreeing with the Andrew Keens, Jaron Laniers, Nicholas Carrs, Evgeny Morosovs, and Douglas Rushkoffs of the world, worrying that the internet is nothing more than a corporate Trojan horse that ransacks our most precious and secret belongings when we welcome them into the privacy of our homes, or that we're becoming gadgets, mere appendages of the technologies that ought to be serving us, or that the easy retrieval of concise snippets of decontextualized information is hurting our ability to think deeply and critically, or that rather than liberating us, the internet is morphing into a tool of government surveillance and oppression, or that the chaotic and constantly changing nature of digital information is destroying whatever remnants of a unifying and coherent narrative our culture ever had. And all of these dystopian worries, I still believe, are valid.

Furthermore, the utopian hopes and dreams of the Kevin Kellys, the Ray Kurzweils, and the Nicholas Negropontes of the world never resonated with me for even a moment. I find it difficult (and, to be completely honest, a bit creepy) to ascribe to technologies human characteristics, or to see anything like the hand of God involved in something manufactured by imperfect human hands (and minds), or to believe that the losses incurred in the transformation of local economies to global ones will be offset by the conveniences of voice-activated machines, or that the human psyche is reducible to circuitry on silicon chips. On the whole, then, I am forced to admit that I've always found myself more skeptical than enthusiastic about both the internet and the digital revolution generally.

Yet at the same time, I've watched as the walls of enclosed power and privilege have been breached by the power of uncontrolled information. I've watched and listened as once marginalized voices have found their place among establishment voices that had only until recently enjoyed a position of absolute dominance. I've watched and participated as political and social movements that were only recently unimaginable have asserted themselves in the face of previously impervious political and economic restraints. And I've had years to think about the lessons of information theory, the need for balance between the forces of redundancy and of entropy, the value of entropy in the learning of new information, and the need for openness to new and uncomfortable perspectives if we are ever to learn.

So in concluding this book, I find that I'm not really sure what to say other than to remind you, the reader, of both your power and your responsibility to take control of our shared information environment. We all have a part to play in this unfolding drama, and our present and future actions can (and will) make the difference between hope and despair. Like Ellul, I reject the imperatives of any technological determinism, and believe that wherever propaganda 2.1 leads us is wholly up to us. This belief fills me, alternately, with hope and despair.

Clearly, propaganda 2.1 implies risks no people have ever been required to face before. The emergence of "fake news" has been one of them. However, let's remember that, aside from the quality of the information content of any given piece of news, fake or otherwise, this emergence has been at the expense of older forms of news, arguably equivalently fake, but too dominant and widely accepted as "real" to ever be labeled so. As far back as 1985, still firmly in the mass-information, propaganda 2.0 environment, Neil Postman was already warning us of the effects of fake news on our culture. Americans, he said, had become "the best entertained and quite likely the least well-informed people in the Western world."[1] Americans live in an information environment, he said, that delivers "information that creates the illusion of knowing something but which in fact leads one away from

---

1. Postman, *Amusing Ourselves to Death*, 106.

knowing."[2] In the mass culture of the late twentieth century we were customarily presented "not only with fragmented news but news without context, without consequences, without value, and therefore without essential seriousness; that is to say, news as pure entertainment."[3] Clearly, Postman is describing what can only be called fake news.

The monopoly of knowledge represented by the organized force of older mass media, a monopoly that facilitated and supported the twentieth-century development of total propaganda, has been under attack by the disorganized forces seeking to establish a new monopoly of knowledge based on digital media. The older monopoly was based on centralized control of information and acted as an agent of stasis, redundancy, and total propaganda. The newer monopoly—at this moment at least—is based on decentralization of power, an absence of control over information flow, and is an agent of entropy. The older one amused us and made us comfortable. The newer one provokes us, challenges us, frightens us, and often infuriates us. The older one made us feel as though everything is as it should be. (It wasn't.) The newer one makes us feel as though nothing will ever be the same again. (It won't—but why would we believe it ought to be?)

"Minerva's owl begins its flight only in the gathering dusk," Harold Innis told us,[4] referencing Hegel's message that we don't really understand a culture until that moment when its dominant monopoly of knowledge—and perhaps the culture itself—begins its collapse. That may be an apocalyptic allusion, but it doesn't have to be. We're witnessing not only the collapse of a once stable system, but of a destructive global ideology as well. That ideology was based on unthinking adherence to expansive consumption of commodities—commoditized information as well as material commodities. Minerva's owl provides an opportunity to step back and think not only about where we've been, but where we want to go and what kind of information system and society we want to build. What many are calling fake news is an unfortunate but inevitable by-product of the collapse of the old. But many who are urging us to reject fake news are no more than a reactionary rear guard of the old monopoly, desperately fighting to remain relevant in a culture that has largely abandoned them, rather than embracing the opportunities afforded by the late-day flight of Minerva's owl.

I have no prescriptions to offer other than those I suggested in the previous chapter. My purpose has been only to examine and describe our situation using principles of information theory as a critical tool. But there

2. Postman, *Amusing Ourselves to Death*, 100.

3. Postman, *Amusing Ourselves to Death*, 100.

4. Innis, *Bias of Communication*, 3.

is one response to the problem of fake news that I would urge us all to avoid: censorship. We should not allow our newly liberated information environment to be closed and controlled again. Censorship, whether corporate, governmental, or structural, will only be an attempt to buttress the shuddering walls of propaganda 2.0. As human beings, we are perfectly competent to modify our information intake for ourselves. Algorithms and fact-check websites are poor substitutes for broad knowledge founded in deep literacy, and function only as crutches for the aliterate. When you see a story that is patently false, avoid it, and advise your friends to avoid it. When you encounter a piece of information that looks as though it might be real but runs counter to your assumptions about reality, read it. Investigate it. Consider it. Question it. And make your own damned decision. It really can be as simple as that. Lies, innuendoes, and fake news did not arise only with the emergence of the internet. We need to be intellectually prepared to confront them under any circumstances.

Likewise, the new media environment must be seen for what it is—a venue not only for the consumption of information produced by others, but for our own production and distribution of information. Protecting net neutrality and denying the access of powerful elites and corporations to positions of information control is the key to ensuring that everyone—nationally and globally—can be heard. Even the purveyors of fake news.

In January of 1939, only months before he died, the Irish poet William Butler Yeats had one of his final poems published in *The Atlantic Monthly*. It was called "The Man and the Echo." In it, the man—who we must presume to be the poet himself—reflects ruefully on some of his writing, and in desperation asks a cliff-faced mountain a painful question about the moral consequences of his words and works in the years leading up to the Easter Uprising and consequent Irish War of Independence from Britain. He wonders if his poems and plays incited violence—"Did that play of mine send out / Certain men the English shot?"—and, wracked with guilt, anguishes over the evil he might have done "until I / Sleepless would lie down and die."[5] And the echo responds, "Lie down and die."

Our new information environment confronts us with challenges and risks as well as opportunities. Many of these are moral challenges. We shouldn't shy away from them. We should hold others accountable for irresponsible behavior anywhere—on a public street, in the workplace, and on the internet. These moral challenges and risks (and opportunities) demand a high degree of responsibility, including what we might call an "intellectual vigilance." These responsibilities will not allow us to get too comfortable

5. Yeats, "Man and the Echo," 383.

or remain complacent in our lives. The alternative to accepting them is to lay ourselves down and die—morally and intellectually. The alternative to accepting our responsibilities is to abdicate them and let others control what information we are allowed to receive, and what information we are allowed to share with others. We need to choose either easy, comfortable, redundant complacency or the difficult, painful entropy of social responsibility. There is really no other choice. "Nothing really worth doing will ever be easy," my father used to tell me. "Do it anyway."

Bibliography

"11 Facts about Sweatshops." DoSomething.org (2017). https://www.dosomething.org/us/facts/11-facts-about-sweatshops.

"18 revelations from Wikileaks' hacked Clinton emails." BBC.com (2016). http://www.bbc.com/news/world-us-canada-37639370.

"1960s Creativity and Breaking the Rules." *Ad Age* (2005). http://adage.com/article/75-years-of-ideas/1960s-creativity-breaking-rules/102704/.

"2012 Republican Party of Texas Report of Platform Committee." http://www.texasgop.org/wp-content/themes/rpt/images/2012Platform_Final.pdf.

Abnett, Kate. "Styling Politicians in the Age of Image Wars." The Business Of Fashion (2016). https://www.businessoffashion.com/articles/intelligence/styling-politicians-donald-trump-theresa-may-hillary-clinton.

Acar, Adam. *Culture And Social Media*. Newcastle upon Tyne: Cambridge Scholars, 2015.

Ackerman, Spencer. "James Clapper: Obama Stands By Intelligence Chief As Criticism Mounts." *The Guardian* (2013). https://www.theguardian.com/world/2013/jun/12/james-clapper-intelligence-chief-criticism#_=_.

Anderson, Nate. "France Attempts to 'Civilize' the Internet; Internet Fights Back." Ars Technica (2011). https://arstechnica.com/tech-policy/2011/05/france-attempts-to-civilize-the-internet-internet-fights-back/.

Aristotle. *The "Art" Of Rhetoric. By John Henry Freese*. Translated by John Henry Freese. New York: G. P. Putnam's Sons, 1926.

Armitage, John. "Resisting the Neoliberal Discourse of Technology: The Politics Of Cyberculture In the Age of the Virtual Class | Ctheory." *Journals.Uvic.Ca* (2020). https://journals.uvic.ca/index.php/ctheory/article/view/14620/5486.

Ashby, W. Ross. *An Introduction To Cybernetics*. 2nd ed. London: Chapman & Hall, 1957.

Assange, Julian. "The Banality Of 'Don't Be Evil.'" *The New York Times* (2013). http://www.nytimes.com/2013/06/02/opinion/sunday/the-banality-of-googles-dont-be-evil.html?pagewanted=all.

Associated Press. "Edward Snowden's Cautious Approach to Post Reporter Barton Gellman." Politico (2013). https://www.politico.com/story/2013/06/edward-snowden-barton-gellman-washington-post-092490.

———. "Snowden's Return to US Could Be Legal Battle." AP News (2013). https://apnews.com/article/947cf044f50b448297894bedcd311d36.

Aston, Margaret. *The Fifteenth Century: The Prospect Of Europe, Etc.* London: Thames & Hudson, 1968.

Barlow, John Perry. "A Declaration of the Independence of Cyberspace." Electronic Frontier Foundation (2020). https://www.eff.org/cyberspace-independence.

Barstow, David. "Behind TV Analysts, Pentagon's Hidden Hand." *The New York Times* (2008). http://www.nytimes.com/2008/04/20/us/20generals.html.

Bass, Thomas A. "Being Nicholas." *Wired* (1995). https://www.wired.com/1995/11/nicholas/.

Bateson, Gregory. *Steps to an Ecology of Mind.* New York: Ballantine, 1972.

Beckett, Lois. "Yes, Companies Are Harvesting—and Selling—Your Facebook Profile." ProPublica (2012). https://www.propublica.org/article/yes-companies-are-harvesting-and-selling-your-social-media-profiles.

Bernays, Edward L. *Crystallizing Public Opinion.* With an introduction by Stuart Ewen. Brooklyn, NY: IG, 2011.

———. *Propaganda.* With an introduction by Mark Crispin Miller. Brooklyn, NY: IG, 2005.

Berners-Lee, Tim. "Frequently Asked Questions by the Press." The World Wide Web Foundation (2012). https://www.w3.org/People/Berners-Lee/FAQ.html.

Berry, Chip, and Maggie Woodward. "Average Number Of Televisions In U.S. Homes Declining." EIA.gov (2017). https://www.eia.gov/todayinenergy/detail.php?id=30132.

Birkerts, Sven. *The Gutenberg Elegies.* New York: Fawcett Columbine, 1994.

Blake, Aaron. "A Record Number of Americans Now Dislike Hillary Clinton." *The Washington Post* (2016). https://www.washingtonpost.com/news/the-fix/wp/2016/08/31/a-record-number-of-americans-now-dislike-hillary-clinton/?utm_term=.72b8ff777f2d.

Bobic, Igor. "Senate Staffer Tried To Scrub 'Torture' From Torture Report's Wikipedia Entry." HuffPost (2014). https://www.huffpost.com/entry/senate-torture-wikipedia_n_6308292.

Boorstin, Daniel J. *The Image: A Guide to Pseudo-Events in America.* New York: Harper & Row, 1964.

Bowerman, Mary. "Julian Assange: Russian government not the source of leaked emails." *USA Today,* January 3, 2017. https://www.usatoday.com/story/news/nation-nation/2017/01/03/julian-assange-russian-government-not-source-leaked-emails/96106052.

Brainard, Lori A. *Television : The Limits Of Deregulation.* Boulder, CO: Lynne Rienner, 2004.

Brande, William Thomas, Joseph Cauvin, Joseph Gwilt, John Lindley, and J. C. Loudon. *A Dictionary Of Science, Literature, And Art.* London: Longmans, Green, and Co., 1875.

Brasunas, Tony. "Only Voter Suppression Can Stop Bernie Sanders." HuffPost (2016). http://www.huffingtonpost.com/tony-brasunas/only-voter-suppression-can-stop-bernie-sanders_b_9780128.html.

Brazile, Donna. "Russia DNC Hack Played Out Exactly as Hoped." *Time* (2017). http://time.com/4705515/donna-brazile-russia-emails-clinton/.

Breitman, Kendall. "Hillary Clinton Explains Why She Really Lost to Trump." NBC News (2017). http://www.nbcnews.com/politics/hillary-clinton/hillary-clinton-explains-why-she-really-lost-trump-n743581.

Brown, David. "Julian Assange a high suicide risk, extradition case told." *The Times* (2020). https://www.thetimes.co.uk/article/old-bailey-told-assange-is-a-high-suicide-risk-86t6rz3rt.

Butler, Smedley D. *War Is a Racket*. Lexington, KY: Aristeus, 2014.

Calugareanu, Ilinca. "Opinion: 'VHS vs. Communism.'" *The New York Times* (2014). https://www.nytimes.com/2014/02/18/opinion/vhs-vs-communism.html?smid=pl-share&_r=2.

Caren, Neal, and Sarah Gaby. *Occupy Online: Facebook and the Spread Of Occupy Wall Street*. Chapel Hill, NC: University of North Carolina at Chapel Hill, 2011. https://ssrn.com/abstract=1943168 or http://dx.doi.org/10.2139/ssrn.1943168.

Carol Wilding, et al., Plaintiffs, v. DNC Services Corp, d/b/a, Democratic National Committee, et al., Defendants. 2017, Transcript of Hearings CASE NO. 16-61511-CIV-WJZ. United States District Court Southern District of Florida Fort Lauderdale Division.

Carol Wilding, et al., Plaintiffs, v. DNC Services Corp, d/b/a, Democratic National Committee, et al., Defendants. 2017, Final Order of Dismissal CASE NO. 16-61511-CIV-ZLOCH. United States District Court Southern District of Florida.

Carr, Nicholas G. *The Shallows: What the Internet Is Doing to Our Brains*. 2nd ed. New York: W. W. Norton, 2011.

Cavanagh, Sean. "Common-Core Testing Contracts Favor Big Vendors." *Education Week* (2014). http://www.edweek.org/ew/articles/2014/10/01/06contract.h34.html.

Cawthorne, Cameron. "David Ignatius: Trump Has Restored 'Credibility Of American Power.'" *The Washington Free Beacon* (2017). http://freebeacon.com/national-security/david-ignatius-trump-has-restored-credibility-of-american-power/.

Chomsky, Noam. *Media Control: The Spectacular Achievements Of Propaganda*. 2nd ed. New York: Seven Stories, 2002.

———. "Necessary Illusions." *CIA.gov* (1989). https://www.cia.gov/library/abbottabad-compound/52/526D2E781AC9EBBB13346BDF7693E1BB_CHOMSKY_Noam_-_Necessary_Illusions.pdf.

Chubbuck, Kay. "Wright's 'Nonzero'—naivete of evolution." *The Baltimore Sun* (2000). https://www.baltimoresun.com/news/bs-xpm-2000-02-20-0002190405-story.html.

CNN.com. "Clinton Condemns Leak as 'Attack on International Community.'" https://cnn.com/2010/US/11/29/wikileaks/index.html.

Coakley, Michael. "Blue Jeans: Uniform for a Casual World—Levi Strauss Considers Its Product a 'Great Equalizer.'" *The Chicago Tribune* (1988). http://archives.chicagotribune.com/1975/05/05/page/1/article/column-1#text.

Cohen, Bernard C. *The Press And Foreign Policy*. Princeton, NJ: Princeton University Press, 1963.

"Collateral Murder". WebCite (2010). https://www.webcitation.org/500VO9f9A?url=http://www.collateralmurder.com/.

Contorno, Steve. "James Clapper's Testimony One Year Later." PolitiFact (2014). https://www.politifact.com/article/2014/mar/11/james-clappers-testimony -one-year-later/.

Conway, Madeline. "Clinton: I don't recall joking about droning Julian Assange." Politico (2016). https://www.politico.com/story/2016/10/hillary-clinton-julian-assange-229123.

Cook, Amy. "The Perils Of Whistleblowing: My Interview With Edward Snowden." *Entrepreneur* (2017). https://www.entrepreneur.com/article/294958.

Creel, George. *How We Advertised America: The First Telling of the Amazing Story of the Committee on Public Information that Carried the Gospel of Americanism to Every Corner of the Globe.* New York: Harper & Brothers, 1920.

Dickens, Arthur Geoffrey. *Reformation and Society in Sixteenth-Century Europe.* London: Thames, 1966.

Dishneau, David, and Pauline Jelinek. "Witness: Manning Said Leak Would Lift 'Fog Of War.'" Boston.com (2011). http://archive.boston.com/news/nation/washington/articles/2011/12/19/letter_suggests_manning_wanted_to_make_history/.

"DNC Lawsuit—Google Search." Google.com (2017). https://www.google.com/search? site=webhp&q=dnc+lawsuit+&oq=dnc+lawsuit+&gs_l=psy-ab.3..35i39k1j0l3.35 524.37768.0.40368.14.14.0.0.0.0.163.1408.5j8.13.0....0...1.1.64.psy-ab..1.13.1397. DN-IXEkpZdw.

Doctorow, Cory. "Saying Information Wants To Be Free Does More Harm Than Good." *The Guardian* (2020). https://www.theguardian.com/technology/2010/may/18/information-wants-to-be-free.

Easley, Jonathan. "Poll: Bernie Sanders Country's Most Popular Active Politician." *The Hill* (2017). http://thehill.com/homenews/campaign/329404-poll-bernie-sanders-countrys-most-popular-active-politician.

East, Kristen. "Top DNC staffer apologizes for email on Sanders' religion." Politico (2016). http://www.politico.com/story/2016/07/top-dnc-staffer-apologizes-for-email-on-sanders-religion-226072.

Editorial Board. "Using Political Flacks as News Analysts Erodes Faith in Journalism. TV Directors: Build That Wall!" *The LA Times* (2016). http://www.latimes.com/opinion/editorials/la-ed-trump-clinton-cnn-fox-20161101-story.html.

Eisenstein, Elizabeth L. *Divine Art, Infernal Machine: The Reception of Printing in the West from First Impressions to the Sense of an Ending.* Philadelphia: University of Pennsylvania Press, 2011.

———. *The Printing Press as an Agent Of Change: Communications and Cultural Transformations in Early-Modern Europe.* 1st ed. Cambridge: Cambridge University Press, 1980.

Ellul, Jacques. "The Betrayal by Technology: A Portrait of Jacques Ellul." *Second Nature.* (2014). https://secondnaturejournal.com/the-betrayal-by-technology-a-portrait-of-jacques-ellul/.

———. "The Ethics Of Propaganda." *The Ellul Forum* (37) 3–8 (2006). https://journals.wheaton.edu/index.php/ellul/issue/viewIssue/62/62.

———. *The Presence Of the Kingdom.* 1st ed. Colorado Springs: Helmers & Howard, 1989.

———. *Propaganda.* Translated by Konrad Kellen and Jean Lerner. 1st ed. New York: Vintage, 1968.

———. *The Technological Bluff.* Grand Rapids: William B. Eerdmans, 1990.

————. *The Technological Society*. 1st ed. New York: Alfred A. Knopf, 1964.

————. *The Technological System*. New York: Continuum, 1980.

————. *Violence: Reflections from a Christian Perspective*. Translated by Cecelia Gaul Kings. New York: Seabury, 1969.

Entertainment Software Association. "2017 Essential Facts about the Computer and Video Game Industry." *TheESA.com* (2017). https://www.theesa.com/resource/2017-essential-facts-about-the-computer-and-video-game-industry/.

Ewen, Stuart. *PR! A Social History of Spin*. New York: Basic Books, 1996.

Fallon, Peter K. *The Metaphysics of Media*. Scranton, PA: University of Scranton Press, 2009.

Febvre, Lucien, Henri-Jean Martin, and David Gerard. *The Coming of the Book*. London: Blackwell Verso, 1997.

Filene, Edward A. *Successful Living in This Machine Age (Classic Reprint)*. London: Forgotten Books, 2015.

Foran, Clare. "Meet the Lifelong Republicans Who Love Bernie Sanders." *The Atlantic* (2015). https://www.theatlantic.com/politics/archive/2015/11/the-lifelong-conservatives-who-love-bernie-sanders/417441/.

Free Snowden. "Political interference." https://edwardsnowden.com/political-interference/.

————. "Threats overview." https://edwardsnowden.com/threats-overview/.

————. "Transcript: ARD Interview With Edward Snowden." https://edwardsnowden.com/2014/01/27/video-ard-interview-with-edward-snowden/.

"Fox News' Bob Beckel Calls For 'Illegally' Killing Assange: 'A Dead Man Can't Leak Stuff.'" HuffPost (2010) https://www.huffpost.com/entry/fox-news-bob-beckel-calls_n_793467.

Gallup. "Americans' Trust in Mass Media Sinks to New Low." Gallup.com (2016). http://www.gallup.com/poll/195542/americans-trust-mass-media-sinks-new-low.aspx.

Gayle, Damien. "CIA concludes Russia interfered to help Trump win election, say reports." *The Guardian* (2016). https://www.theguardian.com/us-news/2016/dec/10/cia-concludes-russia-interfered-to-help-trump-win-election-report.

Giedion, Siegfried. *Mechanization Takes Command: A Contribution to Anonymous History*. Minneapolis: University of Minnesota Press, 2013.

Gilens, Martin, and Benjamin I. Page. "Testing Theories Of American Politics: Elites, Interest Groups, and Average Citizens." *Perspectives On Politics* (2014). https://www.cambridge.org/core/services/aop-cambridge-core/content/view/62327F51 3959D0A304D4893B382B992B/S1537592714001595a.pdf/testing_theories_of_american_politics_elites_interest_groups_and_average_citizens.pdf.

Goebbels, Joseph. "Knowledge and Propaganda." Calvin University German Propaganda Archive (1928). https://research.calvin.edu/german-propaganda-archive/goeb54.htm

Goodman, Alanna. "EXCLUSIVE: Ex-British ambassador who is now a WikiLeaks operative claims Russia did NOT provide Clinton emails - they were handed over to him at a D.C. park by an intermediary for 'disgusted' Democratic whistleblowers." *The Daily Mail* (2016). http://www.dailymail.co.uk/news/article-4034038/Ex-British-ambassador-WikiLeaks-operative-claims-Russia-did-NOT-provide-Clinton-emails-handed-D-C-park-intermediary-disgusted-Democratic-insiders.html.

Greenstein, Fred I. "Can Personality and Politics Be Studied Systematically?" *Political Psychology* 13.1 (1992) 105–28. doi:10.2307/3791427).

Greenwald, Glenn. "Glenn Greenwald: Detaining My Partner Was a Failed Attempt at Intimidation." *The Guardian* (2013). https://www.theguardian.com/comment isfree/2013/aug/18/david-miranda-detained-uk-nsa.

———. "US Threatened Germany Over Snowden, Vice Chancellor Says." The Intercept (2015). https://theintercept.com/2015/03/19/us-threatened-germany-snowden-vice-chancellor-says/.

Greydanus, Steven. "September 11 And Hollywood: How Movies Can Help Make Our Past Real—Or Unreal." Decent Films (2017). http://decentfilms.com/articles/september-11-and-hollywood.

Guccione, Darren. "What Is the Dark Web? How to Access It and What You'll Find." CSO Online (2020). https://www.csoonline.com/article/3249765/what-is-the-dark-web-how-to-access-it-and-what-youll-find.html.

Hagopian, Amy, Abraham D. Flaxman, Tim K. Takaro, Sahar A. Esa Al Shatari, Julie Rajaratnam, Stan Becker, and Alison Levin-Rector. "Mortality In Iraq Associated with the 2003–2011 War and Occupation: Findings from a National Cluster Sample Survey by the University Collaborative Iraq Mortality Study." *PLOS Medicine* (2013). https://journals.plos.org/plosmedicine/article?id=10.1371/journal.pmed.1001533.

Hattem, Julian. "House Staffer Edited Wikipedia Page to Label Snowden a 'Traitor.'" *The Hill* (2014). https://thehill.com/policy/technology/214365-house-staffer-edits-wiki pedia-to-call-snowden-traitor.

Havelock, Eric A. *Preface To Plato.* Cambridge, MA: Belknap, 1982.

Hawkins, Derek. "Brian Williams Is 'Guided by the Beauty of Our Weapons' in Syria Strikes." *The Washington Post* (2017). https://www.washingtonpost.com/news/morning-mix/wp/2017/04/07/beautiful-brian-williams-says-of-syria-missile-strike-proceeds-to-quote-leonard-cohen/?utm_term=.d27bc8aa7fc1.

Hazen, Don, and Kali Holloway. "Patriarchy and Toxic Masculinity Are Dominating America Under Trump." Salon.com (2017). http://www.salon.com/2017/08/01/patriarchy-and-toxic-masculinity-are-dominating-america-under-trump_partner/.

Hedges, Chris. *Empire of Illusion: The End of Literacy and the Triumph Of Spectacle.* 1st ed. New York: Nation, 2009.

Henig, Jess. "'Climategate.'" FactCheck.org (2009). http://www.factcheck.org/2009/12/climategate/.

Hensch, Mark. "CNN Host: 'Donald Trump Became President' Last Night." *The Hill* (2017). http://thehill.com/homenews/administration/327779-cnn-host-donald-trump-became-president-last-night.

Hersh, Seymour. "The Coming Wars." *The New Yorker* (2005). http://www.newyorker.com/magazine/2005/01/24/the-coming-wars.

Hogan, William, Stephen Frost, Lissa Johnson, Thomas G Schulze, E. Anthony S. Nelson, and William Frost. "The ongoing torture and medical neglect of Julian Assange." PMC (2020). https://www.ncbi.nlm.nih.gov/pmc/articles/PMC7316471/.

"How Much Money is Behind Each Campaign?" *The Washington Post* (2017). https://www.washingtonpost.com/graphics/politics/2016-election/campaign-finance/.

Human Rights Watch. "Race to the Bottom: Corporate Complicity in Chinese Internet Censorship." https://www.hrw.org/reports/2006/china0806/index.htm.

Hyde, Cheryl A., and Betty J. Ruth. "Multicultural Content and Class Participation." *Journal Of Social Work Education* 38.2 (2002) 241–56. doi:10.1080/10437797.2002.10779095.

Iceland Review. "U.S. Authorities Ask Iceland to Extradite Snowden." https://www.icelandreview.com/news/u-s-authorities-ask-iceland-extradite-snowden/.

Innis, Harold A. *The Bias of Communication*. Toronto: University of Toronto Press, 1951.

International Association of Democratic Lawyers. "Written Statement Submitted by International Association Of Democratic Lawyers (IADL), a Non-Governmental Organization in Special Consultative Status." *Documents-dds-NY.UN.org* (2019). https://documents-dds-ny.un.org/doc/UNDOC/GEN/G19/049/42/PDF/G1904942.pdf?OpenElement.

International Bar Association. "IBA—IBAHRI Condemns UK Treatment of Julian Assange in US Extradition Trial." https://www.ibanet.org/Article/NewDetail.aspx?ArticleUid=C05C57EE-1FEE-47DC-99F9-26824208A750.

"Iraq Body Count." IraqBodyCount.org (2017.) https://www.iraqbodycount.org/.

Jaspers, Karl. *Way To Wisdom*. New Haven, CT: Yale University Press, 1976.

"Julian Assange: Russian Government Not Source Of Leaked DNC And Podesta Emails —Wikileaks Editor Contradicts CIA Claims In New Interview." *The Belfast Telegraph* (2016). http://www.belfasttelegraph.co.uk/news/world-news/julian-assange-russian-government-not-source-of-leaked-dnc-and-podesta-emails-wikileaks-editor-contradicts-cia-claims-in-new-interview-35300175.html.

Keen, Andrew. "Andrew Keen on Media, Culture and Technology." *Web.archive.org* (2020). https://web.archive.org/web/20060228161226/http://andrewkeen.typepad.com/akfiles/aboutak.htm.

———. *The Internet Is Not the Answer*. 1st ed. New York: Atlantic Monthly, 2015.

Kehoe, André. *Christian Contradictions and the World Revolution*. The Curragh, Kildare: Glendale, 1991.

Kelly, Kevin. *What Technology Wants*. 1st ed. New York: Viking, 2010.

Kloc, Joe. "Is a U. S. senator trolling Snowden's Wikipedia page?" *The Daily Dot* (2013). https://www.dailydot.com/debug/wikipedia-senate-snowden-nsa-traitor/.

Kornberger, Martin. *Brand Society: How Brands Transform Management and Lifestyle*. Cambridge: Cambridge University Press, 2010.

Kurzweil, Ray. *The Singularity Is Near*. New York: Viking, 2005.

Lanier, Jaron. *You Are Not a Gadget*. 2nd ed. New York: Vintage, 2011.

Lasswell, Harold D. *Propaganda Technique in the World War*. New York: Peter Smith, 1938.

Layton, Lyndsey. "How Bill Gates pulled off the swift Common Core revolution." *The Washington Post* (2014). https://www.washingtonpost.com/politics/how-bill-gates-pulled-off-the-swift-common-core-revolution/2014/06/07/a830e32e-ec34-11e3-9f5c-9075d5508f0a_story.html?tid=a_inl&utm_term=.063468557ca4.

Le Bon, Gustave. *The Crowd*. Mineola, NY: Dover, 2002.

Leiserowitz, A. A., E. W. Maibach, C. Roser-Renouf, N. Smith, and E. Dawson. "Climategate, Public Opinion, and the Loss of Trust." School Of Forestry & Environmental Studies (2010). http://environment.yale.edu/climate-communication-OFF/files/Climategate_Opinion_and_Loss_of_Trust_1.pdf.

Lieberman, Joseph. "State of the Union." Transcripts.CNN.com (2010). http://transcripts.cnn.com/TRANSCRIPTS/1006/20/sotu.01.html.

Lippmann, Walter. *Public Opinion*. Blacksburg, VA: Wilder, 2010.

Lutz, Ashley. "These 6 Corporations Control 90% of the Media in America." Business Insider (2012). http://www.businessinsider.com/these-6-corporations-control-90-of-the-media-in-america-2012-6.

MacAskill, Ewen, and Laurence Topham. "'They Wanted Me Gone': Edward Snowden Tells Of Whistleblowing, His AI Fears And Six Years In Russia." *The Guardian* (2019). https://www.theguardian.com/us-news/ng-interactive/2019/sep/13/edward-snowden-interview-whistleblowing-russia-ai-permanent-record.

MacAskill, Ewen. "Julian Assange Like a Hi-Tech Terrorist, Says Joe Biden." *The Guardian* (2020). https://www.theguardian.com/media/2010/dec/19/assange-high-tech-terrorist-biden.

Maher, Stephen, and Michael Corcoran. "The Corporate Media's Attempt to Kill the Occupy Movement." Truthout (2012). https://truthout.org/articles/the-corporate-medias-attempt-to-kill-the-occupy-movement/?tmpl=component&print=1.

Mander, Jason. "Daily Time Spent on Social Networks Rises to Over 2 Hours." Global Web Index Blog (2017). https://blog.gwi.com/chart-of-the-day/daily-time-spent-on-social-networks/.

Manning, Jennifer E. "Membership of the 116th Congress: A Profile." Washington, DC: Congressional Research Service, 2020. https://crsreports.congress.gov/product/pdf/R/R45583.

Marshall, Brad. "No Shit." WikiLeaks (2016). https://wikileaks.org/dnc-emails/emailid/7643.

Marty, Martin E. *Martin Luther*. New York: Viking, 2004.

McGovern, Ray, and William Binney. "Emails Were Leaked, Not Hacked." *The Baltimore Sun* (2017). http://www.baltimoresun.com/news/opinion/oped/bs-ed-hacking-intelligence-20170105-story.html.

McGuire, Michael. *Into the Web of Profit: An In-Depth Study of Cybercrime, Criminals and Money*. Cupertino, CA: Bromium, 2018. https://www.bromium.com/wp-content/uploads/2018/05/Into-the-Web-of-Profit_Bromium.pdf.

McLuhan, Marshall, Paul Benedetti, and Nancy DeHart. *Forward Through the Rearview Mirror*. Cambridge, MA: MIT Press, 1997.

———. *The Gutenberg Galaxy*. Toronto: University of Toronto Press, 1962.

———. *Understanding Media*. 2nd ed. New York: Mentor, 1964.

Meiklejohn, Alexander. "The First Amendment Is an Absolute." *The Supreme Court Review* (1961) 256. doi:10.1086/scr.1961.3108719.

"Mobile Fact Sheet." Pew Research Center: Internet, Science & Tech (2017). http://www.pewinternet.org/fact-sheet/mobile/.

MOMALearning. "Mathew B. Brady (Studio Of). President Lincoln. C. 1862." MOMA.org. (2018). https://www.moma.org/learn/moma_learning/mathew-b-brady-studio-of-president-lincoln-c-1862.

Mumford, Lewis. *Technics and Civilization*. New York: Harcourt Brace, 1963.

The Museum of Public Relations. "1929: Torches of Freedom" *Web.Archive.org* (2018). https://web.archive.org/web/20140715203652/http://www.prmuseum.com/bernays/bernays_1929.html.

Negroponte, Nicholas. *Being Digital*. 1st ed. London: Hodder and Stoughton, 1995.

The New York Times. "EASTER SUN FINDS THE PAST IN SHADOW AT MODERN PARADE." TimesMachine (2018). https://timesmachine.nytimes.com/timesmachine/1929/04/01/95899706.pdf.

"Obama: Hillary Clinton Most Qualified Presidential Candidate Ever." Chicago Tonight/ WTTW (2016). http://chicagotonight.wttw.com/2016/07/27/obama-hillary-clinton -most-qualified-presidential-candidate-ever.

"Obama: Trump 'Uniquely Unqualified' to Be President." Sky News (2016). http:// news.sky.com/story/barack-obama-donald-trump-uniquely-unqualified-to-be- president-10643266.

"Obama's Remarks On Health Care And Surveillance." *The New York Times* (2013). http://www.nytimes.com/2013/06/08/us/obamas-remarks-on-health-care-and- surveillance.html?pagewanted=4&ref=us.

Office of the Director of National Intelligence. "Assessing Russian Activities and Intentions in Recent US Elections." Office of the Director of National Intelligence. (2017) https://www.dni.gov/files/documents/ICA_2017_01.pdf.

"Bernie Sanders on the issues." BernieSanders.com (2016). https://berniesanders.com/ issues/.

Ong, Walter J. *Orality and Literacy: The Technologizing of the Word*. London: Methuen, 1982.

Pace, Julie. "Obama 'Disappointed' In Russia's Snowden Decision." AP News (2013). https://apnews.com/article/ab636248fa97421795a9f01bb878a43d.

Patterson, Thomas E. "News Coverage of the 2016 Presidential Primaries: Horse Race Reporting Has Consequences." Shorenstein Center For Media, Politics, And Public Policy (2016). https://shorensteincenter.org/news-coverage-2016-presidential- primaries/.

———. "Pre-Primary News Coverage of the 2016 Presidential Race: Trump's Rise, Sanders' Emergence, Clinton's Struggle." Shorenstein Center For Media, Politics, And Public Policy (2016). https://shorensteincenter.org/pre-primary-news- coverage-2016-trump-clinton-sanders/.

Payne, Dan. "Commentary: The Most Qualified Candidate For President In Our Lifetime." WBUR.org (2015). http://www.wbur.org/news/2015/03/19/hillary- clinton-presidential-qualifications.

Perez, Chris. "The 'American Dream' Is Pretty Much Dead." *The New York Post* (2016). http://nypost.com/2016/12/09/the-american-dream-is-pretty-much-dead/.

Perez, Sarah. "U.S. Consumers Now Spend 5 Hours Per Day On Mobile Devices." *TechCrunch* (2017). https://techcrunch.com/2017/03/03/u-s-consumers-now- spend-5-hours-per-day-on-mobile-devices/.

Pilkington, Ed. "Adrian Lamo on Bradley Manning: 'I Knew My Actions Might Cost Him His Life.'" *The Guardian* (2013). https://www.theguardian.com/world/2013/ jan/03/adrian-lamo-bradley-manning-q-and-a.

Plato. *Plato's Gorgias*. Translated by Edward Meredith Cope. Cambridge: Deighton, Bell, and Co., 1864.

Podesta, John. "Fwd: Fwd: Congratulations On Paris." WikiLeaks (2016). https:// wikileaks.org/podesta-emails/emailid/15464.

Postman, Neil. *Amusing Ourselves to Death*. New York: Penguin, 1985.

———. *Building a Bridge to the 18th Century*. New York: Vintage, 1999.

———. *The End Of Education*. 1st ed. New York: Alfred A. Knopf, 1995.

———. "Information." In *Past To Present: Ideas That Changed Our World*, edited by Stuart Hirschberg and Terry Hirschberg, 1st ed., 495–97. Upper Saddle River, NJ: Prentice-Hall, 2003.

————. *Technopoly: The Surrender Of Culture To Technology.* 1st ed. New York: Alfred A. Knopf, 1992.

Powell, Lewis F., Jr. "Attack on American Free Enterprise System." *The Powell Memorandum* (1971). http://law2.wlu.edu/deptimages/Powell%20Archives/Powell MemorandumTypescript.pdf.

Rabe, Barry G., and Christopher P. Borick. "The Climate of Belief: American Public Opinion on Climate Change." *Issues In Governance Studies* 31 (2010). https:// www.brookings.edu/wp-content/uploads/2016/06/01_climate_rabe_borick.pdf.

"Ranking: Military Spending By Country 2015." Statista (2015). https://www.statista. com/statistics/262742/countries-with-the-highest-military-spending/.

"Republican Lite—Google Search." Google.com (2017). https://www.google.com/sear ch?q=Republican+Lite&oq=Republican+Lite&gs_l=psy-ab.3..oi20k1jol2joi22i30 k1.23343.28004.0.29086.19.17.1.0.0.0.161.1867.5j11.16.0....0...1.1.64.psy-ab..2.17 .1863...46j35i39k1joi131k1joi46k1joi67k1joi13k1joi10k1.cpm9Dxgi96M.

Reuters. "NSA Surveillance Exposed by Snowden Was Illegal, Court Rules Seven Years On." *The Guardian* (2020). https://www.theguardian.com/us-news/2020/sep/03/ edward-snowden-nsa-surveillance-guardian-court-rules.

Riotta, Chris. "Was the Election Rigged Against Bernie Sanders? DNC Lawsuit Demands Repayment for Campaign Donors." *Newsweek* (2017). https://www. newsweek.com/bernie-sanders-rigged-hillary-clinton-dnc-lawsuit-donald-trump-president-609582.

Risen, James. "Julian Assange Suffered Severe Psychological and Physical Harm in Ecuadorian Embassy, Doctors Say." *The Intercept* (2020). https://theintercept. com/2019/04/15/julian-assange-health-medical-care/.

Roberts, Georgett. "Park-&-wreck freeloaders." *The New York Post,* October 9, 2011. https://nypost.com/2011/10/09/park-wreck-freeloaders.

Romenesko, Jim. "Memo from 1970: 'A Plan for Putting the GOP on TV News.'" Poynter (2011). http://www.poynter.org/news/mediawire/137673/memo-from-1970-a-plan-for-putting-the-gop-on-tv-news/.

Rossetto, Louis. "Cyberspace vs. the State." Cato Institute (1996). https://www.cato.org/ policy-report/mayjune-1996/cyberspace-vs-state.

Sealy, Geraldine. "Purging the Disloyal at the CIA." Salon.com (2004). https://www. salon.com/2004/11/15/cia_13/.

Shane, Scott. "Ex-C.I.A. Official Says Iraq Data Was Distorted." *NYTimes.com* (2006). http://www.nytimes.com/2006/02/11/world/middleeast/excia-official-says-iraq-data-was-distorted.html.

Shanker, Thom. "Soviets' VCRs Often Wrapped in Yards of Red Tape." *The Chicago Tribune* (1986). http://articles.chicagotribune.com/1986-03-17/news/8601200130_1_vcr-market-bootleg-tapes-video.

Shannon, Claude Elwood, and Warren Weaver. *The Mathematical Theory of Communication.* Urbana, IL: University of Illinois Press, 1999.

Sharkov, Damien. "Julian Assange Denies Russia Fed Clinton Emails to WikiLeaks." *Newsweek* (2016). http://www.newsweek.com/assange-denies-russia-fed-clinton-emails-wikileaks-516945.

Singer, Natasha. "Mapping, and Sharing, the Consumer Genome." *The New York Times* (2012). https://www.nytimes.com/2012/06/17/technology/acxiom-the-quiet-giant -of-consumer-database-marketing.html?pagewanted=all.

"SIPRI Yearbook 2020: Armaments, Disarmament And International Security (Summary)." Stockholm International Peace Research Institute (2021). https://www.sipri.org/sites/default/files/2020-06/yb20_summary_en_v2.pdf.

Smith, Aaron. "Record Shares of Americans Now Own Smartphones, Have Home Broadband." Pew Research Center (2017). http://www.pewresearch.org/fact-tank/2017/01/12/evolution-of-technology/.

Smith, Jackie. "How Elite Media Strategies Marginalize the Occupy Movement." Common Dreams (2011). https://www.commondreams.org/views/2011/12/11/how-elite-media-strategies-marginalize-occupy-movement.

Smith, Matt. "NSA Leaker Comes Forward, Warns of Agency's 'Existential Threat.'" CNN (2013). https://www.cnn.com/2013/06/09/politics/nsa-leak-identity/index.html.

Staff, Unzipped. "Throwback Thursday: Jeans as a Symbol of Freedom in Eastern Europe." Levi Strauss and Company (2017). http://www.levistrauss.com/unzipped-blog/2014/11/throwback-thursday-jeans-as-a-symbol-of-freedom-in-eastern-europe/.

Steel, Ronald. *Walter Lippmann and the American Century*. London: Routledge, 2017.

Stein, Sam, and Jason Cherkis. "The Inside Story of How Bernie Sanders Became the Greatest Online Fundraiser in Political History." HuffPost (2017). http://www.huffingtonpost.com/entry/bernie-sanders-fundraising_us_5952758 7e4b02734df2d92c1.

Steinberg, Saul H., and John Trevitt. *Five Hundred Years of Printing*. London: British Library, 2005.

Strauss, Valerie. "Everything you need to know about Common Core—Ravitch." *The Washington Post*, January 18, 2014. https://www.washingtonpost.com/news/answer-sheet/wp/2014/01/18/everything-you-need-to-know-about-common-core-ravitch/.

Sullivan, Margaret. "Has the *Times* Dismissed Bernie Sanders?" Public Editor's Journal (2015). https://publiceditor.blogs.nytimes.com/2015/09/09/has-the-times-dismissed-bernie-sanders/.

Sweeney, Michael Steven. *Secrets Of Victory*. Chapel Hill, NC: University of North Carolina Press, 2001.

Tarde, Gabriel. *On Communication and Social Influence*.   Edited and with an introduction by Terry N. Clark. Chicago: University of Chicago Press, 1969.

Thoreau, Henry David. *Walden, Or, Life in the Woods*. New York: Dover, 1995.

True Pundit. "Under Intense Pressure to Silence Wikileaks, Secretary of State Hillary Clinton Proposed Drone Strike on Julian Assange." https://truepundit.com/under-intense-pressure-to-silence-wikileaks-secretary-of-state-hillary-clinton-proposed-drone-strike-on-julian-assange/.

"Trump Unqualified to Be President—Google Search." Google.com (2017). https://www.google.com/search?site=&source=hp&q=trump+unqualified+to+be+president&oq=trump+unqualified+to+be+president&gs_l=psy-ab.3...1258.8065.0.87 30.34.30.0.0.0.0.382.3627.13j13j1j2.29.0....0...1.1.64.psy-ab..5.16.2294.0..0j35i39k 1joi131k1joi20k1.1rDpb-swsPY.

Tveten, Julianne. "It's Time to Nationalize the Internet." *In These Times* (2017). https://inthesetimes.com/article/fcc-net-neutrality-open-internet-public-good-nationalize.

UN.org. "Universal Declaration of Human Rights." https://www.un.org/en/universal-declaration-human-rights/index.html.

"US Adults Now Spend 12 Hours 7 Minutes a Day Consuming Media." eMarketer (2017) https://www.emarketer.com/Article/US-Adults-Now-Spend-12-Hours-7-Minutes-Day-Consuming-Media/1015775.

"Vault7—Home." WikiLeaks (2017). https://wikileaks.org/ciav7p1/.

Vogel, David. *Fluctuating Fortunes: The Political Power of Business in America.* New York: Basic Books, 1989.

Vollaro, Daniel R. "Lincoln, Stowe, and the 'Little Woman/Great War' Story: The Making, And Breaking, of a Great American Anecdote." *Journal of the Abraham Lincoln Association* 30 (Winter 2009) 18–34.   http://hdl.handle.net/2027/spo.2629860.0030.104.

Watts, Jonathan. "David Miranda: 'They Said I Would Be Put In Jail If I Didn't Co-Operate.'" *The Guardian* (2013). https://www.theguardian.com/world/2013/aug/19/david-miranda-interview-detention-heathrow.

The White House. "Statement by the Press Secretary on the President's Travel to Russia." https://obamawhitehouse.archives.gov/realitycheck/the-press-office/2013/08/07/statement-press-secretary-president-s-travel-russia.

White, Lynn, Jr. *Medieval Technology and Social Change.* London: Oxford University Press, 1962.

"Who Owns The Media?" Free Press (2017). https://www.freepress.net/ownership/chart.

Wiener, Norbert. *Cybernetics, or Control and Communication in Animal and Machine.* 2nd ed. Cambridge, MA: MIT Press, 1961.

———. *The Human Use of Human Beings.* London: Free Association Books, 1989.

Wilding, et. al. v DNC Services Corporation, d/b/a Democratic National Committee; and Deborah "Debbie" Wasserman Schultz. 2016 16-cv-61511-WJZ. United States District Court Southern District of Florida.

Winner, Langdon. *Autonomous Technology.* Cambridge, MA: MIT Press, 1983.

Wolf, Maryanne. *Proust and the Squid.* New York: Harper, 2007.

"World Hunger, Poverty Facts, Statistics 2016." World Hunger News (2016). http://www.worldhunger.org/2015-world-hunger-and-poverty-facts-and-statistics/.

Yeats, W. B. "The Man and the Echo." In *The Variorum Edition of the Poems of W. B. Yeats,* edited by Peter Allt and Russell K. Alspach, 383. New York: MacMillan, 1977.

Zakrzewski, Cat. "Bernie Sanders Just Made Internet Providers a New 2020 Target." *The Seattle Times* (2019). https://www.seattletimes.com/business/bernie-sanders-just-made-internet-providers-a-new-2020-target/.

Zetter, Kim, and Kevin Poulsen. "'I Can't Believe What I'm Confessing To You': The Wikileaks Chats." *Wired* (2010). https://www.wired.com/2010/06/wikileaks-chat/.

Index

Made in United States
North Haven, CT
25 January 2023

31658911R00129